Jesus the Jew

Geza Vermes was born in Hungary in 1924. After World War II he attended the University of Budapest and subsequently studied at Louvain where he obtained a 'Licence' in Oriental History and Philology in 1952, and a Doctorate in Theology in 1953. He held a research post at the Centre National de la Recherche Scientifique in Paris before being appointed, in 1957, to a lectureship in biblical studies at the University of Newcastle upon Tyne. In 1965 he was elected to the Readership in Jewish Studies at Oxford University. He is Professorial Fellow of Wolfson College and was, from 1971-74, Chairman of the Curators of the Oriental Institute. In 1971 he was Visiting Professor in Judaica at Brown University, U.S.A.

Geza Vermes is one of the pioneers of Qumran research. His first book, *Discovery in the Judean Desert*, was published in 1953. He is also the author of *Scripture and Tradition in Judaism* (1961) and *The Dead Sea Scrolls in English* (1962, revised 1965 and 1968). He has now completed, in association with the Oxford Roman historian, Fergus Millar, the modernization of Volume I of Emil Schurer's *History of the Jewish People in the Age of Jesus*.

Dr Vermes has contributed to the *Cambridge History of the Bible*, to various scholarly periodicals on the Scrolls and other Jewish subjects, and since 1971 has been the Editor of the *Journal of Jewish Studies*.

Jesus the Jew

A Historian's Reading of the Gospels

GEZA VERMES

Reader in Jewish Studies
in the University of Oxford

FONTANA/COLLINS

First published by William Collins Sons & Co. Ltd, London, 1973
First issued in Fontana 1976
Second Impression September 1977

© Geza Vermes, 1973

Made and printed in Great Britain by
William Collins Sons & Co. Ltd, Glasgow

These pages are dedicated to the memory of a friend, the leading Jewish New Testament scholar of his generation, whose outstanding achievement in the field of Gospel research is justly celebrated, and whose death on 9 October 1969 created a large gap in the world of learning and left a perceptible emptiness in the lives of the few who loved him.

PAUL WINTER

1904–1969

IN PIAM MEMORIAM

Contents

Preface

Jesus the Jew is written for those who, like the author, are eager to explore the primitive and genuine significance of words and events recorded in the Gospels in order to obtain a fuller understanding of the historical Jesus. The book is intended to interest Christians and Jews, people of other creeds, and men and women with no religion at all. It is addressed to scholars and laymen alike. Experts requiring references to ancient and modern literatures, and the necessary justification of controversial statements, will find these in the notes. Laymen, on the other hand, may like to know that these notes have been compiled in such a way that they are not indispensable to a comprehension of the text.

In the first three chapters, I insert the Jesus of the Gospels into the geographical and historical realities and into the charismatic religious framework of first-century Judaism, and against this background Jesus the Galilean *hasid* or holy man begins to take on substance. The rest of the book analyses the New Testament titles of Jesus (prophet, lord, messiah, son of man, son of God), and demonstrates that in their original meaning these describe exactly the kind of healer and teacher encountered in the first part of this volume. Some readers may find the examination of the titles difficult, but I hope they will persevere with the study of this complex but crucially important matter. For example, a term such as 'lord' was used in many different senses, from a prosaic 'sir', to the designation of the 'Lord' God Almighty, and it is only through a strict and careful application of the rules of historical and literary criticism that we can discover the nuance most appropriate to the context.

Jesus the Jew is the first part of a trilogy: it sets the scene of Jesus' activity and determines what kind of a Jew he was. A second enquiry, *The Gospel of Jesus the Jew*, will be devoted to a reconstruction of his authentic message. Lastly, in a work still without a title, I intend to investigate the transformation of the man, Jesus of Nazareth, into the divine Christ of the Christian faith in the works of Paul, John and the other New Testament writers.

Martin Buber, one of the foremost religious thinkers of this century and a great admirer of Jesus, wrote: 'We Jews know him in a way – in the impulses and emotions of his essential Jewishness – that remains inaccessible to the Gentiles subject to him.'* I trust that those who accompany me on this voyage of exploration will recognize the truth of Buber's words.

The Oriental Institute,   G.V.
University of Oxford

---

*'Christus, Chassidismus, Gnosis', *Werke*, vol. III (Kösel and Lambert Schneider, Munich-Heidelberg, 1963), p. 957.

Bibliographical aid to the general reader

BIBLE AND APOCRYPHA

Most scriptural quotations are taken from the New English Bible with the Apocrypha (Oxford and Cambridge University Presses, 1970). When the NEB fails to display the nuance of meaning required in my argument, I follow the American Revised Standard Version (Nelson, London and New York, 1952) or present my own rendering. Passages originating from these latter sources are designated *RSV* or *AT* (author's translation).

The standard Hebrew and Greek Bibles are: *Biblia Hebraica* (edited by R. Kittel and P. Kahle); *Septuaginta id est Vetus Testamentum Graece* (edited by A. Rahlfs) and *Novum Testamentum Graece* (edited by E. Nestle and K. Aland). All three works have been published by the Württembergische Bibelanstalt, Stuttgart. The same publishers have also issued the best Gospel parallels in Greek, *Synopsis Quattuor Evangeliorum* by K. Aland (1965). The corresponding English works are: *Gospel Parallels: A Synopsis of the First Three Gospels* by B. H. Throckmorton (Nelson, London and New York, 1949) and *A Synopsis of the Gospels* by H. F. D. Sparks (A. & C. Black, London, ²1970). The former is based on the American Revised Standard Version, the latter on the English Revised Version.

The most popular one-volume commentary on both Testaments is *Peake's Commentary on the Bible*, edited by M. Black and H. H. Rowley (Nelson, London and New York, 1962). A. E. Harvey's useful *Companion to the New Testament* (Oxford and Cambridge University Presses, 1970) follows the New English Bible.

The best introduction to the Hebrew Bible, the Apocrypha and

Pseudepigrapha is *The Old Testament: An Introduction* by O. Eissfeldt (Blackwell, Oxford, and Abingdon, Nashville and New York, 1966). O. Cullmann's *The New Testament: An Introduction for the General Reader* (SCM Press, London, 1968) may serve as a first guide to the New Testament. On a more advanced level, the most widely used volume is W. G. Kümmel, *Introduction to the New Testament* (SCM Press, London, and Abingdon, Nashville and New York, 1975). See also *The New Testament: The History of the Investigation of its Problems* by the same author and publishers (1973).

PSEUDEPIGRAPHA

The only collected edition in English of the non-canonical religious writings known as Pseudepigrapha is R. H. Charles, *The Apocrypha and Pseudepigrapha of the Old Testament* II (Clarendon Press, Oxford, 1913).

DEAD SEA SCROLLS

The non-biblical texts may be read in my translation, *The Dead Sea Scrolls in English* (Penguin Books, Harmondsworth and Baltimore, Md., ²1975). A handy edition of the Hebrew original with a facing German translation is offered by E. Lohse in *Die Texte aus Qumran* (Kösel, Munich, ²1971). For a Select bibliography, see E. Schürer – G. Vermes – F. Millar, *The History of the Jewish People in the Age of Jesus Christ* I (T. & T. Clark, Edinburgh, 1973), pp. 118-22.

JOSEPHUS

A Greek-English edition of the complete work of Flavius Josephus is available in the Loeb Classical Library by H. St. J. Thackeray – R. Marcus – L. H. Feldman (Heinemann, London, and Harvard University Press, Cambridge, Mass., 1926-65). For an introduction and a bibliography see Schürer-Vermes-Millar, *History* I, pp. 43-63.

PHILO

The Loeb Classical Library has also issued a Greek-English Philo, edited by F. H. Colson and G. H. Whitaker (1929-62). Cf. also E. R. Goodenough, *An Introduction to Philo Judaeus* (Blackwell, Oxford, ²1962).

RABBINIC LITERATURE

The following list is limited to general introductions and English (or occasionally French or German) translations of the sources.

Introductions: Schürer-Vermes-Millar, *History* I, pp. 68-118; H. L. Strack, *Introduction to the Talmud and Midrash* (Jewish Publication Society, Philadelphia, 1931); J. Bowker, *The Targums and Rabbinic Literature* (Cambridge University Press, Cambridge, 1969).

Translations: The standard rendering of the Mishnah is that by H. Danby, *The Mishnah* (Oxford University Press, London, 1933). No complete translation of the Tosephta is available in any European language. The Jerusalem Talmud may be read in French, *Le Talmud de Jérusalem* by M. Schwab (Maisonneuve, Paris, 1871-89, reprinted in 1969) and the Babylonian Talmud in the thirty-five volumes edited by I. Epstein, *The Babylonian Talmud translated into English* (Soncino, London, 1935-52). Among the Bible interpretations or Midrash works, there are the ten volumes of *Midrash Rabbah* edited by H. Friedman and M. Simon (Soncino, London, ²1951); *Mekilta deRabbi Ishmael . . . with an English translation* by J. Z. Lauterbach (Jewish Publication Society, Philadelphia, 1933); *The Fathers according to Rabbi Nathan* by J. Goldin (Yale University Press, New Haven, Conn., 1955); W. G. Braude, *Pesikta Rabbati . . . translated from the Hebrew* (Yale University Press, New Haven, 1968); *Siphre zu Numeri* in K. G. Kuhn's German translation (Kohlhammer, Stuttgart, 1959), etc.

TARGUMS

The only complete translation of the Targums is a Latin one

included in Brian Walton's London Polygot Bible (1657). There is a somewhat archaic English rendering of the Targums to the Pentateuch by J. W. Etheridge, *The Targums of Onkelos and Jonathan ben Uzziel on the Pentateuch with the Fragments of the Jerusalem Targum from the Chaldee* (1862-5, reprinted by Ktav, New York, 1968). The edition of a recently discovered codex, *Neophyti 1*, by A. Díez Macho, contains also an English translation. So far Genesis (1968), Exodus (1970), Leviticus (1971) and Numbers (1974) have been published by Consejo Superior de Investigaciones Científicas, Madrid and Barcelona.

ENCYCLOPAEDIAS

The two major works in English are: *Jewish Encyclopaedia*, 12 volumes (Funk and Wagnalls, New York and London, 1901-5), and *Encyclopaedia Judaica*, 16 volumes (Keter, Jerusalem, and Macmillan, New York, 1972).

Note on the use of brackets

In the material quoted from ancient sources square brackets are used to indicate hypothetical reconstructions, while parentheses mark words supplied by the translator to facilitate the understanding of the text.

Introduction: from Christianity to Jesus

> I believe . . . in one Lord Jesus Christ, the only-begotten
> Son of God, begotten of his Father before all worlds, God
> of God, Light of Light, very God of very God, begotten,
> not made, being of one substance with the Father, by whom
> all things were made.
>
> Who for us men, and for our salvation, came down from
> heaven, and was incarnate by the Holy Ghost of the Virgin
> Mary, and was made man, and was crucified also for us
> under Pontius Pilate. He suffered and was buried, and the
> third day he rose again according to the Scriptures, and
> ascended into heaven, and sitteth at the right hand of the
> Father. And he shall come again with glory to judge both
> the quick and the dead: whose kingdom shall have no end.

The Creed, especially the Nicene variety from which the
quotation derives, is regarded by believers and non-believers alike
as a genuine, consecrated, shorthand expression of the quintessence
of the Christian faith. Not unexpectedly, three-fifths of the
document are concerned with the focus of this faith, Jesus the
Messiah, the person thought to be the link between heaven and
earth, and between time and eternity. The remarkable feature,
however, of the resulting portrait of the Jesus of Christianity is
its total lack of proportion between history and theology, fact
and interpretation. In formulating her profession of faith, the
Church shows passionate interest in Christ's eternal pre-existence
and glorious after-life, but of his earthly career the faithful are
told next to nothing, save that he was born and died. For its

historical anchor, the Creed relies, not on Jesus of Nazareth himself, but on the second-rate and notoriously cruel Roman civil servant, Pontius Pilate.

Yet according to basic church doctrine, Christianity is a historical religion in which knowledge of the divine Christ and the mysteries of heaven springs from the words and deeds of a first-century AD Galilean Jew, a man firmly situated in time and space. Everything told about him originates, not in the Creed, but in the Gospels, and specifically – from the point of view of history – in the earlier Synoptic Gospels of Mark, Matthew and Luke. Admittedly, not even they were conceived as an objective record of events, nor even as popular chronicles. Nonetheless they are generally less remote from the Jesus of history in time and style of presentation than the last of the four, the spiritual Gospel of John the Divine.[1]

The believing Christian is convinced that the Jesus of history and the Christ of faith are one and the same. For him there is coherence – identity even – between the Gospel picture and that offered by the Creed: though he may concede that the former is a first sketch preceding the artist's final masterpiece, an imperfect portrayal leading to the perfect by means of an inward, direct and legitimate development.

By contrast to these imperatives of faith, the issues which writer and reader will explore together are concerned with the primitive, genuine, *historical* significance of words and events recorded in the Gospels. What they are *believed* to signify is the business of the theologian; the historian's task is to discover the original meaning of their message. In pursuit of this aim, the utmost use will be made of the literary legacy of Palestinian and Diaspora Jews from the last two hundred years of the pre-Christian, and the first few centuries of the Christian era: the Apocrypha, and Pseudepigrapha, Philo, Josephus and Jewish inscriptions, the manuscript discoveries from the Judean desert and early rabbinic writings. These sources will not be treated merely as a backcloth, however, but as witnesses. They will not be employed simply as aids in answering queries arising from the New Testament, but as independent spokesmen capable, from time to time at least, of guiding the enquiry, either by suggesting the right angle of approach, or even the right questions to ask.

It should be emphasized that the present historical investigation of the Gospels is motivated by no sentiment of critical destructiveness. On the contrary, it is prompted by a single-minded and devout search for fact and reality and undertaken out of feeling for the tragedy of Jesus of Nazareth. If, after working his way through the book, the reader recognizes that this man, so distorted by Christian and Jewish myth alike, was *in fact* neither the Christ of the Church, nor the apostate and bogey-man of Jewish popular tradition, some small beginning may have been made in the repayment to him of a debt long overdue.

PART ONE: THE SETTING

1. Jesus the Jew

Most people, whether they admit it or not, approach the Gospels with preconceived ideas. Christians read them in the light of their faith; Jews, primed with age-old suspicion; agnostics, ready to be scandalized; and professional New Testament experts, wearing the blinkers of their trade. Yet it should not be beyond the capabilities of an educated man to sit down and with a mind empty of prejudice read the accounts of Mark, Matthew and Luke as though for the first time.

The basic Gospel is presented in the form of a record of the life of Jesus from the time of his appearance in public in the company of John the Baptist till the discovery of his empty tomb, a biographical framework into which are incorporated extracts from sayings attributed to him. This primary structure has survived in Mark. The other two evangelists preface it with stories relating to the birth and youth of Jesus which are on the whole theologically motivated; they are distinct from the main Gospel body, which at no stage pays any regard to them. All three Gospels have also an epilogue elaborating on the apparitions of Jesus to his disciples after his resurrection, an afterthought which failed to make its way into the earliest manuscript tradition of Mark,[1] but was inserted without difficulty into Matthew and Luke.

Since it is always an arduous, and often almost hopeless, task to try to establish the historical value of the Synoptic story, the plan here is not to attempt to reconstruct the authentic portrait of Jesus but, more modestly, to find out how the writers of the Gospels, echoing primitive tradition, wished him to be known.

What did they think was important about him, and what second-ary? On what did they expatiate fully, and what did they gloss over? Who, in brief, was the Jesus of the evangelists?

PERSONAL PARTICULARS

The main Gospel – that covered by Mark – provides the following personal information.

Name:	Jesus
Father's name:	Joseph
Mother's name:	Mary
Place of birth:	not mentioned
Date of birth:	not mentioned
Domicile:	Nazareth in Galilee
Marital state:	not mentioned
Profession:	carpenter (?); also itinerant exorcist and preacher

A death certificate can be filled in somewhat more fully.

Place of death:	Jerusalem
Date of death:	'under Pontius Pilate', between AD 26 and 36
Cause of death:	crucifixion by order of the Roman prefect
Place of burial:	Jerusalem

FAMILY BACKGROUND

Apart from the infancy stories,[2] which in any case inject an element of doubt into the issue of paternity, the name of the father of Jesus appears only in Luke and in a variant reading in Matthew.

'Is not this Joseph's son?'[3]

'Is he not [Joseph] the carpenter's son?'[4]

The same passage contains also the Greek form of his mother's name, *Maria* or *Mariam*, and (unless the reader's judgement is affected by the later belief in the perpetual virginity of Mary) the names of his four brothers, Jacob, Joseph, Judah and Simon, and mention of his several sisters.[5]

The main Gospel, as opposed to the birth stories in Matthew and Luke, does not state where Jesus was born. If anything, it implies that his birthplace was Nazareth, the unimportant little Galilean locality where he and his parents lived. The only indirect evidence on his date of birth is concealed in the verse describing him as being of about thirty years of age when John baptized him in the fifteenth year of the reign of Tiberius, probably in AD 28/29.[6]

Although several women were included in his group during his ministry, no wife is ever mentioned. He does not seem to have left one behind at home, as he advised his would-be disciples to do,[7] or as did certain mature Jewish ascetics, the Therapeutae, according to Philo of Alexandria.[8] The Gospels do not depict him as a widower either, so one is to assume that he was unmarried, a custom unusual but not unheard of among Jews in his time, as will be shown in a later chapter.[9]

JESUS THE CARPENTER

His secular profession remains uncertain. Tradition has it that he was a carpenter and learned his trade from his father, but this on the fragile evidence that after his first and last sermon in the synagogue of Nazareth, the townsfolk could not understand how 'the carpenter',[10] or 'the carpenter's son',[11] could have acquired such great wisdom. Was he a carpenter himself, or was he only the son of a carpenter? The confused state of the Greek text of the Gospels usually indicates either (a) a doctrinal difficulty thought by some to demand rewording; or (b) the existence of a linguistic problem in the expression in Hellenistic terms of something typically Jewish. Here the second alternative applies. The congregation in the synagogue voices astonishment.

> 'Where does he get it from?' 'What wisdom is this . . . ?' 'Is not this the carpenter/the son of the carpenter . . . ?'[12]

Now those familiar with the language spoken by Jesus are acquainted with a metaphorical use of 'carpenter' and 'carpenter's son' in ancient Jewish writings.[13] In Talmudic sayings the Aramaic noun denoting carpenter or craftsman (*naggar*) stands for a 'scholar' or 'learned man'.

This is something that no carpenter, son of carpenters, can explain.[14]

There is no carpenter, nor a carpenter's son, to explain it.[15]

Thus, although no one can be absolutely sure that the sayings cited in the Talmud were current already in first-century AD Galilee, proverbs such as these are likely to be age-old. If so, it is possible that the charming picture of 'Jesus the carpenter' may have to be buried and forgotten.[16]

JESUS THE EXORCIST

Whatever he did to earn a living before he entered public life, the New Testament record leaves no room for doubt that during his ministry Jesus practised no secular profession but devoted himself exclusively to religious activities. The Synoptists are unanimous in presenting him as an exorcist, healer and teacher. They also emphasize that the deepest impression made by Jesus on his contemporaries resulted from his mastery over devils and disease, and the magnetic power of his preaching. He is claimed to have once defined his mission in the following words:

'Today and tomorrow I shall be casting out devils and working cures; on the third day I reach my goal.'[17]

In Galilee, such was definitely his main occupation.

They brought to him all who were ill or possessed by devils . . . He healed many who suffered from various diseases, and drove out many devils.[18]

So all through Galilee he went . . . casting out the devils.[19]

In addition to these summary references, the Synoptists list six particular episodes involving exorcism. Four of them, the only ones to appear in Mark, describe as demonic possession what seems to have been mental or nervous illness. The Gerasene demoniac was a dangerous madman who walked about naked, repeatedly wounded himself, and had to be kept on a chain.[20]

The boy whose devil the disciples were unable to cast out was an epileptic and possibly a deaf-mute.[21] The man exorcised in the synagogue of Capernaum shrieked and was seized by convulsions.[22] More vaguely, the daughter of the Tyrian woman was tormented whilst possessed, but lay peacefully on her bed after her unclean spirit had been expelled.[23]

In two other instances, unrecorded in Mark and possibly a double narration of the same story, possession is seen as the cause of dumbness, or of dumbness and blindness combined.[24] The twelve apostles of Jesus,[25] as well as his seventy (or seventy-two) disciples, are also portrayed as generally successful exorcists,[26] and to John's great indignation, even a non-disciple was once seen to cast out devils in the name of Jesus.[27]

Contrary to Jewish folk medicine,[28] the Gospels know nothing of a ritual of exorcism. The actual expulsion is described four times and, with the exception of the one effected *in absentia* by a mere declaration,[29] always follows a direct command:

'Be silent!'[30]

'Out, unclean spirit, come out of this man!'[31]

'Deaf and dumb spirit, I command you, come out of him and never go back!'[32]

The last example is the only instance in which the devil is ordered to stay away permanently and not to return when its desert exile becomes too unbearable.[33] Does this imply that in the other cases, to employ contemporary psychiatric jargon, there was merely a temporary remission? It ought to be mentioned at this juncture that the psychiatrist whom I have consulted on the question whether most of the diseases exorcised or healed in the New Testament could be recognized as hysterical, after giving a qualified affirmative reply, wished to know the success rate of the treatment and the state of health of the patients six months after discharge!

The story of the demon called 'Legion' who sought to bargain with Jesus and obtained a comparatively light sentence (a transfer into the local herd of pigs) may sound extraordinary, but is not unparalleled in ancient Jewish literature, as will appear later.[34] Another curious Gospel feature deserves to be pinpointed here: the excellence of the demonic intelligence service.[35] In the temptation story, Satan challenges Jesus to prove that he is 'the son of God';[36] his underlings are afraid of Jesus, knowing that he is 'the holy one of God',[37] 'the son of God'[38] and the 'son of the Most High'.[39]

JESUS THE HEALER

It is not always easy to draw the line between exorcism and healing in the Gospels, but for practical purposes the most reliable distinguishing factor appears to be the treatment adopted by Jesus in dealing with his patients. Exorcism is always effected by word of mouth alone, but with the exception of the verbal healing of a paralytic,[40] physical cures entail the performance of a rudimentary or occasionally complex rite.

Not counting allusions to mass healing in Capernaum,[41] by the lake-side,[42] and throughout Galilee, where people 'scoured that whole country-side and brought the sick on stretchers to any place where he was reported to be', and in 'farmsteads, villages, or towns', where 'they laid out the sick in the market-places';[43] leaving aside, also, the interesting remark that despite the unbelief of Nazareth, he still performed a few cures there,[44] the Gospels contain twelve particular healing narratives (some of them, however, thought to be duplicates).

Arranged according to illnesses, three refer to cures from blindness,[45] two from leprosy,[46] one each from fever,[47] haemorrhage,[48] a withered arm,[49] deaf-muteness,[50] paralysis,[51] lameness[52] and dropsy.[53]

In most cases the Gospels attest that there was some kind of bodily contact between the healer and the sick. Jesus practised the laying on of hands in Nazareth;[54] he did the same with the cripple woman;[55] he held Simon's mother-in-law by the hands;[56] he touched the leper[57] and the blind men,[58] and was touched by many sick persons[59] and by the woman suffering from haemorrhage.[60] In the last case, Jesus is said to have been aware that 'power had gone out of him'.[61]

In two accounts a ritual is performed privately. In the first, Jesus puts his finger into the ears of a deaf-mute, touches his tongue with saliva and gives the command, 'Be opened!'[62] In the second, the blind man from Bethsaida is cured after Jesus has spat into his eyes and laid his hand on him twice.[63]

It is not said how the man with dropsy was healed, or the ten lepers[64] – whether by means of contact or without it – but three instances are described in which a cure was performed without any exchange of touch between Jesus and the patient. In two of these the miracle is attributed to faith, namely in the healing of the blind beggar from Jericho[65] and that of the servant of the centurion from Capernaum.[66] In the second case, contact was physically impossible since the sick man lay paralysed in his home.

The method of healing by command alone – 'Stretch out your arm!' – is noteworthy since this is the only cure placed by the unanimous Synoptic tradition on a Sabbath day.[67] Speech could not be construed as 'work' infringing the law governing the Jewish day of rest.[68]

It should be added that with their powers of exorcism the twelve apostles also received the gift of healing. Their method of treatment was, however, the more conventional one of anointing the sick with oil,[69] although in the Acts of the Apostles reference is nevertheless made to healing by command and touch.[70]

OTHER MIRACLES

The accounts of the raising from the dead of Jairus's daughter, and of the son of the widow from Nain, scarcely differ from any ordinary healing. Jesus holds the hand of the girl who, in his opinion, was in any case not dead, and tells her in Aramaic to rise.[71] Similarly, he touches the young man's bier and orders him to stand.[72] It is worth remarking, even before the matter is discussed more thoroughly,[73] that Jesus is never depicted as a person concerned with defiling himself ritually through contact with a dead body. No one can be a healer and preserve himself from sickness and death, or an exorcist and be afraid of the devil.

Compared with the massive insistence of the Synoptists on the healing of mental and physical disease, other miracles assigned to Jesus are numerically insignificant. The calming of the storm on the Sea of Galilee,[74] and the feeding of a large crowd with a few loaves and fishes,[75] must be set beside other Jewish miracle tales of a similar kind.[76] Others appear to be secondary accretions: for example, the story of Jesus walking on the water by night,[77] the unexpectedly large catch of fish by Peter and his colleagues,[78] and that most convenient landing by the penniless Peter of a fish with a coin in its mouth of just the right value to allow him to pay the Temple-tax for himself and Jesus.[79]

JESUS THE TEACHER

From the outset the Gospels portray Jesus as a popular preacher and preserve various types of sayings ascribed to him. Some of these may have been handed down intact, but others are reformulations of the originals made by the early Church, and still others are actual interpolations devised to secure the authority deriving from the 'words of the lord' for beliefs in vogue at a subsequent stage of doctrinal development. It is not proposed at this moment even to try to extricate the authentic from the inauthentic, but simply to determine what kind of teacher Jesus was according to the evangelists. The enquiry will be concerned not so much with the contents as with the mode of his preaching, and the impression it left on sympathetic listeners.

Contrary to the Essene practice reserving instruction to initiates only,[80] but imitating John the Baptist, Jesus addressed his preaching in Galilee to all who had ears to hear – or rather, to all Jews with ears to hear, for he never envisaged a systematic mission to Gentiles.

'I was sent to the lost sheep of the house of Israel, and to them alone.'[81]

But even within Israel he preferred the uneducated, the poor, the sinners and the social outcasts.[82] All were called to repentance and told that God's rule over the world was imminent.

'The time has come; the kingdom of God is upon you; repent, and believe the Gospel.'[83]

His ethical message was also aimed at all and sundry, as were also his parables, a form of homiletic teaching commonly used by rabbinic preachers. That he employed them to conceal the meaning of his message[84] is a contorted and tendentious explanation. Non-Jews unaccustomed to Palestinian teaching methods must have found some of them difficult to comprehend, but it would have been they, and not Jesus' direct disciples, who would have needed every detail of a similitude to be spelled out.

The equally traditional Jewish method of preaching in the form of Bible interpretation is less frequently attested in the Gospels, though this may be accidental. Nevertheless, if Jesus was primarily a teacher of morals, he might be expected to have shown a liking for short, pithy, colourful utterances, the kind of rabbinic *logia* with which the pages of the *Sayings of the Fathers* in the Mishnah are filled. He several times taught in synagogues[85] and once delivered the liturgical sermon after reading the prophetic lesson of the day in Nazareth.[86]

Did the preaching of Jesus differ from that of his contemporaries? Yes, the evangelists assert, in so far as, unlike the doctors of the Law, he spoke with authority.[87] New Testament commentators usually see in this a contrast between Jesus' method of teaching and the rabbis' habit of handing down a legally binding doctrine in the name of the master from whom they learned it, which was held to derive from a chain of tradition traceable (ideally) back to Moses. Jesus, however, was no expert in Jewish law, and it is therefore misleading to compare his style of instruction to that of later rabbinic academies. It is more probable that people saw the exorcisms and cures as confirmation of Jesus' teaching. For instance, it was when moved by amazement at his expulsion of a demon that his listeners cried out:

'What is this? A new kind of teaching! He speaks with authority. When he gives orders, even the unclean spirits submit.'[88]

This interpretation appears clearly preferable to that opposing the 'scribal' authority of the rabbis to the 'prophetic' authority of Jesus.[89]

If he adopted a personal style of teaching, was his doctrine itself a novelty? Did he reject or contradict any of the basic beliefs of Judaism? Discounting passages which represent him as speaking lightly of certain non-scriptural customs held to be highly important by other teachers, or as interpreting a biblical verse in a sense different from that habitually ascribed to it there still remains one crucial text apparently showing him 'at variance with his inherited Judaism',[90] namely, that concerned with clean and unclean food.[91]

The argument originates in a complaint lodged by Pharisees that the disciples of Jesus fail to conform to the tradition of ritual hand-washing before meals, the implication being that dirty hands can render food unclean and so cause defilement. Judging from his reply in Matthew, Jesus thought the whole matter of external cleanness trivial compared with moral uncleanness.

> 'Whatever goes in by the mouth passes into the stomach and so is discharged into the drain. But what comes out of the mouth has its origins in the heart; and that is what defiles a man. Wicked thoughts, murder, adultery . . . perjury, slander . . .'[92]

In Mark, however, the text is so modified that it is scarcely possible to avoid the conclusion that Jesus rejected the basic Jewish dietary law.

> 'Do you not see that nothing that goes from outside into a man can defile him, because it does not enter into his heart but into his stomach, and so passes out into the drain?' *Thus he declared all foods clean.*[93]

But if the disciples understood Jesus' words in this sense, why did they, and especially Peter, who put the question to Jesus and was answered by him, react so strongly against the possibility of eating forbidden, non-kosher food? For when the chief of the apostles is ordered in a vision by a heavenly voice to eat every kind of meat, instead of exclaiming, 'Of course, I now remember the words of the lord!' he expresses shock and indignation.[94] Paul, too, might have been expected to have appealed to his lord's recommendation when he himself set aside Jewish cere-monial laws.[95]

In the circumstances it is reasonable to ask whether a phrase meaningful in Aramaic can be discerned beneath the Marcan Greek gloss, 'Thus he declared all foods clean' (literally, 'purifying all foods'). It has already been suggested that the word 'food' is employed metaphorically for 'excrement',[96] but to this it should be added that a possible polite term for latrine, 'the place' (*dukha*), might invite a pun on the verb 'to be clean' (*dekha*): '. . . it does not enter into his heart but into his stomach, and so passes out into "the place" where all excrement "is purged away" . . .' This hypothetical exegesis is indirectly supported by the oldest available Semitic version of Mark, the so-called Sinaitic recension of the Syriac Gospel. Sensing, as it were, the play on words underlying the Greek text, the translator replaces 'drain' with the euphemism 'purge' and renders the phrase: '. . . it goes into his belly and is cast into the purge which purges away all food.'[97]

If this interpretation is accepted, the one apparent doctrinal conflict between Jesus and Judaism is due to a deliberate twist given to a probably genuine saying of Jesus by the redactor of the Greek Mark. By that time Gentile Christianity needed and wel-comed a formal ratification in the teaching of the Gospel of the Church's abandonment of the laws and customs of Israel.[98]

ATTITUDES AND REACTIONS TO JESUS

Exorcist, healer and itinerant preacher, Jesus is portrayed by the Synoptists as a person towards whom his contemporaries rarely, if ever, remained indifferent. Their reactions were by no means always favourable, but on the other hand, they were not generally hostile either.

A small group of devotees, simple Galilean folk, joined him from the beginning – 'after John had been arrested'[99] – and became his travelling companions. The Twelve, an even smaller group, were later chosen to be his disciples *par excellence*.[100] So impressed were they by his powerful personality that they left everything to follow him – work, possessions and family.[101] Yet, heroic though they may have become after Jesus' death, consecrating themselves whole-heartedly to the continuation of his lifework, they are not depicted in the Gospels as particularly quick at understanding the mind and preaching of their master while he was alive,[102] or brave at the time of his ordeal, when they all deserted him.[103] They remained in hiding, in fact, for nearly two months before their first reported reappearance in public.[104]

Among the Galilean crowds Jesus was a great success. Large groups formed and accompanied him when the rumour went round that he was on his way to heal the sick,[105] or simply when he travelled.[106] He preached to multitudes in Capernaum and by the lake-side,[107] and soon acquired such a renown that he 'could no longer show himself in any town, but stayed outside in the open country'.[108]

Although his fame apparently also aroused curiosity outside Galilee,[109] he is not described as a welcome visitor in non-Jewish areas. The inhabitants of Gerasa requested him to leave their country,[110] and as a Jew travelling to Jerusalem he is represented as a *persona non grata* in Samaria.[111] As for Judea, only two cities are said by the Synoptic Gospels – which allude to no more than one brief journey to the southern province – to have surrounded Jesus with great numbers: Jericho[112] and Jerusalem. In two out of three Marcan passages, however, the Jerusalem multitude is found in the precincts of the Temple, i.e. a place where immediately before Passover large groups of people would have gathered irrespective of whether Jesus was there or not.[113] Mark's third story, that of the triumphal entry into Jerusalem, tells of 'many' carpeting the road with their cloaks,[114] and the Matthean parallel refers to 'crowds of people'.[115] Luke, on the other hand, is positive, and this time presumably correct, in attributing the entire happy and noisy welcome, not to the Jerusalem crowd, but to 'the whole company of his disciples'.[116] Whichever way this story is interpreted, the evangelists clearly convey the impression that the popularity of Jesus in Judea and Jerusalem did not match that which he enjoyed in his own country.

JESUS AND JOHN THE BAPTIST

The true relationship between Jesus and his associates, and the company led by John the Baptist, is more difficult to determine. The aim of the Gospel writers was, no doubt, to give an impression of friendship and mutual esteem, but their attempts smack of superficiality and closer scrutiny of the admittedly fragmentary evidence suggests that, at least on the level of their respective disciples, sentiments of rivalry between the two groups were not absent.

That Jesus went to be baptized by John is enough to prove the Baptist's initial impact on him. Mark has little further to say on the matter except to draw a distinction between the two religious circles,[117] and to report the curious belief, shared by the Tetrarch Herod and others, that Jesus was a kind of reincarnation of John, a John *redivivus*.[118] Together with the other Synoptists, he also relates a polemic between Jesus and the chief priests, lawyers and elders regarding the origin, divine or human, of John's baptism in which neither party openly discloses its mind.[119]

Matthew and Luke, in contrast to Mark, put into words John's feelings towards Jesus, as well as those of Jesus towards the Baptist. At their first encounter, according to these two evangelists, John recognizes Jesus' superiority.[120] Later, when he is imprisoned, he is depicted as having despatched two of his pupils to ask for formal admission from Jesus that he was 'the one who is to come', or that some other person was still to be expected.[121] Jesus, busy with healing, was unwilling to give a straight reply and his return message takes the form of a free quotation from various verses of Isaiah, all announcing cure and consolation.[122]

Jesus, for his part, proclaims John as the greatest in the long series of Israelite prophets, the one in whom the words of Malachi have come true, i.e. the returning Elijah, the precursor of the Messiah.[123] At the same time, he is also reported to have said that though John may have been the greatest of men, 'the least in the kingdom of heaven is greater than he'.[124]

It is on the interpretation of this remark by Jesus, and of the Baptist's enquiry concerning Jesus' role, that a correct assessment of the non-Marcan material concerning the two men depends.

For – supposing it to be historically conceivable that messengers were sent to Jesus by the imprisoned John, with the attendant implications of a rather enlightened jail administration under Herod Antipas, visiting hours, and an open line of communication with the outside world – what can be the meaning of 'Are you the one who is to come, or are we to expect some other?'[125] Since, it should be stressed, the question was put after the news of 'what Christ was doing' had reached the Baptist[126] – who, according to Matthew, had acknowledged Jesus' role when he baptized him – the words quoted are bound to express doubt: the Messiah is expected to do better than heal and exorcise, so if you are he, make haste and prove it. Jesus avoids the implied query, reasserts his healing mission, and indirectly reproaches those whose faith in him was small:

> 'Happy is the man who does not find me a stumbling-block!'[127]

The apparent sting in the tail of Jesus' praise of John – 'the least in the kingdom of heaven is greater than he' – has baffled many an interpreter. Some have seen in it a contrast between the future glory of the elect, and John's greatness on earth. Others identify 'the kingdom' as the realm of the spirit resulting from the ministry of Jesus and belonging to a higher sphere than the world of the Baptist. Others still understand the phrase, 'the least in the kingdom', as a description of Jesus as the servant of God. The first two interpretations are too theological for serious consideration by a historian, but the third is plausible at least as far as its acceptance as a reference to Jesus is concerned. The Servant concept itself becomes less relevant when it is recalled that in Aramaic and Hebrew the phrase, 'the least one', 'the smallest one', can be used in the chronological sense to designate the youngest or last person in a series. In the belief of the evangelists, Jesus was God's ultimate envoy, and although it is by no means sure that the words are his own, their significance is: John was very great, but I am greater.

If this explanation is right, it may be inferred that the disciples of Jesus unhesitatingly asserted their master's pre-eminence over John. An echo to this mood of rivalry in the Gospels makes itself heard in the apostles' attempt to silence an outsider who dared to cast out demons in Jesus' name,[128] as well as in the complaint of John's followers, preserved only in the Fourth Gospel, that baptism by Jesus is improper and disrespectful towards their teacher.[129]

The conflict arising from Jesus' admiration for the Baptist, and the jealousy of the two groups of disciples, is resolved in the compromise that John, recognized as the precursor, acknowledges the superiority of Jesus at the time of his baptism, or, better still, when they are both in their mothers' wombs.[130] Yet it is interesting to notice that, in contrast to this laboured insistence on the precedence of Jesus over John, Mark is satisfied with a straightforward presentation of Jesus as John's successor, without discussing their relationship beyond the exegesis, by implication, of Isaiah 40: 3: 'Prepare a road for the Lord through the wilderness, clear a highway across the desert for our God.'[131]

CRITICS AND OPPONENTS OF JESUS

As an exceptional and controversial religious teacher, it was inevitable that Jesus should encounter criticism and hostility as well as respect and love, but strangely enough, the first opposition came from those closest to him, his family and fellow-citizens in Nazareth. When his relatives heard of his cures, exorcism and preaching, they set off to take hold of him, for they said:

'He is out of his mind.'[132]

The scandalous incongruity of this statement is the best guarantee of its historicity, and the Marcan variant, 'For people were saying that he was out of his mind', as well as the absence of Synoptic parallels, are no doubt due to an early 'censorship' tendency in the evolving Christian tradition. Moreover, it is difficult not to see it as a preliminary to the fuller account, a few verses later, of the arrival of Jesus' mother and brothers at the house where he was teaching, their summons that he should join them, and Jesus' subsequent retort that the greater family of those who do the will of God had first claim to his presence.[133]

Whatever the actual outcome of this apparent refusal to submit to his family's control, no further contact is mentioned in the Synoptics between them and Jesus. It is to remedy this unfortunate impression that the Fourth Gospel expressly depicts Mary as her son's first convert, at the wedding feast in Cana,[134] and as standing at the last beside him at the cross.[135] Luke, too, finds Jesus' mother and brothers in the company of the apostles after the Ascension.[136] The family may, of course, have changed its mind at a later stage and made common cause with the disciples; it is in fact a historically reliable tradition that James, 'the brother of the lord', became the head of the Jerusalem Church.[137]

If his immediate kin were shocked by his behaviour, it is not surprising that friends and neighbours were also scandalized.[138] No one is prophet in his own town, Jesus is reported to have commented philosophically,[139] though he was taken aback by their want of faith.[140] Nevertheless, the Lucan story of an attempted lynching is probably an exaggeration.[141]

This unsympathetic reception of Jesus in Nazareth may explain his rhetorical disparagement of the ties of nature compared with those which bound men to him, and through him, to God. Happy the womb that carried him! cried a woman admirer, and was corrected, 'No, happy are those who hear the word of God.'[142] On another occasion he was even more direct:

> 'He who loves father or mother more than me is not worthy of me.'[143]

The conflict between Jesus and the representatives of authority on doctrinal and politico-religious grounds requires several preliminary remarks. Firstly, the identity of the opponents is often unclear because the sources are contradictory regarding them. For instance, the protagonists in what appears to be the same event are described by Mark as Pharisees and Herodians, by Matthew as Pharisees only, and by Luke as lawyers and Pharisees.[144] Secondly, interpretative tradition, both scholarly and popular, is too easily inclined to equate Pharisees, scribes and lawyers, but since Mark and Luke expressly refer to the lawyers of the Pharisees, it would follow that those not so described were not necessarily members of that party.[145] Thirdly, in the various accounts of the plot which led to the arrest of Jesus and his surrender to Pilate for trial and execution, the Pharisees as a class play no part.[146] Lastly, the struggle with the chief priests and elders, and probably with the Sadducees too, is confined to Jerusalem.[147]

As far as basic Jewish beliefs are concerned, the only serious clash reported in the Gospels between Jesus and the established authority finds him opposing the Sadducees in their denial of the resurrection of the dead.[148] Here, as well as in the identification of the greatest commandment – love of God and one's fellow-men – Jesus is represented as sharing the outlook and winning the approval of the Pharisees.[149] Yet it would be a gross overstatement to portray him as a Pharisee himself. Indeed, in regard to those customs which they invested with a quasi-absolute value, but which to him were secondary to biblical commandments, a head-on collision was unavoidable. Jesus ate with sinners and did not condemn those who sat down to table with unwashed hands or pulled corn on the Sabbath.[150] The lawyers who accuse him of blasphemy because of his promise to forgive sins, and those who suggest that his exorcistic power is due to his association with the devil, need not have been Pharisees.[151] The only other person said to have raised a charge of blasphemy against Jesus was the Sadducean high priest during the trial, although the words attributed to Jesus cannot, in fact, be construed as such by virtue of any known Jewish law, biblical or post-biblical. According to the Mishnah, only the misuse of the Tetragram, the sacrosanct name of God, constitutes blasphemy,[152] and no accusation is levelled against Jesus in this respect. Also, even if it could be ascertained that he claimed to be the Messiah or the son of God, there are no grounds for seeing blasphemy in this, or any other capital crime.[153]

There is little doubt that the Pharisees disliked his non-conformity and would have preferred him to have abstained from healing on the Sabbath where life was not in danger.[154] They obviously enjoyed embarrassing him with testing questions, such as whether tax should be paid to Rome.[155] An affirmative answer would have outraged Jewish patriots, and a denial would have been synonymous with preaching rebellion.[156] But Jesus himself was not above employing the same methods:[157] indeed, they were an integral part of polemical argument at that time. There is no evidence, however, of an active and organized participation on the part of the Pharisees in the planning and achievement of Jesus' downfall.

ARREST AND EXECUTION OF JESUS

The Synoptic Gospels know of two main plots to put an end to Jesus' activities: one in Galilee, which failed, and one in Jerusalem, which resulted in the cross. Probably, some individual Pharisees bore a measure of responsibility for this, but in both cases the principal, and certainly the ultimate, guilt lay with the representatives of the political establishment – Herod Antipas and his supporters in Galilee, and the chief priests and Pilate in the capital.[158]

Whether there was a trial of Jesus by the supreme Jewish court of Judea in Jerusalem on a religious charge, and a subsequent capital sentence pronounced and forwarded for confirmation and execution by the secular arm, remains historically more than dubious, as Paul Winter has shown in his magisterial study of the subject.[159] If such a trial did take place, and if it were possible to reconstruct its proceedings from the discrepant, and often contradictory reports of the Gospels, the only justifiable conclusion would be that in a single session the Sanhedrin managed to break every rule in the book: it would, in other words, have been an illegal trial. Yet even those who are able to believe that a real trial occurred are compelled to admit that when the chief priests transferred the case from their court to Pontius Pilate's tribunal, they did not ask for their findings to be confirmed, but laid a fresh charge before the prefect of Judea, namely that Jesus was a political agitator with pretensions to being the king of the Jews.[160] It was not on a Jewish religious indictment, but on a secular accusation that he was condemned by the emperor's delegate to die shamefully on the Roman cross.

THE RESURRECTION OF JESUS

Although founded on evidence which can only be described as confused and fragile, belief in the resurrection of Jesus became an increasingly important, and finally central, issue in the post-Synoptic and especially post-Marcan stage of doctrinal evolution. This development is all the more astonishing since the idea of bodily resurrection played no part of any significance in the preaching of Jesus. Moreover, his disciples did not expect him to arise from the dead any more than their contemporaries expected the Messiah to do so.[161]

All in all, taking into account the disciples' despair after the tragedy in Jerusalem, and their startled incredulity on hearing from their women of the empty tomb, the historian is bound to query whether Jesus in fact prepared them for this extraordinary happening by repeatedly foretelling that he would rise again precisely on the third day. Admittedly, Mark and Matthew make room for five separate announcements by Jesus of his suffering, death and resurrection, but it is generally held even by academic orthodoxy that the references to the resurrection at least constitute prophecy after the event.[162]

It is probably to reconcile this inconsistency between lack of expectation and clear prediction that the evangelists clumsily remark that the apostles could not understand Jesus. Peter rebukes him and is called Satan; they argue about the sense of 'rising from the dead'; they do not grasp what he says and are too frightened to ask; they are filled with grief or utterly bewildered.[163] However, the illogicality disappears if the announcement of the passion alone, without the resurrection, is considered authentic, i.e. the form of the saying preserved in Luke 9: 44:

'The son of man is to be given up into the power of men.'

A frightening statement such as this might well provoke an instinctive rebuke from Peter and explain the bewilderment and sorrow of the disciples.

A further point to take into consideration is that despite Luke and Paul, and the Creed, the resurrection of Jesus 'according to the Scriptures' cannot be seen as a logical necessity within the framework of Israel's prophetic heritage because, as has been indicated, neither the suffering of the Messiah, nor his death and resurrection, appear to have been part of the faith of first-century Judaism.

Following these somewhat disconcerting preliminaries, what exactly do the Gospels yield by way of factual evidence? What light do they throw on how the earliest traditions developed?

The main Gospel narrative reports seven events subsequent to the death of Jesus.

(1) Joseph of Arimathea deposits the body of Jesus in a rock tomb, which he closes with a rolling stone.[164]

(2) On the third day, at dawn, two, three, or several women, find the stone rolled back.[165]

(3) They enter and see a young man (Mark), or two men (Luke), wearing white garments, or an angel (Matthew), sitting (Mark, Matthew), or standing (Luke), in the tomb.[166]

(4) According to Matthew and Luke, but not Mark, they are frightened.[167]

(5) The women are told that Jesus has been raised from the dead and they are shown where his body has rested.[168]

(6) They are further instructed to convey a message to the disciples that Jesus is on his way to Galilee where he will be seen as already arranged. According to Luke, the women are reminded of a prediction made by Jesus in Galilee concerning his passion and suddenly remember.[169]

(7) Their reactions are described differently in each Gospel. They return and report the news (Luke); they run with awe and

joy to make their announcement (Matthew); they rush away from the tomb, beside themselves with terror, saying nothing to anybody (Mark).[170]

The oldest manuscripts of Mark's Gospel end at this point, but Matthew and Luke go on to record several appearances made by Jesus to the women, to two disciples travelling to Emmaus, to Peter and the company in Jerusalem, and to the eleven apostles on a Galilean mountain.[171] It is in these stories that modern New Testament scholars, relying on Matthew and Luke, and especially on the tradition handed down by Paul,[172] find the primary source of faith in the resurrection of Jesus; in their opinion, the narrative concerning the empty tomb is 'completely secondary', an 'apologetic legend' intended to 'prove the reality of the resurrection of Jesus'.[173] This explanation is nevertheless open to serious criticism. Mark, which besides being the most ancient of the Synoptic Gospels is also doctrinally the least developed, alludes to no actual apparition, but is content to present as the somewhat embarrassing basis for belief in the resurrection the evidence of two women that they heard from a white-robed youth that the body was missing from the tomb because Jesus had been raised from the dead.

There is one point in this episode on which Mark and the other Synoptists insist, namely that the tomb found empty on that Sunday morning was the one in which the body of Jesus had been placed on the previous Friday. The women did not go to the wrong grave because having followed Joseph of Arimathea they knew the site of the burial place.

Mark and Matthew are categorical and Luke is even more emphatic:

> Mary of Magdala and Mary the mother of Joseph . . . saw where he was laid.[174]

> Mary of Magdala was there, and the other Mary, sitting opposite the grave.[175]

> The women . . . took note of the tomb and observed how his body was laid.[176]

A hostile version, namely that the disciples deliberately removed the body of Jesus, is recorded by Matthew. To neutralize this accusation, he introduces the story of the guards placed by the Sanhedrin near the tomb who fainted when the angel descended in the middle of the earthquake to remove the stone, but later spread the news – after a substantial bribe from the chief priests – that while they slept his followers had come by night and stolen the body.[177]

The Fourth Gospel preserves a tradition to the effect that the body was taken out of its original burial place and interred somewhere else by people unconnected with Jesus' party. Mistaking Jesus for 'the gardener', Mary of Magdala is supposed to have asked:

'If it is you, sir, who removed him, tell me where you have laid him, and I will take him away.'[178]

From these various records two reasonably convincing points emerge, one positive and the other negative. First, the women belonging to the entourage of Jesus discovered an empty tomb and were definite that it was *the* tomb. Second, the rumour that the apostles stole that body is most improbable. From the psychological point of view, they would have been too depressed and shaken to be capable of such a dangerous undertaking. But above all, since neither they nor anyone else expected a resurrection, there would have been no purpose in faking one.

It is preferable not to speculate on the disappearance of the body of Jesus during the earthquake mentioned in Matthew for it may have been more imaginary than real, a literary cliché indicating the presence of the supernatural. It is equally pointless to conjecture what part an uninvolved or hostile outsider such as 'the gardener' might have played.

The corollary must be, curious though this may sound, that for the historian it is Mark's evidence, the weakest of all, that possesses the best claim for authenticity, the story brought by two women which – to quote Luke – the apostles themselves thought such 'nonsense' that they would not believe it.[179]

Christian tradition has tried to improve the argument. Luke

and John introduce two male witnesses to check the women's report,[180] but this is still not enough. The closest approach to first-hand evidence is the testimony of several trustworthy men who assert that Jesus appeared to them – to the Twelve, to all the apostles, and to over five hundred brethren, in addition to the leaders of the Church, Peter and James.[181] It is their collective conviction of having seen their dead teacher alive, combined with the initial discovery of the empty tomb, that provides the substance for faith in Jesus' rising from the dead.

A final comment, as it were in parenthesis. In addition to the usual concept of resurrection, another notion appears to have existed in Galilee in New Testament times. Already in the Bible, Elisha is said to have inherited a double share of the spirit of Elijah.[182] In the Gospels, John the Baptist and Jesus are both described as Elijah *redivivus*, and Jesus is believed by some to be the risen John the Baptist, or the reincarnation of Jeremiah or one of the old prophets.[183]

It is conceivable that a belief of this sort prevailing among those who continued Jesus' ministry, including healing and exorcism, had a retroactive effect on the formation of the resurrection preaching, and liberal historians have long since seen the 'real Easter miracle', not in a changed Jesus, but in metamorphosed disciples.[184]

But in the end, when every argument has been considered and weighed, the only conclusion acceptable to the historian must be that the opinions of the orthodox, the liberal sympathizer and the critical agnostic alike – and even perhaps of the disciples themselves – are simply interpretations of the one disconcerting fact: namely that the women who set out to pay their last respects to Jesus found to their consternation, not a body, but an empty tomb.

2. Jesus and Galilee

It is generally agreed that, whilst maintaining a definite interest in time, space and circumstance, the Synoptists did not aim to write history proper. Although they adopted the biographical literary form, their life of Jesus was intended principally as a vehicle for the preaching of the early Church. In consequence, however brilliantly analysed, the Gospels cannot be expected to provide more than a skeletal outline of Jesus of Nazareth as he really was.

Is it nevertheless possible to add a little flesh to these bare bones? The answer is that it may be done if, as has been remarked in the Introduction, the Jewish parallel material is used in the right manner and spirit. Instead of treating Jewish literature as an ancillary to the New Testament, the present approach will attempt the contrary, namely to fit Jesus and his movement into the greater context of first-century AD Palestine. If such an immersion in historical reality confers credibility on the Gospel picture, and the patchy portrait drawn by the evangelists begins suddenly to look, sound and feel true, this enquiry will have attained its primary objective.[1]

Within such a plan of reintegration and the corresponding work of detection that it entails, which aspects of Palestinian history and religion are most relevant? First, to reanimate Jesus, his natural background, first-century Galilee, must be filled in. Second, to perceive the truth and purpose of his mission as an exorcist and healer, it must be reinstated in the place to which it belongs: that is, in the charismatic stream of post-biblical Judaism.

At first sight the reinsertion of Jesus into the Galilean Judaism of his day would appear to be not only reasonable and necessary, but also easy, since it is justifiable to suppose that the subject must be familiar to scholars versed in post-biblical Jewish literature. Galilee, after all, produced from the second century AD onwards all the essentials of rabbinic religion: the Mishnah, which is the fundamental code of Jewish laws and customs, its extensive commentary, the Palestinian Talmud, and the earliest interpretative works on the Pentateuch. Nevertheless, an indiscriminate use of these writings for the reconstruction of the atmosphere in which Jesus lived would be mistaken and create utter confusion. For although it was formulated in the province, the real inspiration of rabbinic Judaism was of Judean provenance. More precisely, its source was Jerusalem. Galilee's regional identity was deeply affected by the influx of leading Judean rabbis who managed to survive the Bar Kosiba rebellion against the Roman empire of Hadrian (AD 132–5) and its aftermath, and were compelled by imperial legislation to settle in the North. When the academy of Jamnia (Yavneh) – established by Yohanan ben Zakkai after the Temple was destroyed – was moved around AD 140 to the small town of Usha, about ten miles from Haifa, the place became another Jerusalem; but the Torah propagated from this new Zion under the supervision of the Patriarch, the officially recognized head of all the Jews resident in the Roman empire, was Galilean only by accident.

THE HISTORY OF GALILEE

A much more reliable picture of the Galilee of Jesus is reflected in the writings of Flavius Josephus who, as rebel commander-in-chief of the Northern region during the first Jewish War (AD 66–70), possessed a first-hand knowledge of it. Clearly, it was a territory *sui generis*. Not only did it have its own peculiar past, but its political, social and economic organization also contributed to distinguish it from the rest of Palestine. The conflict between Jesus and the religious and secular authority outside Galilee was at least in part due to the fact that he was, and was known to have been, a Galilean.

Geographically this northernmost district of Palestine was a little island in the midst of unfriendly seas. Westwards it was bordered by the country of Ptolemais (Acre) and the originally Galilean Mount Carmel, both largely populated by Gentiles. To the north were the Syro-Phoenician Tyre, Sidon and their dependencies. On its eastern boundary lay the equally heathen Gaulanitis, Hippos and Gadara. And even in the south it was separated from Judea by the Hellenistic territory of Scythopolis (Beth Shean), and the whole hostile province of Samaria. In consequence, although Transjordan, or Perea, shared the same government as Galilee during the New Testament period, the fact remains that to a large degree the province constituted an autonomous and self-contained politico-ethnic unit.

Its overwhelming Jewishness was a relatively recent phenomenon. In the eighth century BC the prophet Isaiah wrote of the 'District (*Gelil*) of the Gentiles',[2] the phrase from which the name Galilee derives. The colonization of the conquered Northern kingdom of Israel by Mesopotamian peoples[3] can hardly have altered this situation though, clearly, Israelite occupation never ceased altogether. The Jewish minority nevertheless came under such pagan pressure at the time of the outbreak of the Maccabean rebellion, that Simon Maccabaeus, having brought temporary relief by defeating the local Gentiles and their outside allies, decided on a drastic rescue bid and removed the whole of Galilean Jewry to Judea.[4]

The refugees no doubt returned to their homes after the final Maccabean triumph, but it was not until the very end of the second century BC (104–103 BC) that Northern Galilee and its adjacent districts were annexed to the Maccabean-Hasmonean realm as a result of the victory of Aristobulus I over Iturea.[5] Josephus also reports an ultimatum issued by the victors to the vanquished that their presence would only be tolerated if they were prepared to 'be circumcised and to live in accordance with the laws of the Jews'.[6]

In regard to the governmental systems in force in Roman

Palestine during the first half of the first Christian century, the province of Galilee possessed an administrative machine distinct from that of Judea, a fact that cannot have failed to reinforce Galilean self-awareness. After the banishment of Archelaus to Vienna in Gaul in AD 6, the ephemeral rule of Judea by a Herodian ethnarch was replaced by a direct Roman take-over. Following the census ordered in the same year by Publius Sulpicius Quirinius of Gospel fame, the legate of Syria, a Roman knight, Coponius, was appointed prefect of Judea, and as such, made directly responsible to the emperor for the military, financial and judicial administration of the region.[7] Thus, despite the real power still possessed by the Sanhedrin and the aristocratic chief priests and Temple officials, Judea could not help but be humiliated by the presence of imperial Rome.

Galilee was spared this outrage altogether. From 4 BC until AD 39 – throughout the whole life of Jesus – it was administered, together with Perea, by a Herodian tetrarch, Antipas, and after him by a king, Agrippa I (AD 39–44). Rome did not appear on the scene except between AD 44 and 66, and even then the region of Lake Tiberias came under the jurisdiction of Agrippa II between AD 54 and 66. The Herodians were the native aristocracy of the province, and in addition the administrators of the 204 cities and villages of Upper and Lower Galilee and of the Valley, i.e. the Tiberias region,[8] such as the *archon* (chief official) Jairus, described as president of the synagogue (the two functions being the same),[9] were Galileans, as were the tax-collectors whose duty it was to fill the tetrarch's, not the emperor's, treasury.

No direct evidence points to a Galilean senate and high court similar to the Jerusalem Sanhedrin, the principal legal, political and religious institution of Judea, but the council (*synedrion*) set up by the proconsul Gabinius in 57 BC in Sepphoris, the capital of Galilee,[10] may be presumed to have continued until Herodian times, or to have been reinstituted then. It can, in fact, hardly be a coincidence that the Galilean magistrates drawn by Josephus into his military government during the first revolt were, like the members of the Judean Sanhedrin, precisely seventy in number.[11]

The Galilee of Jesus was populous and relatively wealthy. 'Never did the men lack courage nor the country men', writes Josephus.[12] The reason for its economic well-being was the extraordinary fertility of the land and the full use made of it by its people. As Josephus describes it, it is 'so rich in soil and pasturage and produces such variety of trees, that even the most indolent are tempted by these facilities to devote themselves to agriculture'. Although smaller than Perea, its resources were greater, 'for it is entirely under cultivation and produces crops from one end to the other'.[13] One of its products was olive oil, which was exported in large quantities to Jews in Syria, Babylonia, Media, Egypt and Cappadocia, Diaspora regions lacking in this important commodity.[14] This rich farming industry, together with the fishing on the Lake, and employment in the usual crafts demanded by everyday life,[15] gave Galilee a self-sufficiency which, with the legacy of its history and the unsophisticated simplicity of its life, is likely to have nourished the pride and independence of its inhabitants.

GALILEAN REBELS

From the middle of the last pre-Christian century it was the most troublesome of all Jewish districts. Simon Dubnov exaggerates only slightly when he writes:

> From Galilee stemmed all the revolutionary movements which so disturbed the Romans.[16]

In fact, if the identification of Judas the son of Ezekias as Judas of Gamala, known as Judas the Galilean, is correct,[17] the main inspiration of the whole Zealot agitation sprang from the same rebellious Galilean family.

Ezekias, described as a 'chief brigand', was the patriarch of the revolutionaries who in the middle of the first century BC ravaged Upper Galilee. Captured and summarily executed in about 47 BC by the young Herod, the then governor of Galilee,[18] his activities were carried on by his son Judas, a man with royal aspirations, who when Herod died broke into the king's arsenal in Sepphoris in 4 BC and 'became an object of terror to all men'.[19] Ten years

later this same Judas surnamed 'the Galilean' incited his com-
patriots to revolt at the time of the census, enjoining them to pay
no taxes to Rome and, in general, to recognize no foreign masters.
With a Pharisee named Zadok, he thus became the co-founder
not only of a band of agitators, but also of a politico-religious
party, that of the Zealots.[20] Some forty years later still, during
his procuratorship of Judea from AD 46 to 48, the wholly Roman-
ized Tiberius Julius Alexander, nephew of the Jewish philosopher
Philo of Alexandria, tried and sentenced to crucifixion two of
Judas the Galilean's sons, Jacob and Simon.[21] His last surviving
offspring, Menahem, captured from the Romans the stronghold
of Masada and attempted, in AD 66, at the beginning of the first
Jewish War, to assert his supreme authority among the rebels by
entering the Temple in royal apparel. However, he and most of
his followers died in the feud which raged at that time between
the various revolutionary factions in Jerusalem.[22] One of those
who escaped the massacre was another descendant of Judas the
Galilean. This was a nephew of Menahem, Eleazar, the son of
Jairus, the legendary captain of Masada, who at the head of a
few hundred Zealots continued resistance against Rome for four
years after the fall of Jerusalem.[23]

The struggle against the Empire was nevertheless not just a
family business, but a full-scale Galilean activity in the first
century AD. Those pilgrims whose blood Pontius Pilate mingled
with their sacrifices must have been Galilean revolutionaries,[24]
and it was again a group of Galileans who, in AD 49, urged the
Jewish masses in Jerusalem to resort to arms, assert their liberty,
and reject the intolerable slavery imposed on them by Rome.[25]
Furthermore, one of the bloodiest leaders of the AD 66–70 war
was John the son of Levi from Gischala (*Gush Halab*) in Upper
Galilee.[26] He and his supporters, 'the Galilean contingent',
acquired particular notoriety in besieged Jerusalem for their
'mischievous ingenuity and audacity'.[27] Thus, all in all, it is not
surprising that to the first-century AD Palestinian establishment
the word 'Galilean' ceased merely to refer to a particular geographical area and took on the dark political connotation of a
possible association with Judas the Galilean.[28] Even the Mishnah's

'Galilean heretic' is an extreme nationalist who reproaches the Pharisees for including the name of the emperor in the dating of a Jewish legal document, a bill of divorce.[29]

Staunch nationalists and lovers of freedom who, in Josephus's words, had 'always resisted any hostile invasion' and were 'from infancy inured to war',[30] the Galileans according to rabbinic evidence were also quarrelsome and aggressive among themselves;[31] though even their critics admitted that, in contrast to the Judeans who 'cared for their wealth more than for their glory', they preferred honour to financial gain.[32]

GALILEE AND THE GOSPELS

Furnished with this largely contemporary information concerning Galilee and its inhabitants, it is now possible to see the extent to which the Jesus of the Gospels conforms to the specifically Galilean type. He is to begin with an appreciative child of the Galilean countryside. The metaphors placed in his mouth are mostly agricultural ones, as would be expected from a man who spent the major part of his life among farmers and peasants. For him the ultimate beauty is that of the lilies of the field, and the paradigm of wickedness the sowing of weeds in a cornfield, even in one belonging to an enemy.[33] The city and its life occupy scarcely any place at all in his teaching. It is in fact remarkable that there is no mention whatever in the Gospels of any of the larger Galilean towns. Jesus for example is never seen in Sepphoris, the chief city and only four miles distant from Nazareth, or in other regional centres such as Gabara (Araba) or Tarichaeae.[34] The Synoptic Gospels do not even refer to Tiberias, the new town built on the lake-side by Herod Antipas and quite close to the heart of Jesus' ministry.[35] By contrast, Jesus' 'own town' Capernaum,[36] the place which saw most of his activity, is definitely mentioned only once in the entire writings of Josephus; in an idyllic description of the rich district of Lake Gennesaret, he alludes to a 'highly fertilizing spring, called by the inhabitants Capharnaum'![37] Nevertheless this place Capernaum, and the slightly better known, but not much more important, townlet of Bethsaida (Julias), and Corazin – unmentioned by Josephus – were the 'cities' of Jesus. At heart, he was a real *campagnard*. At home among the simple people of rural Galilee, he must have felt quite alien in Jerusalem.

It may have been Galilean chauvinism that was responsible for Jesus' apparent antipathy towards Gentiles. For not only did he feel himself sent to the Jews alone;[38] he qualified non-Jews, though no doubt with oratorical exaggeration, as 'dogs' and 'swine'.[39] When the man from Gerasa (one of the ten Transjordanian pagan cities) whom he had freed from demonic possession begged to be allowed into his fellowship, Jesus replied with a categorical refusal:

'Go home to your own folk . . .'[40]

Moreover, the twelve apostles charged with proclaiming the Gospel were expressly forbidden to do so either to Gentiles or to Samaritans.[41] The authenticity of these sayings must be well-nigh impregnable, taking into account their shocking inappropriateness in an internationally open Church. The attitude that inspired them was in any case clearly inherited by those disciples who, to start with, instinctively rejected the idea of accepting the Roman Cornelius among their ranks,[42] and displayed continuing suspicion towards the supra-nationalist Paul. To quote a modern writer: 'Had Jesus championed or evidenced a point of view where Jew and Gentile stood alike, it is extraordinarily difficult to understand how his followers could have proved so obtuse.'[43] Be this as it may, a slant of such a kind in a man otherwise influenced by universal ideas, a teacher who encouraged his followers to love not only their friends but also their opponents in imitation of the God who causes the sun to rise on good and bad alike, and the rain to fall on the just and the unjust,[44] requires some explanation.

Having confronted the facts and accepted a certain degree of xenophobia in Jesus, is it going too far to suggest that he might have been a Galilean revolutionary, a Zealot? This theory has recently been advanced systematically and with force;[45] yet it still fails to convince. All that is known for sure is that his whole interest was centred on Jewish affairs and that he had no great opinion of the Gentiles, but can this have been equivalent to a serious political involvement?

Zealot or not, Jesus was certainly charged, prosecuted and sentenced as one, and that this was due to his country of origin, and that of his disciples, is more than likely. It appears that in the eyes of the authorities, whether Herodian or Roman, any person with a popular following in the Galilean tetrarchy was at least a potential rebel. Josephus's account of the fate of John the Baptist is most apposite and illuminating. He is depicted as a 'good man' who 'exhorted the Jews to lead righteous lives . . . and so doing join in baptism'. But when large crowds began to be moved by his sermons,

> Herod became alarmed. Eloquence that had so great an effect on mankind might lead to some form of sedition, for it looked as though they would be guided by John in every-thing that they did. Herod decided therefore that it would be much better to strike first and be rid of him before his work led to an uprising.[46]

Far from losing his head because of his criticism of the tetrarch's unorthodox marriage, as the Gospels assert, John owed his down-fall to his powers of eloquence, which, it was suspected, might have been used by himself or others for political aims.[47]

It is hardly a coincidence that the Fourth Gospel ascribes an almost identical motive to the priestly plot against Jesus.

> 'What action are we taking?' they said. 'This man is per-forming many signs. If we leave him alone like this the whole populace will believe in him. Then the Romans will come and sweep away our temple and our nation.'

Whereat the high priest, Caiaphas, remarks:

> 'It is more to your interest that one man should die for the people, than that the whole nation should be destroyed.'[48]

The last saying anticipates, as it were, the controversial legal maxim that any Jew whose extradition on a political charge was demanded by Rome under the threat of an ultimatum was to be surrendered 'lest the entire community should suffer on his account'.[49]

If it is permissible to read between the lines of Josephus's account of Jesus, the famous *Testimonium Flavianum*,[50] a text apparently enlarged in places and shortened in others by Christian copyists, it would seem in effect that during a period of riots in Jerusalem the unspecified charge levelled against Jesus by the civic leaders was that as a teacher he had won over many Jews. From the epithet 'wise man', applied by Josephus to Jesus, and from his use of the word 'outrage' in connection with the crucifixion, it would appear that the historian himself did not find Jesus guilty.[51]

Potential leadership of a revolutionary movement would have afforded sufficient grounds for adopting radical 'preventive measures', but some members of Jesus' movement were bound to have compromised him even further. Among the apostles at least one, Simon the Zealot, bore an ominous political surname;[52] but many of his other Galilean followers appear to have been imbued with a spirit of rebellion and to have expected him to convert his religious leadership into the political role reserved for the royal Messiah. When he entered Jerusalem they greeted him:

> 'Hosanna! . . . Blessings on the coming kingdom of our father David!'[53]

> As he approached the descent from the Mount of Olives, the whole company of his disciples . . . began to sing . . . : 'Blessings on him who comes as king in the name of the Lord!'[54]

Moreover, the very last question put by Luke in the apostles' mouths testifies to the survival of their political aspirations even in the 'post-Easter' period:

> 'Lord, will you at this time restore the kingdom of Israel?'[55]

It would also follow, as will be argued in a later chapter, that the first Jewish-Galilean version of Jesus' life and teaching was conceived in a politico-religious spirit likely to account, at least in part, for its powerful Messianic emphasis.[56]

GALILEE AND RABBINIC LITERATURE

If certain features of the Gospel portrait acquire new life when set within the Galilee described by Josephus, others are provided with fresh meaning when complemented by rabbinic literary sources. The warning must nevertheless be repeated that, although Galilean in geographical origin, the Mishnah may not be employed indiscriminately to describe Galilean life as such prior to the end of the Bar Kosiba rebellion (AD 135). As one of the recently discovered letters dictated by the leader of the second Jewish War indicates, regional differences remained clear-cut until then,[57] but from the middle of the second century AD Galilee was the only lively Jewish centre in Palestine and the distinction between Judean and Galilean became largely anachronistic. Comparative material must therefore be restricted to those sections of rabbinic literature in which Judean and Galilean customs, language and way of life are deliberately contrasted. The texts themselves often show that the situation envisaged in them is that which prevailed before the destruction of the Temple in AD 70.

Josephus's image of the Galilean as the indomitable fighter has little in common with the rabbinic portrait of the Northerner as a figure of fun, an ignoramus, if not both. One of the commonest jibes directed against the Galileans is that they did not speak correct Aramaic: U-Aramaic in other words. According to a well-known anecdote preserved in the Talmud, a Galilean went to the market-place in Jerusalem to purchase something which he called *amar*. The merchants ridiculed him:

> You stupid Galilean, do you want something to ride on (a donkey=*ḥamār*)? Or something to drink (wine=*ḥamar*)? Or something for clothing (wool=*'amar*)? Or something for a sacrifice (lamb=*immar*)?[58]

The distinction between the various gutturals almost completely disappeared in Galilean Aramaic; the weaker guttural sounds, in fact, ceased even to be audible. Put differently, in careless everyday conversation the Galileans dropped their aitches. Third-century AD Babylonian rabbis maintain that it was because of the slipshod speech of Galilee that Galilean doctrine disappeared, whilst Judean teachings, in the precise enunciation of the southern dialect, survived.[59] Apparently people from certain northern towns – Tib'on, Haifa and Beth Shean are singled out – were so notorious for their mispronunciation of Hebrew that they were not called on to read the Bible in public when they were away from home.[60]

Even the Greek New Testament refers to the distinctive dialect of Galilee. In the courtyard of the high priest's house Peter is recognized as a follower of Jesus as soon as he opens his mouth.

'You are also one of them, for your accent betrays you.'[61]

Again, the name Lazarus in one of Jesus' famous parables[62] is the 'incorrect' dialectal form of Eleazar as attested both in the Palestinian Talmud and in Greek transliteration of the name surviving in inscriptions in the celebrated Galilean necropolis of Beth Shearim.[63]

Although the subject of precise dialectal differences is complex and still under debate, there can be little doubt that Jesus himself spoke Galilean Aramaic, the language, that is to say, surviving in the popular and somewhat more recent paraphrase of the Pentateuch, the Palestinian Targum, and in the Talmud of Palestine. Practically all the terms which the Synoptic Gospels preserve in Aramaic before rendering them in Greek point in that direction. In the command addressed to the daughter of Jairus, *Talitha kum*, 'Get up, my child', the noun (literally, 'little lamb') is attested only in the Palestinian Targum.[64] Another Aramaic word, *mamona*, 'money', used in the Sermon on the Mount, in Matthew 6: 24, mostly occurs in the Targums. The rabbis, even in Aramaic phrases, usually employ the Hebrew word, *mamon*. Targumic parallel is similarly decisive in determining that when Jesus said *Ephphetha*, 'Be opened', he spoke Aramaic and not Hebrew.[65] Yet although Jesus expressed himself in dialect, it would be wrong to argue from the misunderstanding of his words on the cross, *Eloi Eloi lama sabachtani*, 'My God, my God, why hast thou forsaken me?' as 'Hark, he is calling Elijah', that he was unintelligible to the people of Jerusalem.[66] Clarity cannot be expected of the cry of a crucified man at the point of death.

Far graver, however, than the criticisms provoked by their regional accent were the accusations levelled at the Galileans by the Pharisees and their rabbinical successors concerning matters related to sacrifices and offerings in the Temple of Jerusalem, to levitical cleanness and uncleanness, and to the rabbinic code of proper behaviour in general. The Mishnah, for example, ordains that imprecisely formulated vows regarding the Temple and its priests are binding in Judea. In Galilee, by contrast, because of the presumed local ignorance of ritual, only those vows were acknowledged valid which included every detail of the undertaking.[67] Furthermore, Palestinian rabbinic sources refer to pious men (*Ḥasidim*) ignorant in the field of ritual purity.[68] Even eminent Galilean rabbis such as Hanina ben Dosa and Yose the Galilean are reported to have disregarded the laws of seemly conduct. Hanina is tacitly criticized for walking alone in the street by night;[69] and Yose has to endure the indignity of a reprimand by a woman for being too talkative when enquiring the way to Lydda.

> You stupid Galilean, have the Sages not commanded: 'Do not engage in a lengthy conversation with a woman!'[70]

In brief, for the Pharisees and the rabbis of the first and early second century AD the Galileans were on the whole boors. Moreover, the epithet '*am ha-arez*, 'peasant', which as Adolph Büchler has shown was generally applied to them,[71] carried, in addition to the expected implication, the stigma of a religiously uneducated person. Though obviously overstatements, the following Talmudic quotations reflect the sentiments prevailing between the 'orthodox' and the '*am ha-arez*.

> No man may marry the daughter of the '*am ha-arez*, for they are like unclean animals, and their wives like reptiles, and it is concerning their daughters that Scripture says:

'Cursed be he who lies with any kind of beast' (Deut. 27: 21 (*RSV*)).

Greater is the hatred of the '*am ha-arez* for the learned than the hatred of the Gentiles for Israel; but the hatred of their wives is even greater.[72]

Strangely enough, the clearest echo of the antagonism between Galileans and Judeans reported in rabbinic writings is to be found in the Fourth Gospel in the New Testament. For motives which are not historical but doctrinal, this late work offers seemingly reliable evidence that attitudes definitely attested in the late first and the second century AD are traceable to the age of Jesus.[73]

According to the same evangelist also, when the Jerusalem crowds proclaim Jesus as the expected prophet, or the Messiah, doubts are voiced:

'Surely the Messiah is not to come from Galilee?'[74]

The subsequent episode of the return of the Temple police to the chief priests is even more characteristic. Asked why they have not brought Jesus, they reply: 'No man ever spoke as this man speaks.' The Pharisees then counter:

'Have you too been misled? Is there a single one of our rulers who has believed in him, or of the Pharisees? As for this rabble, which cares nothing for the Law, a curse is on them.'

When Nicodemus, himself a Pharisee, takes up Jesus' cause, he is silenced by the humiliating question:

'Are you a Galilean too?'[75]

As in the rabbinic quotations, the qualification 'Galilean' is synonymous with a cursed, lawless rabble.

Returning to the evangelists, or simply to the outline of the Gospels given in the preceding chapter, it is obvious that Jesus could have been found guilty of the charge of religious impropriety levelled at the Galileans in general. He surrounded himself with publicans and whores. He accepted the hospitality of people unlikely to have observed all the regulations concerning levitical cleanness and tithing. He took no steps to avoid defilement through contact with a corpse. He was more concerned to keep business dealings out of the precincts of the sanctuary than with the quality of sacrificial victims or the type of currency used for Temple donations. A clash with the Pharisees was, in the circumstances, only to be expected therefore, not because they were obsessed with trivialities, but because for them the trivial was an essential part of a life of holiness, every small detail of which was meant to be invested with religious significance.

The crucial question is: who were these Pharisees with whom Jesus came into conflict? Were they themselves Galileans? They are described at least twice in the Gospels as visitors from Jerusalem.[76] Can it be assumed that they were locals when the contrary is not stated? The answer depends on whether it is accepted that the Pharisees were in fact Galilee's moral rulers in the time of Jesus.

Josephus, in any case, gives no grounds for supposing this to have been so. The only Pharisees in Galilee whom he mentions are members of a deputation from Jerusalem sent by Simeon ben Gamaliel, the chief Pharisee in the capital, with a view to engineering his downfall.[77]

The testimony of rabbinic literature is equivocal. Presidents of the Pharisaic party, Gamaliel the Elder and his son Simeon, are purported to have sent epistolary instructions to the two Galilees,[78] but it is not said how they were received. A recent author claims that the Pharisaic school of the disciples of Shammai, Hillel's opponent at the turn of the eras, was influential in Galilee, and even that Shammai himself was a Galilean; but this brave assertion is backed by no serious evidence.[79]

Fragments from rabbinic literature, on the other hand, point towards a sporadic Pharisee presence in Galilee and an absence of impact during the first century AD. Yohanan ben Zakkai, the leader of Jewish restoration after the destruction of Jerusalem, spent some time in the town of Arab, possibly before AD 50;[80] two of his legal rulings concerning the observance of the Sabbath were enacted there. Yet according to a third-century AD tradition, on realizing that despite eighteen years of effort he had failed to make any mark, he exclaimed:

Galilee, Galilee, you hate the Torah![81]

Whether these words are genuine or not, they show that the Galileans had the reputation of being unprepared to concern themselves overmuch with Pharisaic scruples. If Hanina ben Dosa, a figure to be discussed in the next chapter, is to be recognized as a rabbi and a Pharisee at all, he represented a Galilean blend. Apart from him, the only other first-century AD teacher to be known as a Northerner is Rabbi Yose 'the Galilean'. Bearing in mind that Yose was one of the commonest of names, surely the very fact that he was distinguished by his country of origin, instead of being given the ordinary patronymic designation of 'son of so-and-so', is evidence of his unusual standing in a Southern academy of Pharisaic scholarship.

The long and short of this argument is that Pharisaic opposition to Jesus in Galilee was mostly foreign and not local. Even assuming that the Pharisees had acquired some foothold in one or two Galilean cities – their influence was especially felt among town-dwellers according to Josephus[82] – their authority was little noticed in rural Galilee, the main field of Jesus' ministry and success.

Jesus became a political suspect in the eyes of the rulers of Jerusalem because he was a Galilean. Moreover, if present-day estimates of Jewish historians concerning Galilean lack of education and unorthodoxy are accepted,[83] his same Galilean descent made him a religious suspect also. Should, however, this view of the Galilean character be found tendentious, rabbinic antipathy towards the Galileans and the Pharisees' hostility towards Jesus might justifiably be ascribed, not so much to an aversion to unorthodoxy and lack of education, but simply, as the Israeli scholar, Gedalyahu Alon, insinuates, to a sentiment of superiority on the part of the intellectual *élite* of the metropolis towards unsophisticated provincials.[84]

3. Jesus and charismatic Judaism

'Today and tomorrow I shall be casting out devils and working cures; on the third day I reach my goal.'[1]

According to Luke, Jesus himself defined his essential ministry in terms of exorcism and healing, but even if these words are not Jesus' own, but the evangelist's, they reflect the firm and unanimous testimony of the whole Synoptic tradition. His mission as he saw it was to the sick: to the physically, mentally and spiritually diseased, all these illnesses being then considered to go hand in hand, as will be shown presently. He was the healer, the physician *par excellence*.

'It is not the healthy that need a doctor, but the sick; I did not come to invite virtuous people, but sinners.'[2]

In consequence, if his religious personality is to be reconstructed and his affinities with the spiritual trends of his time determined, the three fundamental aspects of his function must be examined in their natural setting. His roles, that is to say, as healer of the physically ill, exorciser of the possessed, and dispenser of forgiveness to sinners, must be seen in the context to which they belong, namely charismatic Judaism. It is not until he is placed within that stream, in the company of other religious personalities with affiliations to diverse movements and groups, that his work and personality can be seen in true perspective and proportion.

THE PHYSICIAN

What is the relationship in biblical and inter-Testamental Judaism between sickness, sin and the devil? Inversely, how is the role of the physician determined? To find the answers to these two questions is the first necessary step towards a proper understanding.

The Bible is almost completely silent on the subject of professional healing. Egyptian physicians, who were renowned as expert embalmers, are explicitly referred to, but their Israelite colleagues receive only obscure and indirect mention: a man convicted of wounding his fellow is ordered to pay compensation for his victim's loss of earnings and to foot the bill for his medical treatment.[3] On the whole, Scripture considers healing as a divine monopoly.[4] Recourse to the services of a doctor in preference to prayer is held to be evidence of lack of faith, an act of irreligiousness meriting punishment. This attitude is reflected as late as the third century BC in the work of the Chronicler in connection with the grave illness of Asa, king of Judah.

> He did not seek the guidance of the Lord but resorted to physicians.[5]

Needless to add, he soon died.

The only human beings empowered to act as God's delegates were the priests and the prophets. Even so, a priest's medical competence was limited to the diagnosis of the onset and cure of leprosy and the administration of sundry purificatory rites with medical overtones following childbirth, menstruation and recovery from a venereal disease.[6] Less institutional but more effective is the part ascribed to certain prophets. Elijah revived the son of a widow,[7] and Elisha, the son of the Shunemite woman.[8] Elisha also healed the Syrian Naaman from leprosy, not by waving his hand over the diseased part of the body as the patient expected him to do, but by prescribing a ritual bath in the Jordan.[9] Isaiah is said to have restored King Hezekiah's health by means of a fig plaster.[10] In general, it can be asserted that to refer certain matters of health to a priest was a duty; to seek the help of a prophet was an act of religion; and to visit the doctor was an act of impiety.

A compromise allowing the intervention of the professional physician, yet at the same time preserving the religious character of healing, first appeared in Jewish literature at the beginning of the second century BC, when, in a remarkable act of tight-rope walking, the author of Ecclesiasticus, Jesus ben Sira, managed to vest the medical man with respectability.[11] The physician's skill does not, he argues, originate from the regions of darkness; it is a divine gift which confers on him high standing in society and secures the respect of kings and noblemen. The medicinal quality of substances is not obtained by magical means; they have been created as such and their use by the doctor is for God's glory.

> The Lord has imparted knowledge to men, that by their use of his marvels he may win praise; by using them the doctor relieves pain.[12]

The procedure thought irreproachable by the Jerusalem sage, the one which he advises every devout man to adopt when sick, is to pray to God, to repent from sin, to resolve to amend his ways, and to offer gifts and sacrifices in the Temple. Having thus proved his genuine religious disposition, he could then call in the doctor, as though taking out an extra insurance policy:

> There may come a time when your recovery is in their hands.[13]

The physician in turn is also to start with a prayer that God may enable him to diagnose the sickness correctly, alleviate the pain and save the patient's life.

In Ben Sira's clever synthesis the theological link between sickness and sin is maintained, and the cause of the disease as well as the means to cure it are discovered through a God-given insight, a kind of revelation. The corollary of such a concept, even though not expressly stated, is that a man's healing powers are measured, first and foremost, by his proximity to God, and only secondarily by the expertise acquired from study of the divinely ordained curative qualities of plants and herbs. Professional knowledge is an additional asset to the healer's essential requisite, holiness.

DEVILS AND ANGELS

In the world of Jesus, the devil was believed to be at the basis of sickness as well as sin. The idea that demons were responsible for all moral and physical evil had penetrated deeply into Jewish religious thought in the period following the Babylonian exile, no doubt as a result of Iranian influence on Judaism in the fifth and fourth centuries BC when Palestine as well as Jews from the eastern Diaspora were subject to direct Persian rule.

The apocryphal book of Tobit is among the first to testify to the new idea. According to this work, a jealous evil spirit possessed Sarah and killed all seven of her previous husbands, always on their wedding night. The young Tobias, following the advice given him by the angel Raphael, rendered this demon harmless and expelled it by burning the liver and the heart of a fish on smoking incense.[14]

> The smell from the fish held the demon off, and he took flight into Upper Egypt; and Raphael instantly followed him there and bound him hand and foot.[15]

The author of the Ethiopic Book of Enoch depicts the same Raphael as the healing angel to whom God entrusted the reparation of the damage caused on earth by the fallen angels, the teachers of sorcery and harmful magic.[16]

> 'Bind Azazel hand and foot, and cast him into the darkness . . . On the day of the great judgement he shall be cast into the fire. And heal the earth which the angels have corrupted, and proclaim the healing of the earth, that they may heal the plague, and that all the children of men may not perish through all the secret things that the watchers have disclosed and have taught their sons . . . The whole earth has been corrupted through the works that were taught by Azazel; to him ascribe all sin.'[17]

From then on the concept established itself in inter-Testamental Judaism that the proper use of the science of the angels was the most efficacious method of achieving mastery over demons. This was an art reserved to initiates because since time immemorial the arcane formulae on which it was based were concealed in esoterical books available and intelligible only to the chosen few. Noah and Solomon are said to be the principal repositories of these secrets. When the sons of Noah were led astray, blinded, and struck by devils, he prayed God that angels might come and imprison them; but Mastema, the leader of the forces of darkness, successfully appealed to the Creator for clemency, i.e. the deliverance of one tenth of his captured followers. Then the angels, as one of them remarks, were commanded by the Lord:

> that we should teach Noah all the medicines . . . We explained to Noah all the medicines of their diseases, together with their seductions, how he might heal them with herbs of the earth. And Noah wrote down all things in a book as we instructed him concerning every kind of medicine. . . . And he gave all that he had written to Shem, his eldest son.[18]

Josephus's portrait of Solomon is most instructive. As a Hellenistic historian, he describes the Israelite king as a model seeker of wisdom, but accompanies this approach with the more popular ideas of a Palestinian Jew.

> There was no form of nature with which he was not acquainted or which he passed over without examining, but he studied them all philosophically and revealed the most complete knowledge of their several properties. And God granted him knowledge of the art used against demons for the benefit and healing of men. He also composed incantations by which illnesses are relieved, and left behind forms of exorcisms with which those possessed by demons drive them out, never to return.[19]

In New Testament times the Essenes occupied the leading position among the heirs of the esoterical tradition. Josephus points out that one of their chief characteristics was an 'extra-ordinary interest' in reading the books handed down by the great men of past generations.

> They . . . single out in particular those which make for the welfare of soul and body; with the help of these, and with a view to the treatment of diseases, they make investigations into medicinal roots and the properties of stones.[20]

If my interpretation, Essenes=healers, is correct,[21] outsiders were so impressed by their activities, which, like those of the Therapeutae – a cognate religious community in Egypt – were devoted to curing the spirit and the body,[22] that they regularly and familiarly referred to them as 'Healers'.

EXORCISM

Josephus does not enter into the Essene rite of exorcism but it is unlikely to have differed very greatly from the 'manner of the cure' adopted by a certain Eleazar – sometimes surmised to have been a member of the sect – when he expelled demons in the presence of Vespasian and his sons, tribunes and soldiers.

> He put to the nose of the possessed man a ring which had under its seal one of the roots prescribed by Solomon, and then, as the man smelled it, drew out the demon through his nostrils, and, when the man at once fell down, adjured the demon never to come back into him, speaking Solomon's name and reciting the incantations which he had composed.[23]

From the same account of Eleazar it appears, furthermore, that the professional healer-exorcist was concerned to provide concrete proof that the evil spirit had departed.

> Eleazar placed a cup or foot-basin full of water a little way off and commanded the demon, as it went out of the man, to overturn it and make known to the spectators that he had left the man.[24]

Since public exorcism was performed with the help of an

incantation believed to have been revealed and handed over to saints in distant centuries, the naming of the ultimate authority appears to have been part and parcel of the ritual. In the Josephus story, Solomon is quoted. In the Gospels, Jesus asks in whose name the Pharisee exorcists operate.[25] He himself was accused, no doubt because he never invoked any human source, of acting in the name of Beelzebub, the prince of demons.[26] His disciples, and even one of their unaffiliated imitators, drove out spirits in their master's name.[27]

Contemporary sources also suggest that the exorcist's success was believed to depend on a literal and precise observance of all the prescribed rules and regulations; the correct substances were to be employed possessing the right supernatural properties and the appropriate conjurations uttered. This quasi-magical slant to professional exorcism gave rise, despite its common occurrence in inter-Testamental Judaism, to a certain measure of rabbinical embarrassment, but it was never directly outlawed, perhaps partly because it had become too integral a component of life, and partly because its condemnation would have reflected unfavourably on certain ritual customs enjoined by the Bible itself. In fact the acceptability of the peculiar ceremony of the red heifer[28] is argued from the efficacy of formal exorcism! The anecdote is worth reproducing in full as it helps to place the whole problem of the expulsion of demons in perspective.

A Gentile said to Rabban Yohanan ben Zakkai: Certain things you (Jews) do resemble some kind of sorcery. A heifer is brought, it is killed and burned. It is pounded into ashes which are collected. If then one of you is defiled through contact with a corpse, he is sprinkled twice or three times and is told: You are clean.

Rabban Yohanan ben Zakkai replied: Has the spirit of madness ever entered you? No, answered the other. Have you seen a person into whom such a spirit has entered? Yes. What does one do to him? he asked. The Gentile answered: Roots are brought and made to smoke under him, and water is splashed on him, and the spirit flees. Rabban

Yohanan ben Zakkai said: Do your ears not hear what your mouth is saying? This spirit (of madness) is also a spirit of uncleanness; as Scripture says, 'I will cause the (mad) prophets of the spirit of uncleanness to pass out of the land' (Zech. 13: 2 (*AT*)).[29]

The Gentile may, as the pupils of Yohanan commented, have been 'knocked down with a straw', but they themselves were more demanding, and on being pressed by them Yohanan eventually became aware of the speciousness of his argument. A ritual such as that of the red heifer, he confessed, admits of no rational explanation. It is observed simply because God so commanded.

By your life! No dead body defiles and no water cleanses, but this is an ordinance of the King of kings.[30]

THE HOLY MAN

Was Jesus a professional exorcist of this sort? He is said to have cast out many devils, but no rite is mentioned in connection with these achievements. In fact, compared with the esotericism of other methods, his own, as depicted in the Gospels, is simplicity itself.[31] Even in regard to healing, the closest he came to the Noachic, Solomonic and Essene type of cure was when he touched the sick with his own saliva, a substance generally thought to be medicinal.[32]

On the other hand, Jesus cannot be represented as an exorcist-healer *sui generis* either, since, in addition to the practice of the angelico-mystical medicine, contemporary Jewish thought reserved a place in the fight against evil for the spontaneous and unscripted activity of the holy man. The pattern set by the miracle-working prophets Elijah and Elisha was first of all applied by post-biblical tradition to other saints of the scriptural past; they, too, were credited with powers of healing and exorcism deriving not from incantations and drugs or the observance of elaborate rubrics, but solely from speech and touch.

Following the biblical chronology, the first hero to be portrayed as a healer is Abraham in the Qumran Genesis Apocryphon.

The Old Testament itself provides no real precedent.[33] The patient was the king of Egypt and the illness with which he was afflicted after the abduction of Sarah is attributed, as might be expected, to the intervention of an 'evil spirit' sent to scourge him and all the male members of his household and thereby protect Sarah's virtue. The trouble continued for two full years and no Egyptian physician was able to overcome it.

> Not one healer or magician or sage could stay to cure him, for the spirit scourged them all and they fled.

Finally Abraham himself was called in to expel the demon, as is recounted in the following autobiographical narrative.

> I prayed . . . and laid my hands on his [head]; and the scourge departed from him and the evil [spirit] was rebuked away [from him], and he recovered.[34]

This combination of prayer, the laying on of hands, and words of rebuke compelling the devil to depart, deserves particular attention because it provides a striking parallel to Jesus' style of cure and exorcism.[35] There is, however, a noticeable though inessential difference between the Qumran concept and that appearing in the Gospels. In the Genesis Apocryphon exorcism and healing form one process; in the New Testament they are kept separate and each is handled in its own way. Sickness is cured through bodily contact, the laying on of hands;[36] the devil is expelled by means of a rebuke.[37] An illuminating parallel to such a form of exorcism is found in rabbinic literature. Rabbi Simeon ben Yohai and Rabbi Eleazar ben Yose are reported to have exorcised the emperor's daughter by ordering her demon, with whom they were personally acquainted, to leave.

> Ben Temalion, get out! Ben Temalion, get out![38]

Moses, although represented in the Bible as a miracle-worker, is never depicted there as a healer. Yet, as early as the second century BC, the Jewish Hellenist Artapanus, whose history of the Jews survives only in fragments incorporated into Patristic literature, tells the story of a supernatural cure achieved by him.

Finding the gate of the prison into which Pharaoh had thrown him opened by a heavenly hand,[39] he walked straight into the royal bedchamber and awoke the king. Pharaoh was intrigued by this unexpected visit, and angry – no doubt because Moses had disturbed his sleep – and enquired the name of the God of Israel so that he could curse him. When the Tetragram was murmured into his ears he collapsed lifeless. But Moses, anticipating the act of Jesus in raising the daughter of Jairus,[40] lifted him up and revived him.[41]

David, whose musical performance is said to have calmed the evil spirit of King Saul,[42] is the only scriptural hero described as a kind of exorcist. The first-century AD author, Pseudo-Philo, portrays him in accordance with tradition as a harp-player and singer, but also reproduces in his Book of Biblical Antiquities a poem allegedly composed by David to keep the devil under control.[43]

The poetic exorcism, which opens with a sketch of the work of the Creation, reminds the devil of the inferior status of 'the tribe of your spirits' and that the infernal world would one day be destroyed by a descendant of David. The poet then issues two commands:

> Now cease molesting, since you are a secondary creature![44]

> Remember hell in which you walk![45]

Another biblical figure posthumously invested with curative gifts is Daniel, according to a very important, but unfortunately badly damaged, fragment from Qumran Cave 4 known as the 'Prayer of Nabonidus'.[46] Although the name Daniel does not appear in the surviving parts of the document, it cannot be in doubt. The composition is inspired by the story of Nebuchadnezzar in Daniel 4.[47] The most crucial section reads:

> I was afflicted with an evil ulcer for seven years . . . and a *gazer* pardoned my sins. He was a Jew from among the [children of Judah and he said:] 'Recount this in writing to [glorify and exalt] the name of the [Most High God].'

The Aramaic word *gazer* applied here to the Jew who healed

the king and forgave his sins appears four times in the Book of Daniel,[48] where, as it is usually linked to nouns designating magicians and astrologers, it is habitually rendered in the pejorative sense of 'soothsayer' or 'diviner'. In the Qumran text such an imputation is definitely not attached to it. *Gazer* signifies in this work, if A. Dupont-Sommer's suggestion is accepted, an exorcist.[49] Moreover, because the root from which the term derives means 'to decree', a *gazer* is one who exorcises by decreeing the expulsion of the devil. In a story to be considered presently, the same verb is employed in a command addressed by Hanina ben Dosa to the queen of the demons.[50]

It is worth noting that although the devil, sin and sickness are logically combined in the Qumran picture, the story is told elliptically. The narrator mentions the king's illness without referring to its cause; and the exorcist is credited, not with the expulsion of a demon, but with the remission of the sufferer's sins. The three elements were so closely associated that it was natural to jump from the first to the third without recording the intermediary stage: an exorcist pardoned my sins and I recovered from my sickness.

This fragment which has so luckily survived is particularly valuable in that it sheds fresh light on the controversial Gospel episode of the healing of the paralytic.[51] Considered side by side with the Nabonidus story, there is nothing outstandingly novel or unique in the words of Jesus, 'My son, your sins are forgiven.' The scribes think that they are blasphemous, but for Jesus – as for the author of the Qumran fragment – the phrase 'to forgive sins' was synonymous with 'to heal', and he clearly used it in that sense.

> 'But that you may know that the *son of man* has authority on earth to forgive sins' – he said to the paralytic – 'I say to you, rise, take your pallet and go home' (*RSV*).

By comparison with the style of the Qumran text, 'he pardoned my sins', the Gospel use of the passive form, 'your sins are forgiven', strikes a more cautious note. The words are not disrespectful of God, nor do they imply that the speaker claimed for himself divine status. The main reason for the scandal of the scribes must have been that their legal language was very different from that of Jesus. But however this may have been, rabbis of the second and third century AD were still voicing the opinion that no one could recover from illness until all his sins were remitted.[52]

JEWISH CHARISMATICS

The representation of Jesus in the Gospels as a man whose supernatural abilities derived, not from secret powers, but from immediate contact with God, proves him to be a genuine charismatic, the true heir of an age-old prophetic religious line. But can other contemporary figures be defined in the same way?

The answer is yes. Furthermore, far from digressing from the main theme of the present enquiry, it is very pertinent to a search for the real Jesus to study these other men of God and the part they played in Palestinian religious life during the final period of the Second Temple era.[53]

1. *Honi*

One of the prime characteristics of the ancient *Hasidim* or Devout is that their prayer was believed to be all-powerful, capable of performing miracles. The best known of these charismatics, though perhaps not the most important from the point of view of New Testament study, is a first-century BC saint, called Honi the Circle-Drawer by the rabbis, and Onias the Righteous by Josephus.[54]

To understand the figure of Honi it is necessary to remember that from the time of the prophet Elijah[55] Jews believed that holy men were able to exert their will on natural phenomena. Thus, in addition to offering formal, liturgical prayers for rain, in times of drought people urged persons reputed to be miracle-workers to exercise their infallible intervention on behalf of the community. Such a request for relief from their misery is reported to have been addressed to Honi some time before the fall of Jerusalem to Pompey in 63 BC.

> Once they said to Honi the Circle-Drawer: 'Pray that it may
> rain.' . . . He prayed but it did not rain. Then what did he
> do? He drew a circle, and stood in it, and said before God:
> 'Lord of the world, thy children have turned to me because
> I am as a son of the house before thee. I swear by thy great
> name that I will not move hence until thou be merciful
> towards thy children.' It then began to drizzle. 'I have not
> asked for this', he said, 'but for rain to fill cisterns, pits and
> rock-cavities.' There came a cloud-burst. 'I have not asked
> for this, but for a rain of grace, blessing and gift.' It then
> rained normally.[56]

It is easy to misjudge the curious attitude revealed by Honi in
this episode. His behaviour towards God appears impertinent;
indeed, as will be seen, it was frowned on by the authorities of
his own day as well as by subsequent orthodoxy. Nevertheless,
in the last resort even his rabbinic critics likened the relationship
between the saint and God to that of a tiresome and spoiled
child with his loving and long-suffering father. The leading
Pharisee of Honi's time, Simeon ben Shetah, is said to have
declared:

> 'What can I do with you, since even though you importune
> God, he does what you wish in the same way that a father
> does whatever his importuning son asks him?'[57]

Josephus's Onias is rather different. This is an admirable and
heroic character, whose saintly detachment aroused the anger of
political partisans just before Rome first intervened in the affairs
of Judea at the time of the conflict between the two sons of
Alexander Janneus, Hyrcanus II and Aristobulus II. As in the
rabbinic story, the supernaturally efficacious nature of Honi's
intercession is once more accepted as a matter of course.

> There was a certain Onias, who, being a righteous man and
> dear to God, had once in a rainless period prayed to God to
> end the drought, and God had heard his prayer and sent
> rain.

Although he had gone into hiding, he was sought out by the men of Hyrcanus who wished him to 'place a curse on Aristobulus' which they believed would be as effective as his prayer for rain.

> When in spite of his refusals and excuses he was forced to speak by the mob, he stood up in their midst and said: 'O God, king of the universe, since these men standing beside me are thy people, and those who are besieged are thy priests, I beseech thee not to hearken to them against these men nor to bring to pass what these men ask thee to do to those others.'

Incensed by such neutrality, 'the villains among the Jews' stoned him to death.[58]

The shift from the almost openly critical presentation of Honi in the Mishnah to the fully sympathetic portrayal in Josephus for the benefit of a Hellenistic audience is worthy of remark. Compare in particular the rather sinister Hebrew epithet, 'Circle-Drawer', with the Greek, 'righteous man and dear to God'. On the other hand, despite the unfriendly mainstream of rabbinic thought concerning Honi, it would be incorrect to characterize Josephus's point of view as representing Hellenistic Judaism and contrast it with that of Talmudic literature. In effect, fragments exist showing a less antipathetic attitude. For example, Simeon ben Shetah declares that a word of the Bible, Proverbs 23: 23, found its fulfilment in Honi.[59] Again, an anonymous comment on Job 22: 28, described as a message from the members of the Sanhedrin to Honi and assigned to the first or second century AD, reads:

> *Whatever you command will come to pass:* You have commanded on earth, and God has fulfilled your word in heaven.
> *And light will shine on your path:* You have enlightened by your prayer the generation which was in darkness.[60]

Even more pregnant is another anonymous saying from the Midrash Rabbah:

No man has existed comparable to Elijah and Honi the Circle-Drawer, causing mankind to serve God.[61]

The sources contain no further information concerning Honi It is known that he was active in Jerusalem before being killed there, but since both the Mishnah and Josephus date the event close to the feast of Passover, he may as easily have been a pilgrim to the holy city as a citizen of the capital. Two of his grandsons, Hanan, his daughter's son, and Abba Hilkiah, his son's son, were also renowned for their powers as rain-makers.[62] From the viewpoint of geographical connections it is of interest to note that in a parallel text Abba Hilkiah, instead of being mentioned by name, is referred to as 'a Hasid from Kefar Imi', a village otherwise unknown but appearing in a Galilean context in the passage in question of the Palestinian Talmud.[63]

2. *Hanina ben Dosa*

The Galilean connections of his descendants, and even more those of Honi himself, remain purely conjectural. Nevertheless the hypothesis associating charismatic Judaism with Galilee acquires further support in the incontestably Galilean background of Hanina ben Dosa, one of the most important figures for the understanding of the charismatic stream in the first century AD.[64] In a minor key, he offers remarkable similarities with Jesus, so much so that it is curious, to say the least, that traditions relating to him have been so little utilized in New Testament scholarship.[65]

Who then was Hanina ben Dosa? Rabbinic sources report that he lived in Arab, a Galilean city in the district of Sepphoris.[66] Situated about ten miles north of Nazareth, the town, as has been noted, had for its religious leader some time in the first century AD, though definitely before the outbreak of the First War, a figure of no less eminence than Yohanan ben Zakkai. Hanina is once described as his pupil.[67] His family background is undocumented, but it would be a mistake to attach much importance to the Greek name of his father; Dosa (=Dositheus) was not unheard of even among rabbis and to carry this name was not tantamount to favouring Hellenistic ideas.

That Hanina lived in the first century AD may be deduced indirectly but convincingly from the fact that the Talmudic sources associate him with three historical figures who definitely belonged to that period: Nehuniah, a Temple official, Rabban Gamaliel and Yohanan ben Zakkai.[68] If, as is likely, the Gamaliel in question was Gamaliel the Elder, a man claimed by the Apostle Paul to have been his master,[69] and not Gamaliel II, the former's grandson, Hanina's activity would appear to have fallen in the period preceding the year of AD 70. In support of this view, it should be underlined that he is nowhere connected with any event occurring after the destruction of Jerusalem.[70]

Setting aside various secondary accretions according to which he was a wholesale wonder-worker, the primary rabbinic tradition represents Hanina as a man of extraordinary devotion and miraculous healing talents.

His name first appears in a chapter of the Mishnah where the early Hasid is depicted as spending a full hour on directing his heart towards his Father in heaven before starting his prayer proper, his rule of concentration being:

> Though the king salute him, he shall not return his greeting. Though a snake wind itself around his ankle, he shall not interrupt his prayer.[71]

An episode in Hanina's life is chosen to illustrate this injunction.

> When Rabbi Hanina ben Dosa prayed, a poisonous reptile[72] bit him, but he did not interrupt his prayer. They (the onlookers) departed and found the same 'snake' dead at the opening of its hole. 'Woe to the man', they exclaimed, 'bitten by a snake, but woe to the snake which has bitten Rabbi Hanina ben Dosa.'[73]

As might be guessed, nothing untoward occurred to him, and when told later of the frightening event, he is reported to have declared:

May evil befall me if in the concentration of my heart I even felt it.

According to another version of the story, when Hanina was told of the presence of the snake, he asked to be led to its hole and deliberately put his foot on it. Whereupon he was bitten but remained unharmed. The snake, however, died immediately. At which Hanina proclaimed:

It is not the snake that kills, but sin.[74]

The present relevance of the message contained in this story, namely that total trust in God and communion with him render the holy man immune, is realized once it is understood that the ideal fulfilled by Hanina is not unlike that which Jesus set before his disciples.

'Those who believe may take up/step on snakes . and nothing will harm them.'[75]

Hanina's intervention was principally sought in cases of sickness. His fame was such that the outstanding personalities of his own time are portrayed as requesting his help. Nevertheless, though later hailed as the saviour and benefactor of his generation, there are signs that he was in part resented by the leaders of contemporary Pharisaism and by representatives of the later rabbinic establishment.

When the son of his community chief, Yohanan ben Zakkai, fell ill, the father is described as having said to the young man:[76]

'Hanina, my son, pray for him that he may live.' He put his head between his knees and prayed;[77] and he lived.

Although the actual cure is tacitly ascribed to God, Hanina's influence on Heaven is indirectly asserted in Yohanan's subsequent comment:

Though ben Zakkai had squeezed his head between his knees all day long, no attention would have been paid to him.

This humble admission of the superiority of the miracle-worker is, however, counterbalanced by a reassertion of Yohanan's momentarily lost dignity. To his jealous wife's question whether Hanina was greater than he, Yohanan replies:

> No, he is like a servant before the king and I am like a prince before the king.

The principal source of the renown won by this Galilean Hasid was his ability to heal from a distance and to announce from there an immediate cure. In this respect, the best story is that which tells of the cure of the son of the famous Gamaliel. The boy was suffering from a mortal fever. The head of the Jerusalem Pharisees therefore despatched two of his pupils to the far-away home of Hanina, who retired to an upper room and prayed, returning with the words:

> Go home, for the fever has departed from him.

Incredulous and critical, the novice rabbis asked·

> Are you a prophet?

He replied modestly:

> I am no prophet, nor am I a prophet's son, but this is how I am favoured. If my prayer is fluent in my mouth, I know that he (the sick man) is favoured; if not, I know that it (the disease) is fatal.

Unimpressed by the explanation, the envoys sat down and recorded the date and hour of the alleged cure, and reported the matter to Gamaliel, who happily and admiringly confirmed it.

> You have neither detracted from it, nor added to it, but this is how it happened. That was the hour that the fever left him and he asked us for water to drink.[78]

The cure from a distance of the centurion's servant (or the son of the royal official)[79] belongs to the same category and illustrates what seems to have been a recognized charismatic pattern. It is of interest to note that both Hanina and Jesus are said to have sensed the efficacy of their cures – Hanina, by means of the fluency of his prayer, and Jesus, who normally came into bodily contact with the sick, by feeling that 'power had gone out of him'.[80]

In addition to being a healer of the sick, Hanina ben Dosa was venerated as a deliverer of persons in physical peril,[81] in particular that caused by evil spirits. According to a tradition preserved in the Talmud, one night, when, in infringement of the Pharisaic code of etiquette,[82] Hanina walked alone in the street, the queen of the demons met him. Recognizing him in time, she said:

> Had there been no commendation from heaven, 'Take heed of Hanina den Dosa and his teaching!' I would have harmed you.

Hanina's retort was:

> If I am so highly esteemed in heaven, I decree that you shall never again pass through an inhabited place![83]

Like Honi, Hanina was also credited with the ability to influence natural phenomena. Once, during a downpour following a long drought, he said to God, whilst walking home:

> Lord of the universe, the whole world is in comfort whereas Hanina is in distress.

At once the rain stopped, and he reached his house dry. He then prayed:

> Lord of the universe, the whole world is in distress whereas Hanina is in comfort.

And it began to rain again immediately.[84]

One important corollary to this survey of Jewish miracle-workers and holy men is that the popular image of the charismatic was inseparable from the figure of Elijah.[85] Honi's association with this legendary prophet has already been noted.[86] Rab, the great Babylonian teacher,[87] reflects the same notion, albeit elliptically, in regard to Hanina by maintaining that although the prototype of the wicked man is King Ahab, that of the benefactor of mankind is not Ahab's contemporary, Elijah, but the prophet's latter-day heir, Hanina. Commenting on the rabbinic saying that the world was created for the sake of the wholly just and the wholly wicked, Rab concluded:

> The world was created only for the sake of Ahab the son of Omri and of Rabbi Hanina ben Dosa. For Ahab this world, for Hanina the world to come.[88]

In anticipation of a point to be discussed in the next chapter, it is appropriate to recall at this juncture that Jesus, too, was identified by some of his contemporaries with the same Elijah.[89]

Another important feature of Hasidic piety was detachment from possessions, the quintessence of which is expressed in the sentence:

> What is mine is yours and what is yours is your own.[90]

Tradition represents Hanina as one who, to his wife's great displeasure, lived in total poverty.[91] A younger contemporary of his, Rabbi Eleazar of Modiim, saw Hanina and those like him as the incarnation of 'men of truth hating evil gain':[92] those, that is to say, who 'hated their own money, and all the more, the *mammon* of other people'.[93] The same lack of acquisitiveness, indeed the same positive embrace of poverty inspired by absolute reliance on God, is fundamental to Jesus' outlook and practice.

> 'Therefore I bid you put away anxious thoughts about food and drink to keep you alive, and clothes to cover your body.'[94]

> 'Go, sell everything you have, and give to the poor.'[95]

> 'Foxes have their holes, the birds their roosts; but the *son of man* has nowhere to lay his head.'[96]

Again, both Jesus and Hanina, and no doubt the Hasidim in general, showed a complete lack of interest in legal and ritual affairs and a corresponding exclusive concentration on moral questions. Hanina is never quoted as an authority on Jewish law in either the Mishnah or the Talmud. By good fortune, on the other hand, three of his *logia* are reproduced in the tractate, Ethics of the Fathers or *Pirke Aboth*, all of them showing concern for the establishment of a correct order of spiritual priorities[97] and all relevant to the New Testament. It is enough, however, to examine the first.

> Any man whose fear of sin precedes his wisdom, his wisdom will endure; but if his wisdom precedes his fear of sin, his wisdom will not endure.[98]

The saying is modelled on 'The fear of the Lord is the beginning of wisdom'.[99] 'Wisdom' in this context is expertise in the Law, but 'fear of sin' is a more equivocal phrase connoting, not a negative disposition towards asceticism and scruple, but the positive performance of good deeds in such a way that even their potential content of sin is avoided. Thus apropos of alms-giving, for instance, the Mishnah mentions a 'chamber of secrets' in the Temple filled with gifts deposited for the benefit of the more diffident so that they might help themselves 'in secret' without having to confront the donors.[100] Tactful benefactors such as these, determined to exclude even the remote possibility of pandering to their own vainglory or of humiliating their fellow-men, are described as 'sin-fearing'.

Jesus reveals a similar preoccupation and expresses it even more emphatically:

> 'Beware of practising your piety before men in order to be seen by them; for then you will have no reward from your Father who is in heaven. Thus, when you give alms, sound no trumpet before you, as the hypocrites do in the synagogues and in the streets, that they may be praised by men. Truly, I say to you, they have their reward. But when you give alms, do not let your left hand know what your right hand is doing, so that your alms may be in secret; and your Father who sees in secret will reward you.'[101]

JESUS AND CHARISMATIC JUDAISM

For all the precautions imperative to a thesis which, owing to the nature of the sources, must in part remain hypothetical, coincidence cannot reasonably be invoked to account for all the similarities noted in the preceding pages. It would appear, rather, that the logical inference must be that the person of Jesus is to be seen as part of first-century charismatic Judaism and as the paramount example of the early Hasidim or Devout.

It may have been their charity and loving-kindness that inspired the affection felt for these men, but it was through their 'miracles' that they made their strongest impact. When rabbinic tradition attempts to define Hanina, it refers to him as a 'man of deed'.

When Rabbi Hanina ben Dosa died, the men of deed ceased.[102]

There have been recent endeavours to discredit this traditional interpretation of the phrase 'man of deed' in the sense of miracle-worker; nevertheless, it still stands.[103] It is, in fact, corroborated by the Gospels, which invest the Greek word for 'deed' (*ergon*) with a similar meaning when they apply it to the healing miracles of Jesus[104] or describe him as a 'prophet mighty in deed and word'.[105]

It is also noteworthy that in the *Testimonium* of Josephus Jesus is portrayed as a 'wise man' and the performer of 'marvellous deeds'. Both epithets, and especially the latter, fit so well into the historical context that their invention or interpolation into the account by a later Christian forger is unlikely.[106] Indeed, even a somewhat critical early rabbinic mention distinguishes not only Jesus himself, but his disciples as well, by their miraculous healing activities.[107]

That a distinctive trend of charismatic Judaism existed during the last couple of centuries of the Second Temple is undeniable. These holy men were treated as the willing or unsuspecting heirs to an ancient prophetic tradition. Their supernatural powers were attributed to their immediate relation to God. They were venerated as a link between heaven and earth independent of any institutional mediation.

Moreover, although it would be forcing the evidence to argue that charismatic Judaism was exclusively a Northern phenomenon because Jesus, Hanina ben Dosa, and possibly Abba Hilkiah were Galileans, this religious trend is likely to have had Galilean roots. It is, in any case, safe and justifiable to conclude that the unsophisticated religious ambiance of Galilee was apt to produce holy men of the Hasidic type, and that their success in that province was attributable to the simple spiritual demands of the Galilean nature, and perhaps also to a lively local folk memory concerning the miraculous deeds of the great prophet Elijah.

CHARISMATICS AND PHARISEES

The relationship of the Hasidim with mainstream Pharisaism is still a matter for debate, though probably for the wrong reasons. Reacting in 1922 against the then fairly common, but today untenable, theory that the ancient Devout were Essene sectaries, A. Büchler set out, with learning and zeal, to demonstrate that Honi and the other Hasidim were 'strict Pharisees attached to God with all their heart, and serving their fellow-men with all their soul'.[108] Today, scholars are inclined to be less categorical. S. Safrai, for example, is prepared to admit that the religious practice taught by the Hasidim was 'highly individual and sometimes, indeed, opposed to that generally prevailing', and that, although revered by the rabbis, the Hasidim were not identical with them.[109] D. Flusser, in a slightly different context, also speaks of the 'inevitable tension between charismatic miracles . . . and institutional Judaism'.[110]

Considering all the evidence available, this 'inevitable tension', indeed conflict, emerges as a fact. The reasons for the opposition between Jews with basically different attitudes yet a great deal in common appear to have been two in number. The first, though perhaps less important, lies in the Hasidic refusal to conform in matters of behaviour and religious observance. The second reason springs from the threat posed by the unrestrained authority of the charismatic to the upholders of the established religious order. It is hardly surprising that the stories concerning Honi and Hanina – not to mention Jesus – often contain an element of open or veiled disapproval when it is remembered that the entire rabbinic tradition has passed through the channel of 'orthodoxy'.

In regard to the first ground for conflict, Hanina not only flouted the rabbinic code of conduct by walking alone at night, but he owned goats which he should not have done in Palestine according to the Mishnah, and even went so far as to carry the unclean carcass of a snake.[111] Another Hasid, who was also a priest, was found by Rabbi Joshua ben Hananiah to be not only lax in such matters, but ignorant of the existence of a biblical law concerning ritual uncleanness.[112] Yet another is said to have sneered at the Mishnaic rule forbidding the use of liquids kept in an uncovered vessel by night.[113] Jesus of Nazareth would seem very much at home in such company. Some might remark that occasionally the Hasidim were stricter in their ritual observances than the average Pharisee – Hanina was reputed to have begun the Sabbath earlier than the rest and to have paid his tithes most scrupulously[114] – but in truth all this is immaterial because it lies nowhere near the centre of their religious concern. Both laxity and severity were to them peripheral: which is why the traditionalists in charge of the well-being of society imagined that they threatened to undermine and pervert the correct order of values and priorities.

The charismatics' informal familiarity with God and confidence in the efficacy of their words was also deeply disliked by those whose authority derived from established channels. Simeon ben Shetah, the leader of the Pharisees in the first century BC, would have wished to excommunicate Honi, but dared not.[115] Similarly, the jibe, 'Are you a prophet?' addressed to Hanina, as well as the assertion that the 'prince' Yohanan ben Zakkai was superior to him the 'servant', were all aimed at neutralizing and eliminating a power and authority apparently, but unascertainably, of divine origin.

It is perhaps worth observing that the one sphere in which supernatural proof was judged totally inadmissible was the definition of lawful conduct (*halakhah*). Nowhere is this better illustrated than in the legendary account of a doctrinal argument around the end of the first century AD between Rabbi Eliezer ben Hyrcanus and his colleagues. Having exhausted his arsenal of reasoning and still not convinced them, he performed a miracle, only to be told that there is no room for miracles in a legal debate. In exasperation he then exclaimed: 'If my teaching is correct, may it be proved by Heaven!' Whereupon a celestial voice declared: 'What have you against Rabbi Eliezer, for his teaching is correct?' But this intervention was ruled out of order because in the Bible it is written that decisions are to be reached by majority vote.[116]

Since *halakhah* became the corner-stone of rabbinic Judaism, it is not surprising that, despite their popular religious appeal, Jesus, Hanina, and the others, were slowly but surely squeezed out beyond the pale of true respectability.

PART TWO: THE TITLES OF JESUS

The conclusion arrived at so far is that once the Gospel report concerning his person and work is analysed, the secondary traits removed, and the essential features inserted into the context of contemporary political and religious history, Jesus of Nazareth takes on the eminently credible personality of a Galilean Hasid. It remains now to be seen whether the fundamental definition thus established is sufficient in itself, or is to be completed, or even replaced, by applying to Jesus the specific roles and functions ascribed by the Bible or post-biblical Jewish tradition to eschatological figures awaited with intensity by first-century AD Palestine.

The coming of the Messiah was incontestably an article of the Jewish creed at that time, as was the belief that Elijah or some other prophetic figure was to play a part in the great Messianic event. However, apart from the conviction that these envoys were to enjoy a special relation with one another and with Heaven, the exact nature of their connection was undefined and the subject of unending debate.

That the New Testament makes claims in this domain is obvious. But the essential question is: who was responsible for them? Jesus himself? His immediate followers? The later Palestinian Jewish Church? Or the Hellenistic Gentile Church?

One point at least can be cleared up straight away: the first evangelists were more concerned with editing the words and actions of Jesus than with examining and demonstrating his titles. It is the more theological writings of Paul and John which evince a preoccupation with the part he was thought to have played in God's eternal plan of salvation; a preoccupation which, by the time the Christian Creeds were formulated, became to all intents and purposes exclusive.

In the pages that follow only those basic christological titles are scrutinized which appear explicitly in the Synoptic Gospels, i.e. those which could derive either from Jesus himself, or from his Palestinian contemporaries: though it should be emphasized that this equation of Synoptic tradition and primitive Palestinian usage is not meant to exclude the possibility – and in many cases the fact – that the same title was to acquire in the course of the Gospel transmission and redaction more advanced non-Palestinian theological connotations.

The historian's approach to the evolution of the Gospel titles is bound to differ from that of the theologian. The latter may admit that there was a doctrinal development, but will claim that it was *intended*, that the modification he can detect in the New Testament, in Patristic thought, in the Councils and in the Church, is 'genuine', inspired, governed, protected and brought to maturity by the spirit of God. By contrast, the historian's task being to enquire into the metamorphosis of Jesus of Galilee into the Christ of Christianity, he must necessarily attach greater weight to the doctrinally least advanced tradition relating to Jesus and endeavour to trace from that point onward the successive stages of theological change. In doing so, he needs to treat extraneous contemporary parallels with particular care, bearing in mind that the meaning of a religious title depends more on culture and traditional usage than on etymology. Epithets such as 'lord' or 'son of God' uttered in Greek by Gentile Christians in Antioch, Alexandria or Athens, evoked ideas other than those attached to their Hebrew or Aramaic originals by Palestinian Jews. The primary aim must therefore be to determine the import of a title in a first-century AD Galilean milieu. If this can be done, there is a good chance of approaching closer to the thought of Jesus and his first disciples. But even a better acquaintance with the wider Palestinian usage will furnish an insight into the minds of those of his contemporaries who employed or witnessed the employment of the title in question.

For the selection of the titles to be examined in the next five chapters the point of departure has been the dialogue between Jesus and his apostles at Caesarea Philippi, reported in Matthew 16: 14–22. There the Master asks them: 'Who do men say that the *son of man* is?' They answer: 'Some say John the Baptist, others Elijah . . . or *one of the prophets*.' To his further question concerning their own opinion, Peter replies: 'You are the *Messiah*, the *son of* the living *God*.' When immediately after this Jesus speaks of his future martyrdom, the same Peter rebukes him· 'No, *lord*, this shall never happen to you.'

Four dependent epithets are discussed with the principal ones: 'rabbi' and 'teacher' with 'lord'; 'son of David' with 'the Messiah', and 'the son' with 'son of God'.

4. Jesus the prophet

No expert would deny that the Gospels portray Jesus as wearing the mantle of a prophet, but the manner in which the relevant New Testament passages are treated is symptomatic of the difficulty experienced by many a scholar who has to handle the historical evidence on which his religious faith is claimed to rest. Writers are inclined either to be selective in what they read in the Gospels, or to tailor their investigation so that issues not considered pertinent are suppressed altogether. Thus their attention is not centred on whether Jesus was a prophet, and on the meaning of the prophetic function in first-century AD Palestine, but on whether he was the *final* prophet. It is taken for granted, or explicitly argued, that the role of prophet pure and simple is irrelevant in view of his greater function.[1] Few contemporary authors are, in fact, willing to echo R. Bultmann's distinction between the concrete historical figure, Jesus of Nazareth, 'teacher and prophet', and the Messiah of Jewish eschatology.[2]

The truth, however, is that, notwithstanding the reluctance of the theologians to pay attention to one of them, the New Testament attributes two kinds of prophetic mission to Jesus, both of which will be observed equally in the present study, irrespective of their pertinence or usefulness to belief. It is left to others to measure 'the advantages and disadvantages of the prophetic concept for explaining the uniqueness of the person and work of Jesus',[3] or to qualify it as christologically 'abortive' and 'inadequate'.[4]

THE PROPHET JESUS

An unbiased reading of the Synoptic evidence reveals that sympathetic witnesses of his Galilean activity recognized Jesus as either John the Baptist, Elijah or a prophet,[5] a view apparently shared by the entourage of Herod Antipas, with the possible hint at the notion of a prophet *redivivus*.[6] The crowd, on his entry into Jerusalem, also refers to him as 'the prophet Jesus, from Nazareth in Galilee'.[7] It should be added that the characterization 'prophet' is not just a deliberate answer to a specific question, but reflects the spontaneous admiration of people convinced of having witnessed a miracle. The account of the raising of the dead youth in Nain concludes with the comment:

> Deep awe fell upon them all, and they praised God. 'A great prophet has arisen among us', they said.[8]

Popular belief in the prophetic talent of Jesus may furthermore be proved negatively from the doubtful, disapproving, or plainly ironical attitude towards this view manifested by his opponents. His Pharisee host, shocked to see Jesus permitting a prostitute to anoint him, questions his prophetic insight:

> 'If this fellow were a real prophet, he would know who this woman is that touches him, and what sort of woman she is, a sinner.'[9]

In Jerusalem, the chief priests and their advisers dared not arrest him, for although they attached little weight to their opinion,

> they were afraid of the people, who looked on Jesus as a prophet.[10]

Finally, after Jesus has been captured, blindfolded and scourged, the members of the Sanhedrin,[11] or more probably the high priest's men,[12] are credited with the mocking question:

> 'Now, prophet, who hit you?'[13]

The common assumption held by New Testament interpreters appears to be that the prophetic image of Jesus was conceived by friendly outsiders, but that, not being good enough, not sufficiently suitable within the circle of his closer companions, it was replaced by more fitting titles. That this was not, in fact, the case is shown by the obituary attributed to one of the Emmaus disciples two days after Jesus' death. He was, Cleopas says,

> 'a prophet mighty in deed and word before God and all the people.'[14]

Furthermore, one of the earliest 'Christologies' surviving in the Acts of the Apostles, despite signs of doctrinal progress, is still content to envisage Jesus as the prophet similar to Moses.[15]

More important still, the opinion of friends and associates seems to coincide with Jesus' own concept of himself. According to a statement reported by all three evangelists, and an additional saying preserved in Luke alone, he not only thought of himself as a prophet, but also ascribed to his prophetic destiny every unpleasantness that was to happen to him. He shrugs off the disappointment caused by his family's rejection of him in Nazareth with the words:

> 'A prophet will always be held in honour except in his home town, and among his kinsmen and family.'[16]

In the same spirit, he declares irrelevant the news that Herod Antipas, the tetrarch of Galilee, has set out to kill him:

> 'It is unthinkable for a prophet to meet his death anywhere but in Jerusalem.'[17]

Doubtless, it would be an exaggeration to claim that Jesus positively declared himself to be a prophet, since neither saying is an answer to an express question; in fact, both may rely on existing, though not otherwise attested, proverbs. Nonetheless, the indirect nature of the argument has if anything a strengthening effect: Jesus conviction that he was a prophet serves as a premise solid enough to allow him to draw a conclusion from it.

The saying attributed to the disciples on the road to Emmaus – 'a prophet mighty in deed' – and the words following Jesus' prophetic self-appraisal – 'he could work no miracle' in Nazareth[18] – suggest that the terms 'prophet' and 'miracle-worker' were used synonymously by him and his followers. This peculiarity is the more remarkable since the miraculous element is absent from the idea of prophecy when it is used critically by the opponents of Jesus. For the Pharisaic host and the jeering servants of the high priest, prophecy is merely an intellectual gift and implies a knowledge of secrets.

As his prophetic mission consisted essentially in charismatic activity, Jesus ranged himself, and was ranged by his friends, with Elijah and Elisha, two biblical characters primarily conceived as wonder-workers in inter-Testamental Judaism.[19] Apart from the obvious dependence of several evangelical accounts on parallel stories in the Books of Kings – the raising of the son of the widow from Nain may be compared to similar acts attributed to Elijah in Zarephath and to Elisha in Shunem,[20] and the feeding of a crowd by Jesus to Elisha's provision of a hundred men with food[21] – a distinct link with the two prophets is positively acknowledged by Jesus when, in connection with his own departure from Nazareth, he cites Elijah and Elisha as the models of the prophet unrespected at home:

> 'No prophet is recognized in his own country. There were many widows in Israel . . . in Elijah's time . . . yet it was to none of those that Elijah was sent, but to a widow at Sarepta in the territory of Sidon. Again, in the time of the prophet Elisha there were many lepers in Israel, and not one of them was healed, but only Naaman, the Syrian.'[22]

Such a parallel, especially that with Elijah, raises the question of a relationship between the prophetic reputation and self-awareness of Jesus, and the concept of the charismatic Hasid. It will be recalled that Hanina ben Dosa was asked if he was a prophet when he announced from a distance a cure achieved as a result of his prayer.[23] Again, the extraordinary praying position adopted by him – with his head between his knees – apparently

in imitation of Elijah,[24] and the story of his interruption of a
downpour of rain associate him with Elijah still further.[25] In
short, it appears to be almost beyond argument that the miracle-
working Hasid either modelled himself on Elijah, or was at least
seen as another Elijah by the men of his generation. But this
having been established, it is important to stress that the connection was with the real historical character of the biblical past,
and not with the Elijah who was to return in the age of the Messiah,
which would imply that the Hasidic imagery existed – or at least
could have existed – without being tied to eschatological speculation of one kind or another. Placing the parallel New Testament
problem within the framework of charismatic Judaism, it may
in consequence be justly held that for references to Jesus as a
prophet or Elijah to be meaningful, it is not necessary to fall
back on the eschatological concepts of a final mediator of revelation
or of a forerunner of the Messiah.

In fact, the belief professed by his contemporaries that Jesus
was a charismatic prophet rings so authentic, especially in the
light of the Honi-Hanina cycle of traditions, that the correct
historical question is not whether such an undogmatic Galilean
concept was ever in vogue, but rather how, and under what
influence, it was ever given an eschatological twist.

THE PROPHET IN POST-BIBLICAL JUDAISM

The prophetic movement which had flourished in various forms
from the beginning of the Israelite monarchy (tenth century BC)
came to an end in the period following the Babylonian exile
(sixth century BC). Its last representatives, Haggai and Zechariah,
enriched the Bible with works still classified as prophetic, but
with them the genre reached its fulfilment, and apart from the
book of the shadowy Malachi, about whom nothing is known,
the canon of the Latter Prophets was allowed to receive no further
supplement. No doubt the idea prevailed among scholars well
before the turn of the eras that prophecy as such had ceased in
Israel. It is sufficient to note that Daniel was not recognized by
Jews as a prophet, and that the book bearing his name was

accepted only among the Writings, the last section of the tripartite Hebrew Bible, following the Pentateuch and the Prophets. Again, the second-century BC historian of the Maccabean uprising, describing the distress that afflicted Israel after the death of Judas Maccabaeus, writes that it was 'worse than any since the day when prophets ceased to appear among them'.[26]

Spokesmen of the post-prophetic era gladly came to terms with the new situation and, assuming that it was to continue, introduced heirs to the prophets. Josephus, for instance, who regarded the latter as inspired chroniclers, saw historians – himself no doubt included – as their second-rate successors.

> From Artaxerxes to our own time the complete history has been written, but has not been deemed worthy of equal credit with the earlier records, because of the failure of the exact succession of the prophets.[27]

In rabbinic thought, the same supposition is axiomatic, and the indispensable functions of prophecy are provided with other channels. The 'men of the Great Synagogue' replaced the prophets in their capacity as transmitters of the Mosaic 'oral law',[28] and following a more recently attested, though probably antique tradition, the Bible-interpreting Targumists. It was from the prophets Haggai, Zechariah and Malachi that Jonathan ben Uzziel is said to have received instruction before composing his Aramaic paraphrase to the prophetic books of the Old Testament.[29]

On the other hand, although the prophet's secondary roles were maintained in this way, his essential office, the revelation of God's will to men, was not made good by human means because no one was thought worthy to receive the holy spirit, and thus become a prophet. If such a person existed, his generation was unworthy of prophecy. It is said, for example, of Hillel, one of the pillars of Pharisaism in the time of Jesus:

> When the elders came to the house of Gadia in Jericho, a heavenly voice proclaimed to them: There is a man among you worthy of the holy spirit, but this generation is unfit for it. They fixed their eyes on Hillel the Elder.[30]

The only substitute instrument of revelation recognized by rabbinic teaching, an instrument expressly described as having succeeded prophecy, was the 'heavenly voice' (*bath kol*):

> Since the death of the last prophets, Haggai, Zechariah and Malachi, the holy spirit ceased from Israel, but they received messages by means of a heavenly voice.[31]

As has been shown, the 'voice' was allowed no authority, in normal circumstances, in matters relating to *halakhah*, a discipline which was to be constructed, not on new revelation, but on tradition and reason.[32] Its activity was confined to testifying to a person's holiness – as in the case of Hanina and on the occasion of the baptism of Jesus by John – or to conveying a divine command. For example, Jonathan ben Uzziel was forbidden by a *bath kol* to publish the Targum of the Writings.[33]

Needless to say, these were the views of the Pharisaic intellectual *élite* of Jerusalem; for the tendency to dispense with prophetic mediation was neither general, nor even predominant, in the inter-Testamental period. Whereas the Sadducees appear to have associated prophecy with the priestly function,[34] the belief in saints, the bearers of the spirit of God, continued among the simple people, and in those milieux the Gospel tradition concerning the prophet Jesus was not seen as self-contradictory. Indeed, there are also sporadic signs on the level of literature that a prophetic revival was expected.

The First Book of the Maccabees is the earliest post-biblical source to provide evidence of such an outlook. In it the notion is conveyed that the settlement of a very difficult or important issue must be accompanied by a clause foreseeing its possible revision, or cancellation, by an eventual prophet. When the friends of Judas Maccabaeus were undecided about what they should do with the defiled stones of the altar in the Temple, they agreed to leave them in an appropriate place 'until a prophet should arise who could be consulted about them'.[35] Similarly, the appointment of Judas's brother, Simon, to a hereditary ethnarchy and pontificate was made vaguely conditional on future prophetic approval.

The Jews and their priests confirmed Simon as their leader and high priest in perpetuity until a true prophet should appear.[36]

It is worth remarking that the prophet envisaged is a person with insight rather than charismatic activity, and although his coming is placed in the future, the context does not seem positively eschatological.

Josephus is another to express belief in the survival of prophetic gifts among Jews, as he demonstrates in representing John Hyrcanus I, the Hasmonean high priest and ruler, as a man enabled by God 'to foresee and foretell the future'.[37] What is more, he regarded himself as an interpreter of dreams, like the patriarch Joseph, his namesake, and the chronologically less remote Simon of the Essene sect,[38] and spoke of himself as an inspired exponent of 'ambiguous utterances of the Deity'. Above all, he thought he was one whose spirit had been chosen 'to announce the things that are to come',[39] and claimed to have correctly predicted the overthrow of his Galilean headquarters after forty-seven days, his own capture by the Romans, and also the accession of Vespasian and Titus, his captors, to the imperial throne.[40]

Admittedly, Josephus's boasting is one thing, and an immaterial one, and the reality of his claim another; but the very fact that he could write in such a way shows that although prophecy as such was believed to have ended, it was still possible to conceive that a favoured individual might be endowed with the gift of prediction. There is indeed nothing surprising in the survival of the 'intellectual' aspect of prophecy with its professed insight into the future. The real problem is the miraculous element attending it – for educated Jews of the transitional period, like Josephus and the rabbis, were reluctant to invoke miracles and refused to ascribe great importance to them. Neither Hillel, nor Shammai, two older contemporaries of Jesus whose place is among the greatest architects of Judaism, have ever been credited by rabbinic writings with performing wonders;[41] and Josephus himself can hardly conceal his detestation for the self-proclaimed miracle-workers of his own age whom he prefers to designate as charlatans.[42]

ESCHATOLOGICAL PROPHECY

Together with this loosely defined notion of a revival of prophecy and an acceptance of occasional manifestations of prophetic phenomena, the expectation was prevalent in inter-Testamental Judaism of a heavenly messenger who, at the end of time, would deliver God's final words to Israel. This so-called eschatological prophet assumes two different forms in the sources, one dependent on the figure of Elijah and the other on that of Moses, both of them drawn from classic scriptural proof-texts. It is with these two that early Gospel tradition associates the 'prophet' Jesus.

1. *The returning Elijah*

Post-biblical belief in a renewed ministry of Elijah in the last days of the present time – a figure quite different from the miracle-worker seen reflected in Honi, Jesus and Hanina – originated in the prophecy of Malachi identifying the 'messenger' who was to clear a way before God:

> Look, I will send you the prophet Elijah before the great and terrible day of the Lord comes.[43]

In the text itself, and in its expansion by Jesus ben Sira, this Elijah is depicted as a mediator between God and Israel.

> He will reconcile fathers to sons and sons to fathers.[44]

> It is written that you are to come at the appointed time with warnings, to allay the divine wrath before its final fury, to reconcile father and son, and to restore the tribes of Jacob.[45]

The implication here seems to be that Elijah was expected as a redeemer and a peace-maker,[46] rather than as a forerunner of the Messiah. That he was soon to be given such a role is, however, clear from an allegory in the First Book of Enoch in which, symbolized as a ram, he and three angels prepare the final scene during which the Messiah makes his appearance in the shape of a white bull with great horns.[47]

For a certain period of time, therefore, the Jewish expectation of Elijah was twofold. Some awaited an independent agent entrusted with the final restoration of Israel; others, probably the majority, looked for a person whose task was to herald the onset of the messianic age.

It was the first of these hopes that almost certainly led Galileans who were in sympathy with Jesus to believe that he was Elijah,[48] though there is no indication in the Synoptics to suggest that Jesus ever thought of himself in this way.

The second image, that of the forerunner of the Messiah, is deeply embedded in the Gospel tradition which assigns the function to John and thereby reduces the dignity of the Baptist from the status of a Messiah ascribed to him by his own disciples.[49]

In brief, the figure of the Elijah-like prophet was soon dissociated from Jesus, and attached to the person of the Messiah's precursor. As a result, when Jesus was later portrayed as 'the prophet', the title had no longer any direct dependence on Elijah the Messenger, but possessed a totally different scriptural derivation.

2. *The awaited prophet*

The biblical source for the expectation of the eschatological prophet is the Pentateuch, and in particular – to judge from quotations in the New Testament and in the Dead Sea Scrolls – the last two verses of the passage from Deuteronomy in which Moses announces the coming of another mouthpiece of God similar to himself:

> The Lord your God will raise up a prophet from among you like myself, and you shall listen to him. . . . 'I will raise up for them a prophet like you, one of their own race, and I will put my words into his mouth. He shall convey all my commands to them, and if anyone does not listen to the words which he will speak in my name I will require satisfaction from him.'[50]

In the Scrolls the Community Rule discloses that three leading figures were expected to appear in the last days. The men of holiness, it orders,

> shall be ruled by the primitive precepts . . . until the prophet and the Messiahs of Aaron and Israel shall come.[51]

The same eschatological trinity is reflected in the Messianic Anthology or Testimonia from Cave 4: the prophet is associated with Deuteronomy 18: 18–19, the text already cited, and the royal and priestly Messiahs with Numbers 24: 15–17 and Deuteronomy 33: 8–11.[52]

The prophet's actual mission is not clearly defined, but it seems to have been conceived as that of a teacher. There is, moreover, no indication that he was to be subordinate to the Messiahs: in fact, the three figures are represented as being basically equal. One further consideration to be remembered is that if the present writer is correct in suggesting that at a subsequent stage of Qumran doctrinal evolution the 'prophet' was identified as the historical figure of the sect's Teacher of Righteousness,[53] it would follow that in the minds of Jews living in the inter-Testamental period, the fulfilment of the prediction concerning the prophet could be seen as chronologically independent of other more traditional messianic phenomena.

The investment of Jesus with the prophet's role occurs in the Fourth Gospel and the Acts of the Apostles rather than in the Synoptics, where the accent lies on the miraculous feature of prophecy. In John's Gospel the Baptist formally denies, when questioned by a priestly and levitical embassy from Jerusalem, that he is either Elijah or 'the prophet we await',[54] but friendly witnesses twice attribute this dignity to Jesus, both times distinguishing it from that of the Messiah.[55]

But where the Johannine evidence merely alludes to Deuteronomy 18, the author of Acts, in Peter's exhortation to a Jewish crowd in the Temple of Jerusalem, explicitly applies to Jesus this proof-text concerning the eschatological prophet.

'And now, my friends, I know quite well that you acted in

ignorance, and so did your rulers; but this is how God fulfilled what he had foretold in the utterances of all the prophets: that his Messiah should suffer.

'Repent then and turn to God, so that your sins may be wiped out. Then the Lord may grant you a time of recovery and send you the Messiah he has already appointed, that is, Jesus. He must be received into heaven until the time of universal restoration comes, of which God spoke by his holy prophets. Moses said: "The Lord God will raise up a prophet for you from among yourselves as he raised me; you shall listen to everything he says to you, and anyone who refuses to listen to that prophet must be extirpated from Israel." '[56]

The speaker thus appears to establish a distinction between the earthly career of Jesus foretold in prophecies regarding the suffering Messiah, and the exalted figure returning from heaven promised in the Mosaic oracle. In other words, whereas in John the Deuteronomic eschatological prophet is interpreted historically, according to Peter's exegesis formulated by Luke, the fulfilment of the expectation was to await the day of the Parousia.

Nevertheless, the image of Jesus as the final prophet did not endure. The New Testament and rabbinic literature alike provide evidence of the same kind of diminishment of the eschatological function of the Mosaic prophet as that which resulted from the reduction of the originally autonomous mission of Elijah to that of the Messiah's forerunner. In the Transfiguration story of the Gospels, Moses and Elijah are the attendants of the glorified Jesus.[57] Similarly, in rabbinic tradition they are described as arriving together at the end of time,[58] or Moses and the Messiah are described simply as the companions of the Word (*memra*) of God on the final Passover night of salvation.[59]

Whereas the non-success of the concept of the Elijah-like prophet, as well as of other primitive titles like 'the saint' and 'the righteous',[60] can be found attributable to their failure to do justice to the veneration with which Jesus was regarded, the image of the New Moses might have attained permanence: in contemporary Jewish thought, Moses, the first Redeemer, was one of the chief prototypes of the final Saviour, the Messiah.[61] That the title, after promising beginnings,[62] made no further headway, seems to have been due to the coincidence, unfortunate or not, that during the formation of primitive Christian thought there was a plethora in Palestine of pseudo-prophets. These caused untold suffering to the credulous with their promises of supernatural deliverance from the Romans and a repetition of the miracles of the Exodus.[63] Josephus names two of these 'impostors', and refers anonymously to a large number of them. Of one of the most famous, Theudas (also mentioned in the New Testament[64]), he writes that during the procuratorship of Cuspius Fadus

> he stated that he was a prophet and that at his command the river (Jordan) would be parted.[65]

The other notorious troublemaker was 'the Egyptian'. This man, who called himself a prophet and was popularly known as such, announced that at his word the walls of Jerusalem would collapse.[66] Later, Saint Paul was mistaken for him by the Roman tribune after his arrest in the Jerusalem Temple. He was asked:

> 'Are you not the Egyptian, then, who recently stirred up a revolt and led the four thousand men of the Assassins out into the wilderness?'[67]

During the last stages of the siege of Jerusalem yet another of these charlatans foretold immediate deliverance to those prepared to follow him to the Temple court; he thus led six thousand people to their death.[68] There were many prophets, according to Josephus, in the service of the rebel leaders, offering miraculous help to the miserable crowds. The historian's comment on the situation is that

> in adversity man is quickly persuaded; but when the deceiver actually pictures release from prevailing horrors, then the sufferer wholly abandons himself to expectation.[69]

It is clear from these texts, and the Gospel *logion* warning against pseudo-prophets,[70] that from the middle of the first century AD to the end of the first revolt these self-proclaimed wonder-workers found a ready following among the simple victims of the revolutionary activities of the Zealots. But as the promises remained unfulfilled and the miracles failed to materialize, and as the sarcasm and antipathy of their political opponents stripped the pretenders of their repute, the term 'prophet' applied to an individual between the years AD 50 and 70 not surprisingly acquired distinctly pejorative overtones in the bourgeois and aristocratic idiom of Pharisees and Sadducees.

It was no doubt for this reason also, and not merely because of any dogmatic inadequacy, that the title ceased altogether to be applied to Jesus: which is curious in view of the fact that it seems to have been the description he himself preferred.

Excursus: prophetic celibacy

There is complete silence in the Gospels concerning the marital status of Jesus. No wife accompanies him in his public career, or, for that matter, stays at home, as the wives of his followers were expected to do. Such a state of affairs is sufficiently unusual in ancient Jewry to prompt further enquiry, for the Hebrew Bible, though it prescribes temporary sexual abstinence in certain circumstances, never orders a life of total celibacy. Women were declared taboo to soldiers on campaign,[71] and participation in an act of worship entailed abstention from intercourse[72] since it was judged to cause ritual uncleanness lasting till the following evening, as did contact with a menstruating woman.[73] As a result, Temple ministers as well as ordinary people taking part in the cult were obliged to regulate their sexual life carefully.[74]

By contrast, the sect of the Essenes, despite the fact that the Qumran texts do not expressly enjoin the renunciation of marriage (though they order women to be excluded from the camp of the sons of light during the whole forty-year-long eschatological war),[75] appears to have made an institution of celibacy, probably in order to be always in a condition to take part in worship, even if Philo and Josephus prefer to attribute the cause to misogyny.

> They do not, indeed, on principle, condemn wedlock . . .
> but they wish to protect themselves against women's wanton-
> ness, being persuaded that none of the sex keeps her plighted
> troth to one man.[76]

From Josephus's claim that young children were admitted into the sect, it may in addition be inferred that, among some of the communities at least, celibacy may have been lifelong. On the other hand, Philo and Pliny the Elder maintain that the sectaries were mature, and even elderly, persons, widowers perhaps, or men who had segregated themselves from their families in order to pursue holiness.[77] The Egyptian branch of this ascetic move-ment, the Therapeutae, also consisted of celibate men and elderly virgins.[78]

Nevertheless, taking into consideration the very great difference, indeed, diametrical opposition between the spirituality of Jesus and the ritual asceticism of the Essenes, it is unlikely to have been their influence that inspired his own choice, or suggested the rule he imposed, or is reported by the evangelists to have imposed, on his would-be disciples that they should forsake their wives to follow him.[79] More helpful, however, is a glance at traditions surviving in rabbinic literature which imply an incompatibility between prophecy and marriage.

According to the Talmud, Moses freely decided to terminate cohabitation with his wife after he received his call from God. He reasoned that if the Israelites, to whom the Lord spoke only once and briefly, were ordered to abstain from women temporarily, he, being in continual dialogue with Heaven, should remain chaste permanently.[80]

One of the early rabbinic commentaries on Numbers treats the same theme from the woman's standpoint. Moses' sister, Miriam, noticing her sister-in-law's neglected appearance, asked her why she had ceased to look after herself. Zipporah answered:

> 'Your brother does not care about the thing.'[81]

The same passage of the document also notes that when it was announced that the two Israelite elders, Eldad and Medad, had started to prophesy, Miriam overheard Zipporah's muttered remark:

'Woe to the wives of these men!'

The first of these interpretations is anonymously transmitted. The second is attributed to Rabbi Nathan, who flourished in the second half of the second century AD. Nevertheless, the antiquity of the tradition, and its certain existence at the time of Jesus, may be deduced from Philo's use of it. The Alexandrian sage states that to render himself pure, Moses cleansed himself of

all the calls of mortal nature, food and drink and intercourse with women. This last he had disdained for many a day, almost from the time when, possessed by the spirit, he entered on his work as prophet, since he held it fitting to hold himself always in readiness to receive the oracular messages.[82]

Against such a background of first-century AD Jewish opinion, namely that the prophetic destiny entailed amongst other things a life of continence, Jesus' apparent voluntary embrace of celibacy, at any rate from the time of his reception of the holy spirit, becomes historically meaningful. (Due to a total lack of evidence, his sexual situation before his baptism by John, and the significance of a possible perpetual celibacy, must remain outside the realm of historical research proper.)

There is, however, no more directly relevant material in rabbinic literature than the texts cited. As the authors were convinced that prophecy belonged to the past, prophetic abstinence from sex was for them a purely academic question; their own religious duty was marriage for the purpose of procreating children. Rabbi Eliezer ben Hyrcanus even went so far, at the end of the first century AD, as to compare deliberate abstention from procreation to murder; and so did his contemporary, Simeon ben Azzai. As Simeon was himself unmarried, this exposed him to the criticism of his colleagues. To their accusation, 'You preach well, but do not practise your preaching', he pleaded unceasing devotion to biblical study:

> 'My soul is in love with the Torah. The world can be kept going by others.'[83]

This excuse was not found convincing and his view was frowned on by Judaism.

The outlook of the early Hasidim in this respect is not expressed verbally in the sources, though both Honi and Hanina are said to have been husbands and fathers, but one interesting teaching comes from a second-century AD miracle-worker, the Galilean rabbi and saint, Pinhas ben Yair:

> Watchfulness leads to cleanness, cleanness to purity, purity to abstinence, abstinence to holiness, holiness to humility, humility to the fear of sin, fear of sin to devoutness, devoutness to the holy spirit, the holy spirit to the resurrection of the dead, and the resurrection of the dead to Elijah of blessed memory.[84]

This chain of virtues seems to combine mainstream rabbinic piety with ideals proper to the Hasidim. Among these are devoutness, humility and the fear of sin, but also sexual abstinence and the holy spirit which is the hallmark of prophecy. And at the climax of the path of perfection, it will be noted, stands once more the Hasid's model, Elijah.

5. Jesus the lord

'Lord' is a New Testament key-word. Its frequency in the Gospels and Acts, and the use in the Letters of such stereotyped formulas as 'the lord', 'the lord Jesus (Christ)' and 'our lord (Jesus Christ)', suffice to prove it. Yet, paradoxically, whereas Jesus is seldom called 'prophet' despite his approval of this title, he is often referred to as 'lord', notwithstanding the fact that in the Synoptic Gospels he never accepts such a dignity or attributes to himself any 'lordly' function.[1] Even more paradoxical is the apparent indifference of present-day New Testament scholars, usually so keen on the titles of Jesus, to whether he himself believed he was 'the lord'. In any case, only a minority of them concede authenticity to the application of this mode of address to Jesus during his lifetime. It is generally assumed that it was an invention of the 'post-Easter' period and has nothing to do with Jesus himself.

Since this sort of treatment is symptomatic of the kind of doctrinaire paralysis into which students of the Gospels have argued themselves, it will be instructive, as much for the understanding of the New Testament as for that of contemporary New Testament scholarship and its ills, to see in detail how it manifests itself. As the theories relating to historico-doctrinal evolution equal in number the solutions arrived at, it has been thought best to classify them schematically under three headings: (a) the conservative view, (b) the radical view, (c) compromises.

(A) THE CONSERVATIVE VIEW

The conservative approach is well illustrated by the work of an English New Testament specialist, Vincent Taylor.[2] Characteristically, he begins with a feat of mental acrobatics. He maintains, in effect – in conformity with scholarly orthodoxy – that the numerous Gospel examples of the vocative 'lord' are largely irrelevant since they merely represent the manner in which disciples addressed their teacher in Hebrew.[3] The implication of this remark is that as a mode of address, however historically true, it is not worth bothering about. It means simply that Jesus was regarded as a teacher; but even if he were, this would be of no interest to a theologian! Taylor then eviscerates his own critical comment by adding:

> It is hardly to be doubted that in some cases, when (lord) is addressed to Jesus, it is more than an expression of courtesy.[4]

Leaving aside points dependent on 'impressions and suppositions', Taylor claims that the title, 'the lord', though not introduced until after the resurrection, derives from Jesus' own exegesis of the allusion to the Messiah in Psalm 110: 1, not as the son of David, but as his 'lord'.[5] The 'post-Easter' date is deduced from the usage of 'the lord' in Luke,[6] the spurious epilogue of Mark,[7] and John's nine examples in chapters 20 and 21.[8]

The primitive theological use of the title, this author continues, is displayed extensively in the Acts, especially in the first half of the book, which 'probably' represents 'the earliest preaching with fidelity'. As might be expected, however, it is the Pauline evidence that is judged to be decisive. For the Apostle of the Gentiles and the members of the churches founded by him, 'Jesus is preeminently Lord'. Paul applies the phrase indiscriminately to the historical Jesus as well as to the 'exalted', 'coming', triumphant and ruling Christ.[9]

Essential though the Pauline evidence may be, it is further maintained that the title was not coined by him but was inherited from the primitive community of worshippers. The

Maranatha ('Come, our lord!') invocation in 1 Corinthians 16: 22 shows 'unmistakably' that the phrase 'our lord' was 'in familiar use in Aramaic-speaking communities'. Accepting a sequence of unsubstantiated assumptions, it is traceable back to an Easter-day exclamation. These assumptions are: (1) that the frequent mention of 'the lord' in 1 Thessalonians, written in AD 51, implies that the title had a long previous use, during, at least, the decade from 40 to 50; (2) that its liturgical employment in Jewish-Christian circles suggests as an origin the years AD 30–40; and (3) that the cry, 'The lord has risen!' is only negligibly, if at all, anachronistic; 'it is by no means excluded that historically it is the earliest use of the name'.[10] The resurrection is singled out as the most important factor in the development of the 'lord' concept, and with it the expectation of the Parousia, the celebration of the Lord's Supper, the transmission of reinterpreted parables concerning the 'lord of the vineyard' and the 'lord' of the servants, and the Christian exegesis of Psalm 110.[11]

In regard to the relationship of the christological title 'lord' and the Septuagint divine name, *Kyrios*=the Lord, Taylor believes that it is unlikely to have been used in connection with Jesus because of its employment as a designation of God. On the other hand, it is because he is called 'lord' that Old Testament passages are applied to him mentioning the 'Lord=God', and that subsequently a 'Christian' reading of the Bible recognizes Jesus=God in all the 'Jesus=lord' texts.[12] In other words, although originally the title conveyed no identification of Jesus as God, it moved – even independently of the peculiar atmosphere of the Hellenistic world with its many lords and deities – unavoidably in that direction.

> Invocation is next door to prayer and confession to worship. Implicit in the recognition of the lordship of Jesus is the acknowledgement of His essential divinity.[13]

In short, and despite careful beating about the bush, the two crucial assertions are that the title fundamentally comes from Jesus' own definition of the Messiah as lord, and that ultimately it is nothing less than a synonym for his divinity.

(B) THE RADICAL VIEW

Compared with the labyrinthine thought-processes characteristic of the conservative approach, the point of view of radicals such as Wilhelm Bousset or Rudolf Bultmann is refreshingly simple. Jesus did not call himself 'the lord', nor was he so designated by his disciples or any Palestinian Aramaic-speaking believer. The title *Kyrios* was borrowed from pagan Hellenistic terminology and applied to Jesus by Gentile Christians on Greco-Roman soil. They modelled their proclamation, 'Jesus is lord', on the worship of the 'Lord' Osiris (or Sarapis, or Hermes, or the 'Lady' Isis, Artemis, or Cybele) in the mystery religions, and on the apotheosis of the Roman emperors (*Kyrios/Dominus et Deus noster*), especially from the time of Gaius Caligula (AD 37–41) onward.[14] Bultmann systematically rejects even more adamantly than Bousset, whose doctrinal heir he is, every claim to Judeo-Christian antecedents. For him, not even *Maranatha* is proof that the primitive community invoked Jesus as 'lord', for the phrase may originally have been applied to God. As for the description of Christians as 'those who . . . call on the name of our lord Jesus Christ',[15] it belongs not to the Palestinian, but to the Hellenistic Church.[16]

Here the conclusion is brief. Since the *Kyrios* title is alien to the original Gospel and has nothing in common with Palestinian communities, it is a non-issue in a study devoted to Jesus, though essential to the theology of Gentile Christianity.

(C) COMPROMISES

As may be foreseen, attempts have been made to bridge the gulf separating the conservative and radical extremes. One such effort to achieve a scholarly compromise is the theory construed by Ferdinand Hahn.[17] At first sight, it appears the most satisfactory of all contemporary endeavours.

Unlike Taylor and Bultmann, Hahn sees a historical link between the Synoptic form of address and its subsequent conceptual development. He claims that the vocative 'lord!' paved the way to the absolute designation, '*the* lord', in the same way that the appellation 'rabbi!/teacher!' led to the definition of Jesus as '*the* teacher'.

Obeying the unwritten law of New Testament scholarship, Hahn considers as historically admissible only 'lord' invocations made by Gentiles, namely by the Syro-Phoenician woman and the centurion from Capernaum.[18] The first uses the title as a mode of address in the most general sense; the second, as an acknowledgement of Jesus' authority. In neither case is it invested with any 'christological' significance, and even less with a reference, however faint, to divine 'lordship'. The latter notion first emerges in Matthew 8: 2, where the person invoked as 'lord' is also 'worshipped'. This point, incidentally, is most debatable, in spite of Hahn's unhesitating assertion that 'lord' and 'to worship' combine to form a 'divine name of Majesty'.[19] The Greek word used in Matthew renders in the Septuagint the Hebrew verb, 'to prostrate oneself', employed in the Bible in relation to men as well as to God.[20] And who would be prepared to assert that the Matthean parable deifies the royal ruler just because a servant is said to have knelt down and worshipped him?[21]

If Hahn admits that Jesus was occasionally addressed as 'lord' *qua* teacher, he is most firmly opposed to any suggestion that it was a title chosen by the Galilean master to express his 'self-awareness'.

> This was the work of the church . . . faced with the task of defining the reality of the . . . person of Jesus.[22]

The original usage was maintained for a long time parallel with the later theological developments, as is manifest in the Pauline mention of the 'words of the Lord' and 'brothers of the Lord', and even in John's 'teacher and Lord'.[23]

The second stage of the doctrinal evolution of 'lord' took place, according to Hahn, in Palestinian Judeo-Christianity and centred on the expectation of Jesus' return. In addition to the eschatological overtones of the invocation, 'lord, lord!' in the Gospels and the parable of the Ten Virgins,[24] the Aramaic-speaking worshippers'

Maranatha appeal in 1 Corinthians 16: 22 (and in the Doctrine of the Twelve Apostles 10: 6, a late-first-century AD liturgy) testifies to the metamorphosis of 'lord=teacher' into 'Our lord= Universal Judge'. There is here, the reader is told, 'a Christological concept . . . able to include . . . both the earthly and ultimate activity of Jesus'.[25]

The third stage saw the notion come into being of the 'exalted lord', 'sitting on the right hand of God', a title explained as springing from the idea of a 'messianic enthronement'. But whereas in Hahn's view 'the lord' and 'the glorified Messiah' were two separate concepts in Aramaic-Palestinian thinking, Hellenistic Judeo-Christianity brought them together by interpreting Psalm 110: 1:

> 'The Lord (God) said to my lord (the Messiah), "Sit at my right hand . . ." '[26]

This fusion of 'lord' and 'glorified Messiah' preserves the typical Jewish stress on an 'act of inauguration' conferring lordship on Jesus, a sovereignty altogether different from a 'divine dignity';[27] it has nevertheless inevitably contributed to a blurring of the distinction between the two. In addition, besides opening the way to associating with Jesus such biblical ideas as the 'day of the Lord', the 'way of the Lord' and the 'name of the Lord',[28] it has made it possible to introduce the notion of his everlasting presence with believers,[29] and of the redemptive virtue inherent in the proclamation of his title:

> If you confess with your lips that Jesus is lord . . . you will be saved.[30]

The last of the evolutionary stages, according to Hahn, is that which witnessed the transformation of the 'exalted lord' into a Divine Being, a process which took place in the realm of Gentile Christianity. The ultimate Hellenistic-Jewish contribution to this is Paul's hymn to Christ in Philippians 2: 9–11 (*RSV*):

> God has highly exalted him and bestowed on him the name which is above every name, that at the name of Jesus every

knee should bow . . . and every tongue confess that Jesus
Christ is lord, to the glory of God the Father.

But it was under the influence of the mystery religions, and as
a result of a confrontation with the emperor cult, that belief in
the divine lordship of Jesus came into being, a faith so powerful
that the Gentile-Christian martyr refused, even at the price of
his life, to profane it by recognizing Caesar as lord.

The criticisms formulated against Ferdinand Hahn's theory by
fellow New Testament specialists, namely that certain literary
data belong to evolutionary layers other than those he suggests,
have the appearance of a special pleading.

Thus Philip Vielhauer's wholesale assault on Hahn might be
dismissed as unproven except for the fact that it also involves
statements concerning concrete and verifiable data. He reproaches
Hahn with serious shortcomings in the field of Greek and Aramaic
linguistic usage, and judges the first stage of the reconstruction
unreliable because the whole speculation on the significance of
the Aramaic word for 'lord' (*mar*) is based on 'antiquated secondary literature'.[31]

Hahn's understanding of Palestinian linguistic customs is
almost entirely dependent on the studies of Gustaf Dalman, the
leading Aramaic expert at the turn of the century, whose dual
analysis, in the epoch-making work, *The Words of Jesus*, of the
term 'Lord' as applying to God or men, he largely reproduces.[32]
But Dalman's drawback is that he wrote seventy years ago, and
part of his carefully devised argument has since been contradicted
by fresh discoveries.

Vielhauer, in criticizing Hahn and his use of antiquated authors,
relies on an attempt made by Siegfried Schulz to present an
up-to-date picture of 'Lord' in Palestinian and Hellenistic
Jewish thought.[33] This author knows, having read Paul Kahle,
that the replacement of the Tetragram by *Kyrios* attested in Old
Testament codices copied by Christian scribes does not figure in
the relics of Jewish manuscripts of the Greek Bible. In these,
YHWH is not translated but is kept unchanged, i.e. written in
Hebrew letters. The old assumption, still held by Dalman, that

in Hellenistic Jewry YHWH and 'Lord' were synonyms, is no longer tenable. In fact Schulz considers it doubtful whether 'the Lord' was employed at all as a divine name in pre-Christian days. Admittedly, Origen testifies to the Jewish custom in the early centuries of the Christian era of rendering the Tetragram – pronounced in Hebrew *Adonai* (Lord) – as *Kyrios* in Greek.[34] Yet the remains of pre-Christian Hellenistic Jewish literature, i.e. the Letter of Aristeas and excerpts from third- and second-century BC authors preserved by the Church Father Eusebius, show that in these works 'the Lord' never occurs. By the first century BC, however, the Greek Apocryphon, the Wisdom of Solomon, employs it frequently; and thereafter it serves as a regular title of God in the first-century AD writings of Philo and Josephus. Consequently, Schulz maintains, the change took place in the first century BC.[35]

He begins his outline of Aramaic linguistic usage with the Elephantine papyri dating from the fifth century BC which contain only one reference to God as 'the Lord of heaven', but numerous instances in which 'lord' is employed in connection with human authorities, and in particular as a courteous form of address.[36] Moving then to the language of the Book of Daniel, God is found depicted there as the 'Lord of kings' and the 'Lord of heaven', and Nebuchadnezzar is referred to as 'my lord',[37] which implies that the style of the fifth century BC remained unchanged for the next three hundred years or so.

The sector of Jewish literature treated least satisfactorily by Schulz is that of Qumran, with its substantial quota of new information. Here, he proceeds with unsure steps, misses references and misinterprets fresh data. As for the Targums and rabbinic documents, from them he deduces that they use 'lord' rarely, or very rarely, and when they do, they mean 'rabbi'.

What does he conclude from this survey? Apart from the obvious fact that in addition to its application to God, 'lord' was used in connection with men in authority (king, prefect, husband, etc.), and that the predominant feature of 'my lord' as a style was judicial dignity, Schulz's main finding is that it is in the Qumran writings that God is addressed for the first time as 'my

Lord' in Aramaic.[38] To underline its novelty, he points out the total absence of a similar invocation 'in the entire Aramaic material' from the fifth to the first century BC.[39]

This argument looks much stronger than it is since the 'entire Aramaic material' amounts, in fact, to very little, and in this quantitatively small literary source God is addressed only once.[40] In other words, the invocation, 'my lord', had little opportunity for expression, and the truth is that it is not known whether it was often, seldom, or never used in prayer.

Turning to the New Testament, Schulz argues that the 'lord' title designates the Universal Judge in the 'post-Easter' eschatology. The prayer *Maranatha* is an invitation to this apocalyptic envoy of God to come and exercise his judicial function. Here, the traditional Jewish 'messianology, Toralogy [sic] and apocalyptic' are actualized, leading to a Kyriology [sic] in which the community hails the self-revealing God by inspired acclamation.[41] This means that in the New Testament the Hellenistic 'acclamation-*Kyrios*' was linked to the Hellenistic-Jewish 'Tetragram-*Kyrios*' and the originally purely apocalyptic *Mara*=Lord, the whole of which occurred in the pre-Pauline stage of doctrinal evolution, that is to say, within twenty years of the death of Jesus!

To sum up, the systematizing efforts of contemporary New Testament scholarship appear to agree on two points: (1) The title, 'lord', postdates the historical Jesus; (2) its use as an acknowledgement of divinity arises from a Hellenistic milieu. Little regard has been paid during the last few years to the opening phase of its evolutionary movement. In this respect, therefore, the most useful and constructive step would seem to consist in a reconsideration of the nature of the Aramaic (and Greek) speech of Jews in New Testament times, a study to be performed for, as it were, its own sake, and not, as in the past, for New Testament exegetical purposes.

THE PHILOLOGICAL BACKGROUND

What then is actually and factually known about the use of the term '(the) lord' in Jewish writings during the period extending roughly from 200 BC to AD 300, i.e. from Daniel to the rabbis of the Talmud? Was it, to begin with, commonly applied to God?

Disregarding the negative view prevailing until now,[42] it is necessary to start with the document the discovery of which has completely altered the linguistic situation, namely the Genesis Apocryphon from Qumran Cave 1, published in 1956.[43] This is the first Aramaic inter-Testamental document to represent the right kind of comparative literature. In it the frequency of 'Lord' (*marah*) is striking: of the twenty-six Aramaic titles of God used in the part of the work published so far, twelve include 'Lord'. Mostly, it figures in composite expressions coined on the pattern of biblical Aramaic language, such as 'Lord of greatness', 'Lord of heaven' and 'Lord of heaven and earth'. The Tetragram YHWH in Genesis 13:4, it is worth noting, is rendered 'Lord of the worlds', or 'Lord of the ages', in the Apocryphon.[44]

Twice the mention of 'Lord' comes very close to a titular or absolute use in the context of a prayer. In the first instance the text reads:

> Blessed art thou, O Most High God, Lord of all the worlds, thou who art Lord and ruler over all things.[45]

In the second example, the prayer runs:

> Thou art the Lord of all the kings of the earth.[46]

Moreover, God is addressed no less than four times by this title. Abraham invokes him as 'my Lord', and 'my Lord God', and confesses:

> Thou art God Most High, my Lord.[47]

Thus the first fact to emerge from the Genesis Apocryphon is that in literary Aramaic little older than the New Testament the term 'Lord' appears to have been commonly applied to God, both descriptively and as an invocation. The essentially parallel usage in later rabbinic literature can therefore scarcely be treated as an innovation:

> My Lord, cause the land to produce!
> My Lord, cause the land to prosper!

> My Lord, may the Temple be built!
> My Lord, when will the Temple be built?[48]

In regard to contemporary Hebrew style, the Qumran writings confirm that in the inter-Testamental period the worshipper thought of God almost instinctively as 'Lord'; in the psalms composed by the sectaries, the Thanksgiving Hymns, he is most frequently addressed as *Adonai*.[49] Furthermore, in addition to Aramaic and Hebrew, the Jewish Greek usage points in the same direction. In the Greek version of Ecclesiasticus, not only the Tetragram, but also 'Lord' (*adon*), are rendered as *Kyrios*;[50] and in the free composition of the Wisdom of Solomon, God is addressed or described as 'Lord' no less than twenty-seven times.[51] The Greek linguistic custom, like the Semitic, remained unchanged in subsequent centuries, as is proved by a funereal inscription from the famous Galilean necropolis of Beth She'arim (third century AD):

> Lord, remember thy maidservant, Primosa!
> Lord, remember thy servant, Sacerdos![52]

Finally, completing the full circle, the Greek *Kyrios* entered the Galilean Aramaic dialect as a loan-word and became a name for God! The most curious example of this, perhaps, is contained in the Palestinian Targum (Pseudo-Jonathan) to Numbers 11: 26, which renders in an extraordinary Greco-Aramaic glossolalia the prophetic message of the two elders, colleagues of Moses, who were seized by the holy spirit:

> The Lord (*Kiris*) is present (*etimos=hetoimos*) to them in the moment of distress (*aniki=ananke*).

It may be wondered whether this bilingual 'prophecy' (three words in Greek and the remainder in Aramaic) should not be used to interpret the charisma of 'speaking with tongues' described in Acts 2: 4–13. In fact a mixture of Aramaic and Greek would have been more or less intelligible to most Jews in the first century AD.

In brief, any objective survey of the philological evidence, Aramaic, Hebrew and Greek, is bound to acknowledge that the term 'Lord' occupies an important position in the religious language of the Jews from Daniel to the rabbis of the third century AD.[53]

'Lord' (*mar/kyrios*) is no less well attested as a human form of address. Taking once more the Qumran Genesis Apocryphon as a primary guide, the style, 'my lord', is employed when a wife speaks to her husband and a son to his father. It occurs also as the title of a ruler, i.e. a man wielding political power. Pharaoh is called 'my lord' by one of his princes, and Abraham by the submissive king of Sodom.[54] In rabbinic terminology, also, the Roman emperor is addressed as 'Our lord the King': Judah the Prince destroyed a letter written by his secretary which opened, 'From Judah, the Patriarch, to our lord the King Antoninus'. He substituted for it the following style: 'To our lord the King, from Judah, your servant.'[55]

Once again, the Greek of Beth She'arim furnishes a distinct echo to the Qumran terminology and a clear link with Talmudic Aramaic. Two brothers, signing familiarly as Iako and Thino, refer to their deceased parents as 'my lord father' and 'my lady mother'.[56] This manner of designating a dead father is in harmony with the rabbinic rule recommending the replacement, in such circumstances, of *abba* ('father') by *abba mari* ('father, my lord').[57]

In the same way that in the previous section the adoption of *Kyrios* as an Aramaic word allowed a full circle to be drawn, the same process is possible here, though in the opposite direction, for to judge from another Beth She'arim inscription, the Aramaic *mar* could be used as a Greek title in *Mar* Thietetus.[58]

There is, moreover, indirect evidence testifying to a current association of the Aramaic and Greek titles, namely the famous mimicry of Galilean mispronunciation of certain words, which resulted in a Gentile judge being addressed as 'my lord slave' (*mari cheiri*) instead of 'my lord, my lord' (*mari kiri*).[59] Also, the story reported by Rab Kahana in the third century AD concerning the onomatopoeic *kiri kiri* ('lord! lord!') greeting of King Herod by all his doves save one (a Galilean pigeon?) which called, 'lord slave!'[60] further demonstrates that the equation of *mar* and *kyrios* was so familiar among Jews that the same pun could receive parallel formulations. It may therefore be safely deduced from the evidence extending from Qumran to the Talmud that the application of the mode of address, 'lord', to Jesus, contrary to academic opinion, is not only possible, but very likely.

If such is the case, it should be asked how the title 'lord' and the office of an authoritative teacher relate to one another. This would require a careful checking of the statements made by New Testament experts since Dalman[61] regarding the interchangeability of 'lord' and 'teacher' (*rabbi*, *rabbuni*), and the consequent synonymity of *rab/rabbun* and *mar*.[62]

In the light of the full evidence, this view seems misleading unless accompanied by further comments. (1) In spite of John 20:16, where *rabbuni* is interpreted as teacher, the primary significance of this Aramaic invocation is 'lord' (*kyrie*).[63] (2) In the Palestinian usage, the term maintained its basic meaning of a person wielding authority, even if it is true that in the terminology of third-century rabbis in Babylonia *mar* was to become the title of a teacher.[64] (3) It is correct that in Palestinian speech *mar* and *rab* are normally accompanied by a pronominal suffix (my, thy, etc., lord or teacher), but the much-repeated claim concerning the impossibility of an absolute use of 'lord' resulting from the consciously felt relationship between addresser and addressee appears to be excessive. Though no first-century AD evidence is available, it can be proved that in the following centuries the style, 'my teacher' (*rabbi*), had become a title in which all awareness of a personal bond had disappeared. From a form of address, *rabbi* became descriptive of a function. In the necropolis of Beth She'arim various rabbis are commemorated on their tombs as *Rabbi* X both in Hebrew and Greek, this really signifying, not '*my* teacher', but '*the* teacher' X.[65] As an external linguistic parallel, it may also be pointed out that the possessive pronoun *mon* has so completely lost its meaning in the French *monsieur* that it is possible to speak of *le monsieur*.

In other words, when the comments (1) and (2) are taken into account, it will no longer be certain that those addressing Jesus as 'lord' really meant 'teacher'. Furthermore, the third remark indirectly queries the axiomatic claim that the phrase, 'the lord', was inapplicable because *mar* was never used without a possessive pronoun.[66] But above all, it should be asked whether the development implied in the polite form of Aramaic speech might affect in any way the understanding of the use of *mar*, and its New Testament parallel, *kyrios*.

In his Aramaic grammar, Gustaf Dalman notes that in addresses of particular courtesy directed to a venerable person, or persons, the Galilean dialect substitutes for the direct 'thou' or 'you' a phrase composed of 'my lord' or 'our lord', and a verb in the third person singular.[67]

'May my lord (*mari*) not be angry with me!' is a standard formula of this sort.[68] Elsewhere, 'you' and 'thou' in the same dialogue are replaced by 'our teachers' (*rabbanan*) and 'our lord' (*maran*). Rabbi Abbahu asks his two junior colleagues, Rabbi Jonah and Rabbi Yose:

> Would our teachers care to discuss something from the Torah?

They retort:

> Would our lord care?[69]

It is but a short step from this Galilean Aramaic speech-form, in which the possessive pronoun has already lost its semantic value, to its complete omission. Instead of using the circumlocution, 'my lord', the speaker refers to the honoured person as *mar*, (the) lord. In a famous legend concerning Joshua ben Levi (a third-century AD Palestinian rabbi) and a reappearing Elijah, the prophet is asked by Joshua:

> Why did *mar* stay away?[70]

This Palestinian linguistic phenomenon is even better attested in the Babylonian Talmud and seems to have been characteristic of both dialects of Jewish Aramaic. Another story reports a conversation between the same Joshua ben Levi and the Messiah. Joshua greets him, 'Peace be upon you, my teacher and my lord!' and is saluted in return with, 'Peace be upon you, Levite'. Joshua then continues with greater awe and timidity, 'When is *mar* coming?' and is told, 'Today'.[71]

In addition to its application to the Messiah, this combination of *mar* and the third person singular is used in the Babylonian Talmud to address highly respected rabbis. The messengers sent to the prospective head of the Yavneh academy, Rabbi Eleazar ben Azariah, by those plotting the deposition of Gamaliel II, are reported to have asked him:

> Would it be agreeable to *mar* to become the head of the academy?[72]

Abayye questions Rabbi Avia:

> Why did *mar* not come to the lecture? . . . Does *mar* not think . . . ?[73]

Requesting Rabbi Isaac the Smith to discuss a legal issue, Rabbi Ammi asks:

> Would *mar* expound *halakhah*?

But Rabbi Asi, preferring doctrinal instruction, ripostes:

> Would *mar* expound *haggadah*?[74]

Finally, a distinction between straightforward and circumlocutory speech is expressly commented on in an exchange between Rabbi Jeremiah bar Abba and Rab, two third-century AD masters. The former asks:

> Have you recited the Havdalah prayer (at the end of the Sabbath)?

To which Rab replied:

> Yes, I have.

The Talmudic narrator of the episode then remarks:

> Rabbi Jeremiah did not say, 'Has *mar* recited the Havdalah prayer?' but 'Have you . . . ?'[75]

He then explains that, despite the informality of the phrasing, the style employed by Jeremiah was not improper because the two were students together and were consequently on friendly terms.

Several important points emerge from the evidence so far

collected. Firstly, an absolute use of 'lord' was possible in Jewish Aramaic, and its employment as a method of addressing a high-ranking person is at least probable. Secondly – and as far as is known this has never yet been pointed out – when the titles 'rabbi' and 'lord' occur together but refer to different persons, far from being synonymous, they reflect a hierarchical order in which *mar* is the superior. The dialogue in which Jonah and Yose are referred to as 'our rabbis', and Abbahu as 'our lord' has already been cited.[76] All three dramatis personae are established teachers and both parties employ courtesy forms, but it is the senior and most celebrated of them, Abbahu, who is called *mar*.

The apparently most significant illustration has however been left for the end, namely the story of the first-century BC miracle-working Hasid, Abba Hilkiah.[77]

> Abba Hilkiah was the son of Honi the Circle-Drawer's son. When the earth needed rain, our teachers (*rabbanan*) were in the habit of despatching envoys to him. He prayed and it rained. Once the earth was in need of rain, so our teachers (*rabbanan*) sent two of our teachers (*rabbanan*) to him that he might pray and rain might fall.

Abba Hilkiah was not at home when the messengers called. They found him labouring in the fields and saluted him, but as he did not return their greeting they waited, and in the evening followed him to his house. Allowed indoors, but not invited to share his table, they watched him eat. Then, when the family had finished, Abba Hilkiah, still ignoring the rabbis, said to his wife:

> We know that our teachers (*rabbanan*) have come because of the rain. Let us go to the roof and pray. Perhaps the Holy One, blessed be he, will be merciful and it will rain. But we shall not credit this blessing to ourselves.

They went up to the roof and he stood in one corner, and his wife in the other. When the first clouds rose, they came from his wife's direction.[78] He then came down and said to the rabbis:

> Why have our teachers (*rabbanan*) come? They said: Our

teachers (*rabbanan*) have sent us to *mar* that he might pray
for rain. He said to them: Blessed be God that he did not
allow you to need Abba Hilkiah. They said to him: We know
full well that the rain has come on account of *mar*.[79]

They then interrogated him concerning his strange behaviour,
calling him always *mar* – thirteen times in all – and he as regularly
addressed them as 'our teachers' (*rabbanan*).[80]

There is no doubt that in this account, as in the previous one,
mar is a title superior to that of *rabbanan*, but in the first case it
designates a higher-ranking rabbi, whereas here it serves to
underline the pre-eminence of a holy man over ordinary teachers.

It might be argued that even though the Abba Hilkiah story
purports to describe an episode of first-century BC Jewish history,
it survives only in the much later compiled Babylonian Talmud.
Is it methodologically proper to antedate the linguistic use to the
first century BC (Abba Hilkiah's time), or even only to the time
of Jesus? Clearly, in the absence of direct evidence, no degree of
certainty can be reached, but it seems that a good case can be
made out in favour of such a hypothesis.

In addition to the evidence established in the previous pages,
of a straight evolutionary line in regard to the use of 'lord' in
Aramaic, as well as that showing that neither the employment of
mar nor the reverential third person form of address can be discarded as exclusively Babylonian features, it must especially be
emphasized that both stylistic peculiarities are well-attested in
biblical Hebrew and consequently belong to the common domain
of Jewish speech. Even more remarkable, they occur there in the
same linguistic context, i.e. in the form of a question, and apropos
of the miracle-working prophets, Elijah and Elisha.

Obadiah, speaking to Elijah, asks:

'Has it not been told my lord (*adoni*) what I did when
Jezebel killed the prophets of the Lord?'[81]

Likewise, Elisha is asked by Hazael:

'Why does my lord (*adoni*) weep?'[82]

The questioner using the courteous circumlocution is, it should be noted, the future king of Damascus; the prophet, by contrast, answers directly:

> 'Because I know the evil that *you* will do to the people of Israel.'

In other words, there is no reason to consider the form in which the Abba Hilkiah story has been transmitted as anachronistic in an era between the first century BC and the first century AD. Moreover, the appellation, *mar*, directed to Abba Hilkiah by professional teachers, can only be explained by the assumption that, in the mind of the narrator at least, they recognized his miraculous power. There is no other reasonable explanation for the use of such a title and style in connection with a man engaged in one of the humblest of trades, for Abba Hilkiah was an agricultural worker.

It is now possible, with the help of these observations, to define the linguistic situation into which the New Testament's use of 'lord' is to be integrated.

(1) It is a fact that God was depicted as 'Lord' throughout every stage of Jewish Aramaic literature. In so far as the quantitatively negligible amount of evidence permits any conclusion at all, it appears that such phrases as 'Lord of heaven', 'Lord of Abraham', or 'my Lord', 'our Lord', were more common than the absolute 'the Lord', but the Genesis Apocryphon approaches very close to the latter, and in addition, provides the earliest example of God addressed as 'my Lord' (*mari*). Finally, a parallel Jewish-Greek usage attested at Beth She'arim, and the naturalization of *Kyrios* in Jewish-Aramaic, complete a picture showing that 'Lord' as a designation of God enjoyed universal familiarity among Jews.

(2) The same literary sources bear witness equally firmly to the continued application of the Aramaic noun, 'lord', to persons of authority in the family (husband, father), or in society at large (judge, governor, king). Here again, there are signs indicating linguistic interpenetration, with *mar* being used as a title in Greek,

and the vocative of *kyrios* employed in Aramaic, either on its own as *kiri*, or coupled with the corresponding native term, *mari kiri*.

(3) There is little doubt that some degree of synonymity exists between 'lord' and 'teacher'. The two words are not infrequently linked, and in the Babylonian dialect, at least, 'lord' was a common designation of rabbis in general. But any claim concerning a quasi-automatic identification of the two must be judged an exaggeration.

(4) In examples in which 'rabbi' and 'lord' are used in conjunction with one another but refer to different persons, the two titles are definitely not of equal dignity. The person alluded to as *mar* is more distinguished than the one simply described as rabbi.

(5) In the story of Abba Hilkiah, where both *mar* and rabbi are used, the first title is employed exclusively on the basis of miracle-working powers.

(6) In the surviving Palestinian documents a lord is generally lord of something or someone; though as far as the suffixes, 'my', 'our', etc., are concerned, analysis of the illustrations demonstrates a trend towards semantic redundancy. 'Our rabbis' really means 'the rabbis'.

(7) The circumlocutory form of address of a venerable person as 'my lord' followed by a verb in the third person – a form modelled on biblical Hebrew – appears to mark the beginning of a process of emancipation for the term 'lord'. It is very probable that in Galilean Aramaic, and certainly in the Babylonian dialect, *mar* without the emphatic ending, i.e. without the Aramaic substitute for the definite article, acquired the meaning of '*the* lord', and was employed in deferential speech as a replacement for 'you' when the persons addressed were influential teachers, or supernatural figures such as Elijah and the Messiah.

Thus in Jewish Aramaic the designation, '(the) lord', is appropriate in connection with God, or a secular dignitary, or an authoritative teacher, or a person renowned for his spiritual or supernatural force. The field in fact – and contrary to the opinion generally held by New Testament experts – is entirely open. Everything tends to suggest that from a purely linguistic point of view Jesus could have been both addressed and described as 'lord' in a number of senses. The real problem is to determine whether he was actually so addressed and depicted by Aramaic speakers, and, if so, in what capacity he merited the title 'lord'.

THE USE OF 'LORD' IN THE GOSPELS

It is plain from the philological survey just completed that the linguistic foundations of the various theories advanced by interpreters of the New Testament are insufficient and unsafe. It is in consequence imperative to reconsider the whole literary evidence with fresh eyes. Each Gospel is to be scrutinized for its use of the invocation, 'lord!' and its employment of the absolute, 'the lord'.[83]

(1) Mark

If scholarly opinion is to be believed, this oldest Gospel gives no hint whatever that Jesus was addressed as 'lord' in Palestine. The one example of the employment of the title is that of the Syro-Phoenician woman who, when told by Jesus that the children's bread is not for dogs, retorts:

'Yes, lord; yet even the dogs under the table eat the children's crumbs.'[84]

But is it true that the vocative 'lord!' figures no more than once in the Marcan Gospel? If by 'Mark' one is to understand the text printed by scholarly editors, the answer must be in the affirmative. But if, in addition to the choice made by them, variant readings from manuscripts and ancient versions are also consulted, matters begin to look different.

Thus, according to some of the oldest codices, a Galilean leper begs Jesus in Mark 1: 40:

'Lord, if you will, you can make me clean.'[85]

Similarly, in Mark 9: 22, the prayer addressed to Jesus by the father of the boy possessed by an evil spirit reads in one of the textual traditions:

'*Lord*, if you can do anything, have pity on us and help us.'[86]

Although the precise geographical location of the story is not given, the context of chapter 9 of Mark would suggest that it may also have been Galilee.

Finally, in Mark 10: 51, Bartimeus, the blind beggar from Jericho, when asked by Jesus, 'What do you want me to do for you?' answers, according to some manuscripts:

'*Lord*, I want my sight back.'

In addition to these vocative cases, there is also one Marcan example of the absolute form, 'the lord': when Jesus instructs his disciples to untie a donkey and bring it to him, he tells them to inform anyone who might object that 'the lord has need of it'.[87] Most exegetes contend, either that 'lord' here means 'owner', or that the phrase is not genuine but a later Church creation.[88]

The first alternative is, of course, possible; though it is natural to wonder in that case why, if the owner was one of Jesus' group, he did not fetch the animal himself. To the second alternative, with its somewhat arbitrary overtones, it might be retorted that, in referring to himself as 'the lord', Jesus was simply repeating the style by which his disciples customarily knew him.

To conclude, if all the Marcan witnesses are allowed to testify, the old axiom that 'lord' appears only in the mouth of Gentiles in the earliest Gospel tradition[89] will have to be discarded. On the contrary, the evidence of this Gospel suggests that the appellation was the regular mode of address to a miracle-worker, and the peculiar style employed by the disciples when mentioning or speaking to their master.[90]

(2) *Matthew*

Examination of Matthean passages containing the term 'lord' reveals the same predominant usage as in Mark: *kyrios* is principally employed in miracle-stories. To those with Marcan parallels[91] must be added the episodes of the centurion from Capernaum and of the two blind men from Galilee.[92] The novelty in Matthew's employment of 'lord' is that in this same miraculous setting it is found not only in the mouths of strangers, but also four times in those of his regular companions. During the storm on the lake, the disciples exclaim:

'Save, lord; we are perishing.'[93]

Wishing to join his master walking on the water, Peter requests:

'Lord, if it is you, tell me to come to you over the water.'[94]

When subsequently he begins to sink, he cries out:

'Save me, lord.'[95]

Matthew furthermore confirms that Jesus was regularly addressed by his disciples as 'lord'. A would-be follower petitions him:

'Lord, let me go and bury my father first.'[96]

His listeners, when asked whether they understand an explanation of the parables, reply:

'Yes, *lord*.'[97]

Elsewhere Peter asks:

'Lord, how often shall my brother sin against me . . . ?'[98]

And all the disciples wonder during the Last Supper:

'Is it I, lord?'[99]

There are moreover three examples of a similar mode of address in a context with supernatural or prophetic overtones. At the Transfiguration, Peter is represented as saying:

'Lord, how good it is that we are here! If you wish it, I will make three shelters here, one for you, one for Moses, and one for Elijah.'[100]

The same Peter remonstrates after the prediction by Jesus of his suffering and death:

'No, lord, this shall never happen to you.'[101]

Finally, emphasizing in one of his sayings that his teaching demands more than a simple imitation of his charismatic activity, Jesus comments:

> 'Not everyone who calls me "lord, lord" will enter the kingdom of heaven . . . when that day comes, many will say to me, "Lord, lord, did we not prophesy in your name, cast out devils in your name, and in your name perform many miracles?" '[102]

(3) *Luke*

By comparison with Mark and Matthew, the title 'lord' in a miraculous context is much less evident in the third Gospel. In fact, discounting verses with Marcan parallels and the story of the centurion appearing in Matthew,[103] only three examples exist with this particular association. Awestruck after a miraculous fishing expedition, Peter exclaims:

> 'Go, lord, leave me, sinner as I am!'[104]

John and James seek permission to bring down punishment on a Samaritan village:

> 'Lord, may we call down fire from heaven to burn them up?'[105]

On their return from their first mission of exorcism, the disciples proudly announce:

> 'In your name, lord, even the devils submit to us.'[106]

In all the thirteen remaining cases, however, 'lord' always implies teacher, with the occasional suggestion that he is the head of a group, the master of a circle of disciples.[107] One other tradition, unparalleled elsewhere in the Gospels, but well-attested in Aramaic parlance, also appears in Luke, or at least in one of the Lucan manuscripts: Jesus, the royal 'lord'. One of the criminals crucified with him says:

'*Lord*, remember me when you come into your kingdom.'[108]

Where Luke completely departs from the traditional style is in his substantial use of the absolute form of the title. In the third Gospel, Jesus is called 'the lord' no less than eighteen times.[109] Of these, 'the lord' equals the Messiah twice, and twice designates the risen Jesus.[110] Two instances can be included in the category of the miraculous;[111] six represent an amalgam of miracle-worker, prophet and teacher;[112] and another six describe Jesus in his function as teacher.[113]

Phrased differently, an unbiased analysis of the evangelical text indicates that the first two Gospels mostly apply the title 'lord' to Jesus in his capacity as a performer of miracles, Mark and Matthew, that is to say, preserve in Greek what appears to have been one of the original meanings of the Aramaic form of address. Matthew, however, testifies to an extension of the meaning to include other aspects of Jesus' personality – those of teacher and religious leader – aspects which increase in importance, and in Luke finally predominate.

(4) *John*

The consensus among serious New Testament scholars is general: the Fourth Gospel, theologically the most developed of the New Testament writings and an exemplary mixture of Jewish and Hellenistic elements, mirrors to perfection the full extent of the evolution of the use and significance of 'lord'.

A scrutiny of John discloses no established pattern. Only one of his accounts is reminiscent of the Synoptic style, the story of the miraculous cure of the son of the royal official from Capernaum, parallel to that of the centurion in the earlier Gospels.[114] The meaning of the Johannine 'lord' mostly varies between a quite prosaic 'Sir' and 'teacher'.[115] But the evangelist, for whom Jesus is patently the Messiah, places on the lips of Martha the following confession:

'Yes, lord; I believe that you are the Christ, the *son of God*, he who is coming into the world.'[116]

It is, however, in the words that Thomas addresses to Jesus that the climax is reached:

'My lord and my God!'[117]

The New Testament career of 'lord' reflects the various uses of the term listed in the survey of Aramaic terminology. That it was widely employed will from now on be difficult to contest, for the objections raised against its applicability to the historical Jesus have been shown to be specious. The title primarily links Jesus to his dual role of charismatic Hasid and teacher, and if the stress is greater in the earlier strata of the tradition, this is no doubt due to the fact that his impact as a holy man preceded that of teacher and founder of a religious community.

Excursus: 'lord' and the style of the Gospel of Mark

As has been seen, strong emphasis is laid by interpreters of the New Testament on the general scarcity of the use of 'lord' in Mark and its limitation to non-Jews. From this dual premise, based on what is claimed to be the best text, the following conclusion is deduced:

The fact that the Church's use of the title 'Lord' with reference to Jesus is not reflected in this Gospel as it is in Matthew and Luke is . . . significant.[118]

It is further argued – could ever an argument be more circular? – that the fact that Mark does not employ the expression shows that the word 'lord' in Mark 1: 40 is 'unlikely' to belong 'to the original text, since it is not characteristic of Mark . . . *in spite of the strong* (manuscript) *attestation*'.[119]

To avoid hasty inferences, it will help to approach the issue, not from a dogmatic, but from a literary angle for once, that of the Greek style of Mark. One of its distinctive features is bluntness and brevity. Thus, direct, and purportedly literal, dialogue in the other Synoptics is given in Mark indirectly.

Matthew 12:38	*Mark 8:11*
Some of . . . the Pharisees said,	The Pharisees came out and . . . they asked him for
'Master, we should like you to show us a sign.'	a sign from heaven.

Bearing this style in mind,[120] it is clear that there can be in any case little room for the employment of 'lord' or any other title. The two following episodes will serve as examples.

Mark 1:40 (AT)	*Mark 1:40 var. (AT)* (*Matthew 8:2*)
A leper . . . knelt down and said to him, 'If you will . . .'	A leper knelt down and said: 'Lord, if you will . . .'
Mark 7:25 (RSV)	*Matthew 15:22 (RSV)*
Immediately a woman, whose little daughter was possessed by an unclean spirit, heard of him, and came and fell down at his feet.	A Canaanite woman . . . came out and cried, 'Have mercy on me, O lord, son of David; my daughter is severely possessed by a demon.'
Mark 7:26 (RSV)	*Matthew 15:25 (RSV)*
And she begged him to cast the demon out of her daughter.	But she came and knelt before him, saying: 'Lord, help me.'

One other point emerges from a comparison of these parallels. If an Aramaic oral tradition underlies them both – as it is legitimate to suppose – the Matthean version, with its typical repetitive Semitic style, resembles it more nearly. Its reproduction of 'lord' is therefore likely to be more authentic than the absence of the title in Mark. This view is not tantamount to declaring Matthew's priority over Mark. Mark is more primitive in outlook and thought; Matthew more faithful to the original Aramaic genre of story-telling.

6. Jesus the Messiah

Whatever significance is ultimately ascribed to the title 'the Christ', 'the Anointed', one fact is at least certain: the identification of Jesus, not just with *a* Messiah, but with *the* awaited Messiah of Judaism, belonged to the heart and kernel of the earliest phase of Christian belief. So central and vital was this designation in the life of the primitive Church that within a generation of the crucifixion a Greek neologism, 'Christian', could be coined in the Judeo-Hellenistic community of Antioch in Syria.[1] A little later, King Agrippa II uses the name with familiarity in his rejoinder to Paul:

> 'You think it will not take much to . . . make a Christian of me.'[2]

Indeed, the original style, 'Jesus the Christ', or 'the Christ Jesus', became so generally employed and so much part of everyday language that in the Gentile circles evangelized by Paul it contracted into the double-barrelled 'Jesus-Christ' and even the shortened 'Christ'. From indicating a function, it was thus transformed into a personal name.[3]

Such a universally favourable and prompt response to the title of Messiah leads to the need, firstly to know precisely what Messianism meant to Jesus' contemporaries, and secondly, to discover from the Gospel evidence whether he himself and his immediate followers believed he had fulfilled these expectations.

I. MESSIANISM IN ANCIENT JUDAISM

Modern research has tended to blur the traditional Jewish view
of the Messiah as King Messiah, Messiah son of David. The
study of inter-Testamental literature has resulted in such statements as, 'The word Messiah has no fixed content',[4] and, 'Even
if there may have been . . . a tendency to connect the word
(Messiah) especially with the expected Son of David, . . . there
still remained a wide range of variety in details'.[5] These conclusions are correct if each single usage of the term in the Pseudepigrapha, Dead Sea Scrolls and early rabbinic sources is taken
into account and accorded identical importance. 'Messiah' will
then be found to designate a future Saviour or Redeemer in
various forms and guises. It is however debatable whether this
is the angle from which the problem should be tackled. It would
seem more appropriate to bear in mind the difference between
the general Messianic *expectation* of Palestinian Jewry, and the
peculiar Messianic *speculations* characteristic of certain learned
and/or esoterical minorities.

(1) *Messianic expectation*

What was the Messianic hope of Israel in the inter-Testamental
age? What kind of Redeemer figure was expected?

A reliable answer is to be found in the least academic, and at
the same time most normative, literary form: prayer.[6] In this
respect, two significant sources have been preserved: the Psalms
of Solomon, and the ancient synagogal prayer, *the* Prayer (*Tefillah*)
par excellence, the Eighteen Benedictions. Their content of Messianic belief will be compared, with a view to verification, with that
of a Qumran liturgical Blessing and with the rabbinic interpretation
of classic Messianic prophecies.

Psalms 17 and 18 of Solomon derive from a first-century BC
collection of poems inspired by mainstream Jewish religious
ideology with a pronounced anti-Hasmonean political tendency.[7]

The title of Psalm 18, as well as verses 6 and 8 (or 5 and 7), mentions God's Anointed who will be raised up on 'the day of mercy and blessing' and will use his 'rod' to instil the 'fear of the Lord' into every man and direct them to 'the works of righteousness'. This prayer, inspired by chapter 11 of Isaiah, is preceded by the celebrated supplication in Psalm 17 concerning the coming of the 'son of David', described also with words borrowed from the same prophet and explicitly referred to as 'the Anointed'.

> Behold, O Lord, and raise up unto them their king, the son of David . . .
> And gird him with strength, that he may shatter unrighteous rulers . . .
> With a rod of iron he shall break in pieces all their substance,
> He shall destroy the godless nations with the word of his mouth . . .
> And he shall gather together a holy people . . .
> He shall have the heathen nations to serve him under his yoke . . .
> And he shall be a righteous king, taught by God . . .
> And there shall be no unrighteousness in his days in their midst,
> For all shall be holy and their king the Anointed (of) the Lord.[8]

There can be no doubt that for the author of these two prayers the Messiah was not a shadowy figure. His contours follow the traditional image. He was expected to be a king of David's lineage, victor over the Gentiles, saviour and restorer of Israel. He is of course not depicted merely as a 'warrior-king', as has been rightly pointed out,[9] but his care for the establishment of God's justice reflects the picture of the final ruler portrayed by Isaiah 11 and Jewish Messianic thought in general. It is nevertheless more than doubtful whether, in his prayer for the Messiah's coming, the man in the street in ancient Jerusalem would have positively excluded the idea of a future triumphant king.

The substance of the so-called 'Blessing concerning David' in the Eighteen Benedictions, a composition surviving in a dual

Palestinian and Babylonian recension after undergoing several ancient modifications, is generally dated to not later than the first century AD.[10]

Palestinian recension

Be gracious, O Lord, our God, according to thy great mercies
To Israel thy people, and Jerusalem thy city,
And Zion, residence of thy glory;
And to thy Temple and dwelling-place;
And to the kingdom of the house of David, thy righteous Messiah.
Blessed art thou, O Lord, God of David, Builder of Jerusalem.[11]

Babylonian recension

Make the Branch of David soon spring forth,
And let his horn be exalted by thy salvation,
[For we await thy salvation (always).]
Blessed art thou, O Lord, who makest salvation spring forth.[12]

Some aspects of this Benediction are still subject to debate. It is, for example, uncertain whether the Palestinian antedates the Babylonian version, or vice versa, and whether the clause 'thy righteous Messiah' refers to the historical David or to his ultimate heir. One point is clear and is of prime importance: namely, that in what may be described as the most essential ancient Jewish prayer, the one and only Messianic citation is formulated in terms of royalty.

Further evidence, indirect in nature, may be adduced. In the Blessing of the Prince of the Congregation, the leader-to-be of the Qumran sect at the end of days, it is still the royal, and probably Davidic, concept and terminology of Isaiah 11 that predominate, despite the absence of the word 'Messiah' and the contextual difference arising from the belief in more than one Anointed.

The Master shall bless the Prince of the Congregation . . .
that he may establish the kingdom of his people for ever . . .
May the Lord raise you up to everlasting heights . . .
May you ravage the earth with your sceptre!

May you bring death to the ungodly with the breath of your
  lips!
[May he shed upon you the spirit of counsel] and everlasting
  might,
the spirit of knowledge and of the fear of God . . .
You shall be as a lion . . .[13]

The correctness of the conclusion that Jews of the inter-
Testamental period, when entreating God to send the Messiah,
thought of him as the son of David, is further confirmed by a
glance at Messianic Bible exegesis in ancient Judaism. Four very
disparate examples are presented here, two from the Dead Sea
Scrolls, one from the Palestinian Talmud and one from Philo; yet
they all testify to the same ideology.

In the Commentary on Jacob's Blessing from Qumran Cave 4,
the famous biblical verse, 'The sceptre shall not depart from
Judah', from Genesis 49: 10 (*RSV*), is paraphrased and interpreted of the Davidic Messiah.

> *The ruler shall not depart from Judah.* Whenever Israel rules,
> there shall [not] fail to be a descendant of David upon the
> throne . . . until the Messiah of Righteousness comes, the
> Branch of David . . .[14]

Recalling the comments on the Isaiah terminology of the
Psalms of Solomon, it will cause no surprise to find in a Qumran
commentary on Isaiah 11: 1–3 that the same Branch of David is
expected to be the Messiah who will subjugate the Gentiles.

> [Interpreted, this concerns the Branch] of David who shall
> arise at the end [of days] . . . [God will put a sceptre] in his
> hand and he shall rule over all the [nations]. And Magog . . .
> and his sword shall judge [all] the peoples.[15]

The Messianic metaphor of the 'Star' that was to arise from
Jacob according to Numbers 24: 17 was not only regularly
related to the King Messiah, but was even thought to have been
fulfilled in the person of Simeon bar Kosiba, renamed by his
followers bar Kokhba, 'Son of the Star'. Bar Kosiba, who was

the leader of the second Jewish War against Rome under the emperor Hadrian, was hailed by the greatest rabbi of his age as the Messiah.

> Rabbi Akiba interpreted, 'A star has come forth out of Jacob' as '[Kosiba] has come forth out of Jacob'. When Rabbi Akiba saw bar [Kosiba], he said: This is the King Messiah. Rabbi Yohanan ben Torta replied: Akiba, grass will grow out of your cheek-bones before the son of David comes.[16]

Finally, Philo, in his book on *Rewards and Punishment*, a popular treatise addressed to farmers,[17] interprets from the Greek Bible Numbers 24: 7, another section of Balaam's prophecy, generally seen as Messianic in ancient Judaism, in the same vein.

> For 'there shall come forth a man', says the oracle, and leading his host to war he will subdue great and populous nations, because God has sent to his aid the reinforcement which befits the godly, and that is dauntless courage of soul and all-powerful strength of body, either of which strikes fear into the enemy and the two if united are quite irresistible.[18]

To conclude, ancient Jewish prayer and Bible interpretation demonstrate unequivocally that if in the inter-Testamental era a man claimed, or was proclaimed, to be 'the Messiah', his listeners would as a matter of course have assumed that he was referring to the Davidic Redeemer and would have expected to find before them a person endowed with the combined talents of soldierly prowess, righteousness and holiness.

(2) *Messianic speculation*

Without disagreeing with the opinion of a leading New Testament expert that the expectation of a Redeemer – whether called 'Messiah' or anything else – is 'not an essential part of Jewish eschatological thinking',[19] it remains an observable fact that, during the turbulent centuries starting with the Maccabees and finishing with the bar Kosiba war, a wide range of Messianic ideas and images arose in the various religious-social circles of Palestinian Jewry.[20]

In addition to the royal concept, Messianic speculation in ancient Judaism included notions of a priestly and prophetic Messiah, and in some cases, of a Messianic figure who would perform all these functions in one. On occasions, furthermore, Messianic brooding and reflection went hand in hand with the belief that the Anointed had already come. The concealment 'in heaven' and subsequent revelation of a 'pre-existent' Messiah are also alluded to, and although the attestation is late, the figure of a 'slain' Messiah, too. These all require at least cursory treatment.[21]

(a) *The Priest Messiah*

During the Persian and early Hellenistic eras, roughly from 500 to 170 BC, the importance of the priesthood in general, and the eminence of the high priest in particular, were taken for granted. Because of the ban by the foreign overlords on any exercise of power by the family of David or any of the aristocrats, it was they who wielded not only religious, but also political authority. Jewish autonomy was regained by the priestly Maccabean-Hasmonean rulers in the second century BC, and out of the amalgamation in their persons of both pontifical and royal offices, a new situation arose, and with it a fresh doctrine to the effect that the levitical priests had inherited the mantle of the Davidic princes. Simon, the first Hasmonean to be invested with dynastic leadership, is celebrated in the First Book of the Maccabees with royal praises reminiscent of Messianic terminology.[22]

> His renown spread to the ends of the earth.
> He established peace in the land, and Israel rejoiced with
>   great joy.
> Each man sat under his vine and his fig tree . . .
> And the kings were crushed in those days.
> He strengthened all the humble of his people;
> He sought out the Law, and did away with every lawless and
>   wicked man.

He made the sanctuary glorious, and added to the vessels of
the sanctuary.[23]

By the time the Testament of Levi came into being, not later
than the first century BC,[24] a new synthesis was achieved, as is
manifest from a famous hymn which, with its more recent
Christian interpolations, forms chapter 18 of the Greek version
of the document.

Then shall the Lord raise up a new priest . . .
And he shall execute a righteous judgement upon the
earth . . .
And his star shall arise in heaven as of a king . . .
And there shall be peace in all the earth . . .
And the knowledge of the Lord shall be poured forth . . . as
the water of the seas . .
And the spirit of understanding and sanctification shall rest
upon him . . .[25]

The image of the Priest-King incorporates features from the
Messianic prophecies of Balaam ('the Star') and Isaiah 11
('knowledge of the Lord', 'spirit of understanding'). Thoroughly
anti-traditional though this teaching may have been, the fully
committed champions of the Hasmonean cause must have found
it perfectly satisfactory.

The less adventurous chose to keep the two functions apart,
but acknowledged superiority to the priestly leader. For instance,
the author of the Testament of Judah 24: 2–5 asserts Levi's right
to the priesthood and Judah's to the royal throne, but claims that
God set the latter below the former. The same tendency is
revealed in the Testament of Naphtali 5: 3–5 which compares
Judah to the moon and Levi to the sun.

A similar dual leadership with sacerdotal superiority is attested
in several of the Dead Sea Scrolls. The Community Rule speaks
of 'the Messiahs of Aaron and Israel', and the same two figures
are hinted at elsewhere as the 'Interpreter of the Law' and the
'Branch of David', 'the Priest' and 'the Messiah of Israel', and
probably 'the Priest' and 'the Prince of the Congregation'.[26]

The Damascus Rule, on the other hand, introduces a certain amount of confusion into the terminology of the Scrolls for although it refers to both the 'Interpreter of the Law' and the 'Prince of all the Congregation' as two distinct characters,[27] it regularly substitutes for the plural 'Messiahs' of the Community Rule the singular 'Messiah of Aaron and Israel'.[28] Moreover, from the yet unpublished fragments from Qumran Cave 4 it appears that this is the genuine reading and not a doctrinal correction effected by a late copyist.

(b) *The Prophet Messiah*

Since the matter has been examined in detail in Chapter 4, it will suffice to recall briefly the solidly established Jewish expectation of a prophetic Precursor of the Messiah (the returning Elijah) and of a final Prophet similar to Moses. The Dead Sea sect, according to the Community Rule, envisaged the appearance of three Messianic figures:

> Until there shall come the Prophet and the Messiahs of Aaron and Israel.[29]

The same trio is mentioned in the Messianic Anthology, which appeals to the three biblical proof-texts of Deuteronomy 18: 18–19 (the Prophet), Numbers 24: 15–17 (the King), and Deuteronomy 33: 8–11 (the Priest).[30] Despite his eschatological function and clear association with the two other christological figures, the Prophet is, however, never designated as the Messiah.[31]

(c) *The hidden and revealed Messiah*

Another important strand of Messianic speculation turning on the verb, 'to be revealed', was in great vogue from the latter part of the first century AD onward. Needless to say, the 'revelation' of the Messiah demanded a previous concealment either on earth or in heaven.

According to the first theory, the Messiah was to remain unknown and unrecognized on earth until the divine plan reached maturity. A third-century AD rabbinic legend sees him biding God's time in Rome itself.[32] Another legend claims that this hidden existence of the Christ began on the day of the destruction of the Temple in AD 70.

> It happened that while a Jew was labouring in the fields, his cow started to low. An Arab passed by and hearing the noise said: Son of Judah, son of Judah, untie your cow, untie your plough, for behold the Temple is destroyed. Then the cow lowed again and the Arab said: Son of Judah, son of Judah, re-tie your cow, re-tie your plough, for the King Messiah is born . . .[33]

Yet another description of the Messiah's hidden existence, handed down by Justin Martyr in the middle of the second century AD, makes his opponent, the Jew Trypho, state that the Messiah would himself be unaware of his future dignity until the moment of his actual anointing.

> Even though the Messiah has been born and is living somewhere, yet he is still unknown. Indeed, he does not even know himself, nor has he any power until Elijah comes, anoints him, and reveals him to all.[34]

The second belief, that the Messiah was to be concealed in heaven before being revealed to men on earth, underlies the statement in 2 Baruch 30: 1 that after accomplishing his earthly mission, he 'shall *return* in glory' – presumably to heaven whence he came. More clearly, Pseudo-Ezra of 4 Ezra 14: 9 was to be 'taken up from among men' and remain with the Messiah ('my Son').

Some may be tempted to see in this Messiah an eternally pre-existent, heavenly Christ; but no such conclusion is warranted. The surviving sources are concerned only with a kind of notional pre-existence of the Messiah in so far as his 'name', i.e. his essence and nature, preceded the formation of light by God on the first day of Creation. The name of the Messiah was, according to rabbinic tradition, one of the seven things created before the world itself was made, the other six being the Torah, repentance,

Paradise, Gehenna, the throne of glory, and the Sanctuary.[35] The reality of the Christ, his actual existence following this pre-existence, would begin only with his birth on earth.[36] But before leaving the topic of the Messiah concealed in heaven, it will also be well to bear in mind that in 2 Baruch and 4 Ezra he is identical with the son of David and not a substitute for him.[37]

Finally, let there be no mistake. In Jewish thought the celestial pre-existence of the Messiah does not affect his humanity. The Christ preserved in heaven until the end of time was expected, according to 4 Ezra, to share the common lot of mankind:

> It shall be, after these years, that my servant the Messiah shall die . . .[38]

(d) *The slain Messiah*

Sporadic relics survive in rabbinic literature of speculation concerning a Messiah who was to be slain on the eschatological battlefield. This figure, known as the Messiah son of Joseph or the Messiah son of Ephraim, is projected as the unsuccessful commander-in-chief of Israel in the first phase of the war against the final enemy, Gog.

Exegetically, the notion is connected with Zechariah 12: 10-12, 'They shall look on me, on him whom they have pierced . . . The land shall wail . . .'.

> What is the cause of this wailing? Rabbi Dosa and the rabbis disagree.[39] One says: It is on account of the killing of the Messiah son of Joseph. Another says: This is on account of the killing of the evil inclination. But the former interpretation is to be adopted, for it is written, 'And they shall look on him whom they have transpierced; and they shall wail over him as over an only child.' Why should he who says that it is on account of the killing of the evil inclination be sorrowful? He should rejoice rather than weep.[40]

Also in an early example of rabbinic interpretation of Psalm 2, when the Messiah son of David 'who is to be revealed soon in our days' witnesses the death of the Messiah son of Joseph, he begs God to save his life.

> *Ask me and I will give you the nations to be your inheritance:* 'Lord of the universe, I ask you only that I may live.'[41]

Similarly, the Targum of Zechariah 12: 10 comments:

> Afterwards the Messiah son of Ephraim shall go forth to engage in battle with Gog, and Gog shall kill him before the gate of Jerusalem.

Thus the main rabbinic tradition concerning this Messiah embraces the element of chronological priority in regard to the Davidic Redeemer, together with the foreseen military failure in the war against the ultimate foe.[42] The origin of this ideology is totally uncertain, but since there is no evidence of it prior to the second Jewish War, it is reasonable to infer that the tragic fate of Simeon bar Kosiba, killed in AD 135, may have been the cause, or one of the causes, of the elaboration of the image of a slain Messiah.[43]

II. THE TESTIMONY OF THE NEW TESTAMENT

That Jesus never asserted directly or spontaneously that he was the Messiah is admitted by every serious expert, even such a conservative scholar as Vincent Taylor. The traditional claim is therefore based, at best, on circumstantial evidence. This state of affairs is astonishing enough in itself, and to understand and assess it four problems have to be settled, the last of them crucial.

(1) What part, if any, did the figure of the Messiah play in the thought and teaching of Jesus?

(2) How did his alleged Messianic office strike his opponents?

(3) Was he believed to be the Messiah by his friends and companions?

(4) How did Jesus react towards those who proclaimed or challenged his Messiahship?

1. *The teaching of Jesus*

Strange though it may seem, Jesus' own teaching on the subject
of the Messiah, even if the obviously inauthentic passages are
included, amounts to very little. The most important text is his
interpretation of the famous verse of Psalm 110: 1:

> The Lord said to my lord . . .

The commentary given by the three Synoptists is essentially
the same, but the setting of the *logion* differs in each Gospel.

According to Mark 12: 35–7, Jesus publicly questions the
doctrine propounded by the professional Bible interpreters:

> 'How can the teachers of the Law maintain that the Messiah
> is "son of David"? . . . David himself calls him "lord"; how
> can he also be David's son?'[44]

Although no subsequent debate is recorded, an altercation
having been excluded in advance by the opening statement –
'nobody ventured to put any more questions to him' – the words
have a definite polemical edge.

Matthew's scene in 22: 41–6 is a direct confrontation between
Jesus and the Pharisees; Jesus takes the initiative but his opponents
show themselves to be no match for him and are obliged to stay
quiet thereafter. The redaction of Luke 20: 41–4 is a clumsy
conflation of Mark and Matthew, and, as a secondary development dependent on the other two Gospels, should be discounted.

It is unimportant whether the direct attack conveyed by
Matthew, or the indirect challenge of Mark, represents the original
form of the saying. Either way, the primary and possibly exclusive
aim of the question was to embarrass Jesus' antagonists. That he
did not disdain the easier weapon of dialectics is clear from the
insoluble dilemma thrust at the chief priests, lawyers and elders
when he preferred not to reply to their doubting of his authority.

> 'I have a question to ask you too; and if you give me an
> answer, I will tell you by what authority I act. The baptism of

John: was it from God, or from men? Answer me.' This set
them arguing among themselves: 'What shall we say? If we
say, "from God", he will say, "Then why did you not believe
him?" Shall we say, "from men"?' – but they were afraid
of the people, for all held that John was . . . a prophet. So
they answered, 'We do not know.' And Jesus said to them,
'Then neither will I tell you by what authority I act.'[45]

There is no evidence in the son of David *logion* of any open or
secret endeavour by Jesus to identify himself as the Messiah,
but every reason to believe that the issue was an *ad hominem*
exegetical argument.

The eschatological discourse in which Jesus' disciples are
repeatedly warned of the imminent danger of political upheavals
during which many 'false Messiahs' would appear in his name
is another sermon with a Messianic content.

'Take care that no one misleads you. Many will come claiming
my name, and saying, "I am [the Messiah]"; and many will
be misled by them.'[46]

If these words are authentic, they imply that in the final days the
disciples of Jesus would still be awaiting the coming of the
Messiah. Nothing is said to the effect that such an idea was futile,
as would be expected of those who believed that the Messiah
had already come. In fact Mark's deliberate omission of 'the
Messiah' in the elliptic 'I am . . .' – copied slavishly by Luke 21: 8
– is most likely due to the disturbing realization that the mention
of the word 'Messiah' would have necessitated some adverse
comment on the part of Jesus and demanded a plain declaration
of his own Messianic self-awareness. If, on the other hand, the
discourse is not genuine, but rather reflects the chaotic politico-
religious situation in Palestine in the fifties and early sixties of
the first century AD,[47] then it cannot be used to illustrate Jesus'
own doctrine concerning the Christ.[48]

Of the remaining three passages in which Jesus is supposed to
refer to the Messiah, two are placed on the lips of the risen Jesus
speaking to the Emmaus disciples and echo Paul's teaching on

the necessary suffering of the Christ.[49] The third, Mark 9: 41, is generally acknowledged to be corrupt and interpolated, and in consequence irrelevant:

> 'If anyone gives you a cup of water to drink in a name [*sic*] because you are Christ's, truly I tell you that his reward shall not perish.'[50]

Of the five texts considered, only the first can be counted as authentic; the genuineness of the eschatological discourse is most improbable, and that of the last group, practically nil. It is clearly not an exaggeration, therefore, to suggest that Messianism is not particularly prominent in the surviving teaching of Jesus. Furthermore, it is reasonable to suppose that the early Church, for which Jesus was the Messiah, would have produced additional evidence to support her faith if such had existed. The deliberate omission of words proving her case does not make sense.

2. *Hostile opinion*

According to all three Synoptics, no one accused Jesus of Messianic pretensions before the moment of the passion. Moreover, discarding the suspect account of the mockery and beating of the prisoner by some, if not all, of the members of the Sanhedrin[51] – or was it the military guard?[52] – whose insults culminate in the contemptuous sneer, 'Prophesy to us, you Christ! Who is it that struck you?'[53] the only literary context in which Jesus is treated as a self-proclaimed King Messiah is the story of his appearance before Pilate and the sequel to that meeting.[54]

Mark and Matthew imply, and Luke, attempting to improve the narrative, explicitly asserts, that Jesus was handed over to the Roman governor as a royal pretender.[55] No proof is offered, no proper indictment is laid against him; yet Pilate always refers to him as 'king of the Jews', 'the man you call king of the Jews', and Jesus 'called Messiah'.[56] According to the *titulus* on the cross, he was executed as 'king of the Jews'.[57] Soldiers, chief priests and scribes are said to have laughed at the 'king of the Jews', the 'king of Israel', 'the Messiah, the king of Israel', or simply, 'the Messiah'.[58]

In the absence of any substantial Messianic preaching on the part of Jesus or debate concerning his Messiahship, how is this accusation to be explained? Everything seems to suggest that failing to discover a non-political cause to condemn him, but panicking at the prospect of a popular upheaval in the overcrowded Jerusalem which this dangerous Galilean, whom many acclaimed as the son of David, might easily have brought about, those responsible for the maintenance of law and order saw in the capital charge of rebellion the simplest means of eliminating him.[59]

Apart from the leaders of Judea, only the devils – their counsellors, in the opinion of the evangelists – proclaim Jesus the Messiah, or the son of God.[60]

In brief, conflict concerning Jesus' Messiahship is attested in Jerusalem alone. It has no polemical antecedents in the Synoptic Gospels.

3. Sympathetic opinion

Did the entourage of Jesus think of him as the Messiah? It is undeniable that he is presented as such in the infancy narratives, that the author of Matthew refers to him in an editorial clause simply as 'Christ', and that the titles of the Gospels of Mark and Matthew give the composite name 'Jesus-Christ'.[61] However, all these texts patently belong to a late stage of the evolutionary process and reflect the primitive Christian beliefs expressed in the Acts of the Apostles.[62]

More reliable proof of a focusing of Messianic hope on Jesus is afforded by the impertinent and selfish request put to him by James and John, or their mother, the wife of Zebedee, when they demand places of honour in the 'glory' or 'kingdom' of Jesus.[63] That such hopes endured is suggested by the question attributed by Luke to the apostles on the way to the mountain of the 'Ascension':

'Lord, will you at this time restore the kingdom to Israel?'[64]

It is nevertheless the confession of Peter at Cesarea Philippi that provides the best insight into the disciples' belief that their master was the Messiah. To a direct question by Jesus, 'Who do you say I am?' Peter is reported to have answered:

'You are the Messiah.'[65]

From these texts, the apostles' faith may be taken as established. Some New Testament interpreters – though not the more enlightened, such as C. K. Barrett[66] – argue that the so-called triumphal entry into Jerusalem was arranged by the followers of Jesus as a royal procession to fulfil the prophecy of Zechariah 9: 9. The simpler and more likely explanation is that Jesus entered the capital on the back of a donkey because he found this mode of transport more suitable and convenient than walking. It was only at a later stage that Jesus' ride was seen against a background of Messianic prophecy. The Greek Matthew even misunderstands the Hebrew parallelism of Zechariah (an ass = the young of a she-ass) and makes the disciples produce two animals, a colt and its mother, lay their cloaks on both, and seat Jesus on 'them'.[67]

4. *Jesus' own view*

What action did Jesus adopt when, despite his own unwillingness to confront the Messianic issue, he was compelled to make his position clear? The first and least important of four such situations finds him proclaimed Messiah by demons.

As has been pointed out earlier,[68] sick people identified as 'possessed by the devil' are frequently described in the Gospels as shouting and screaming during exorcism, and the issue of a command for silence was part of the ritual.[69] Similarly, in the episode under consideration, when the expelled devils shout, 'You are the son of God', in Luke's version Jesus 'rebuked them and forbade them to speak, because they knew that he was the

Messiah'.[70] Manuscript variants in Mark 1: 34 support the same specific statement, whilst the main textual tradition explains that 'he would not let the devils speak, because they knew who he was'.

This silencing of the demoniacs may be interpreted in three ways. Either Jesus may have wished his status as Messiah to remain secret: but in that case, if the expulsion of demons was believed to be part of the Messiah's task, was it not somewhat illogical to fulfil it publicly, and simultaneously aim at secrecy? A second alternative could be that the command to keep quiet had no particular meaning as the exorcist would have silenced the patient no matter what he was shouting about. Or Jesus' rebuttal of what the devils were saying may signify that he disagreed with them: in which case, as in the previous one, the evangelists' words, 'because they knew that he was the Messiah', would supplement – and distort – the historical record.

Far more representative than this encounter with the demons is Jesus' reaction to the confession of Peter.[71] The first point to note is that he himself solicits the apostles' opinion. But when their spokesman subsequently declares that in their view he is the Messiah, all he does, according to the earliest form of the tradition, is to forbid them to announce this in public. He makes not a single comment on the truth or untruth of their belief:

> Then he gave them strict orders not to tell anyone about him.[72]

> He then gave his disciples strict orders not to tell anyone that he was the Messiah.[73]

> Then he gave them strict orders not to tell this to anyone.[74]

It would admittedly not be correct to deduce that Jesus thereby denied that he was the Messiah. It is nonetheless easy to imagine how odd his instruction must have sounded in the ears of the first generation of Christians whose main confessional formula was precisely Peter's, namely that Jesus *was* the Messiah.

According to Matthew 16: 17, the final injunction to keep quiet in public is preceded by a private congratulation:

'Blessed are you, Simon Bar-Jona! For flesh and blood has
not revealed this to you, but my Father who is in heaven'
(*RSV*).

Yet it is much easier to conceive that the saying was interpolated
by the first evangelist to remedy an embarrassing situation than
to account for its omission in the more primitive Marcan version.
The saying would be entirely acceptable if it had been followed
up by a modifying clause such as, 'You are right, but for the
time being keep this to yourselves', or, 'This is correct, but you
must make sure that people understand my idea of the Messiah'.
The earliest tradition, however, fails to provide such an escape.

As the Marcan narrative stands, not only did Jesus abstain
from approving Peter's words, but he possibly dissociated himself
from them. His immediate reference to future suffering was, in
fact, seen by the angry Peter as a definite rejection of his Messianic
creed. 'At this Peter took him by the arm and began to rebuke
him', only to receive the shattering rejoinder, 'Away with you,
Satan!'[75]

The final two examples belong to the passion story. It is a very
tall order to expect anyone to accept as historical the dialogues
between Jesus and the high priest and Pilate, but since his
recorded answers scarcely vary – although anything but useful
from the viewpoint of apologetics – it is reasonable to infer that
they are modelled on his standard reply when asked whether he
was the Messiah.

The Synoptic presentation of the exchange with the high
priest runs as follows.

Mark 14:61–2	*Matthew 26:63–4*	*Luke 22:67–70*
Again the high priest questioned him:	The high priest then said,	They (the members of the Council) said,
'Are you the Messiah, the son of the Blessed One?'	'Are you the Messiah, the son of God?'	'Tell us, are you the Messiah?'
Jesus said,	Jesus replied,	He replied, 'If I tell you, you will not believe me . . .'

Mark 14:61-2	Matthew 26:63-4	Luke 22:67-70
		They all said, 'You are the son of God, then?'
'I am.'	'It is as you	He replied:
[Variant: 'You say that I am.']	say.'	'It is you who say I am.'

If the Marcan formulation of the answer as given by the main textual tradition is accepted – that is, if Jesus is assumed actually to have replied, 'I am' – it not only clashes with the Synoptic parallels and with Jesus' reaction to Peter's confession in Mark, but is also the one and only occasion in the first three Gospels where Jesus openly admits that he is the Messiah. Such a unique occurrence is all the more improbable since it is supposed to have taken place 'precisely at the moment at which it is inconceivable that anyone should believe him'.[76] It was the passion story with its doctrinal tenets that required that Jesus should confess that he was the Messiah; and without doubt, the author of Mark made the Master's words conform to the Church's expectation.

The more primitive of the three forms are those transmitted by Matthew and Luke, 'It is as you say', or 'It is you who say I am'. Certainly, they possess no advantage which would have justified their substitution for 'I am'. But what do these less straightforward answers mean? It has been argued that they are wholly affirmative: It is as you say=I am.[77] Others claim that they correspond to a form of admission under pressure.[78] Other scholars construe the phrases to represent an evasion, or even a veiled denial: 'It is as *you* say, not I.' Appeal is made also to a difficult rabbinic text concerning an argument between two late-first-century AD teachers.

> A man may advance between the porch and the altar (in the Temple) without washing his hands and feet, according to Rabbi Meir, but not according to the sages. Rabbi Simeon the Modest said to Rabbi Eliezer (ben Hyrcanus): 'I advanced between the porch and the altar without washing my hands and feet.' He replied: 'Who is more eminent, you or the high priest?' Rabbi Simeon kept silent. Rabbi Eliezer said to him:

'Demean yourself and admit that the high priest's dog is more eminent than you.' Simeon answered: 'Rabbi, you have said it.'[79]

Although the last reply is understood by Dalman as an ac-quiescence,[80] it is more likely to be a denial.[81] There is no reason why Simeon should have altered his conviction of the rectitude of his behaviour simply because Eliezer insulted him. In his modesty, he answers the first jibe with silence, and the second, with a courteous refusal to become involved in a further exchange of words.

All in all, the only legitimate deduction is that the expression is equivocal.[82] This would mean that Jesus is not claimed positively to have asserted that he was the Messiah, even as the result of a direct and solemn challenge. It may have been realized that whatever he said would make no difference:

'If I tell you, you will not believe me . . .'[83]

Finally, all three Synoptists report that he replied, 'It is as you say', to Pilate's enquiry whether he was the king of the Jews.[84] Mark and Matthew leave the meaning open. Luke, however, seems to suggest that Pilate understood him to be denying the charge, since he immediately concludes:

'I find no case for this man to answer.'[85]

In fact, since the figure of the Messiah appears not to have been central to the teaching of Jesus, and since no record has survived of any hostile challenge concerning his Messianic status before his last days in Jerusalem; since, moreover, he deliberately withheld his approval of Peter's confession and, in general, failed to declare himself to be the Christ, there is every reason to wonder if he really thought of himself as such.

The Acts of the Apostles
A very different construction emerges from the Acts of the Apostles. At the stage represented by this work, i.e. the early

years of Christianity, Jesus was unquestionably identified as the Messiah;[86] although it should be added that there is still no attempt to attribute the claim to Jesus himself. The Acts rather imply that he became the Messiah, not during his lifetime, but through his elevation to a throne on God's right hand after his resurrection from the dead:

> 'Let all Israel then accept as certain that God has made this Jesus, whom you crucified, both Lord and Messiah.'[87]

Nevertheless, in the more technical area of Bible interpretation, and in the fulfilment type of exegesis familiar from the Dead Sea Scrolls,[88] the historical Jesus becomes 'the Messiah of the Lord' whom 'the kings of the earth' and 'the rulers' – Herod and Pilate – conspired together to destroy, as predicted in Psalm 2: 2.[89]

Basically, Jesus' Messianic status was the main issue of primitive preaching. Philip proclaimed 'the Messiah' to the Samaritans; after his vision, Saul 'silenced the Jews of Damascus with his cogent proofs that Jesus was the Messiah', and in Corinth, Saul-Paul 'devoted himself entirely to preaching, affirming before the Jews that the Messiah was Jesus'. Likewise, in Achaia, the scholarly Alexandrian, Apollos, demonstrated 'from the Scriptures that the Messiah is Jesus'.[90]

One specifically fresh element in the Christology of the Acts is that of the suffering Messiah. It was not despite, but because of, his passion that Jesus was the Christ. This is given as a bare statement without the backing of biblical evidence, as Peter illustrates in his address to the Jews of Jerusalem.

> 'And now, my friends, I know quite well that you acted in ignorance, and so did your rulers; but this is how God fulfilled what he had foretold in the utterances of all the prophets: that his Messiah should suffer.'[91]

Paul, too, appeals to Scripture, but without citing chapter and verse, when he demonstrates to the Thessalonian Jews or to King Agrippa II the necessary passion of the Christ.[92]

With the idea of suffering leading to death went, as part of the Christian message, the theme of the foreordained resurrection of the Messiah. This also is predicted in (unnamed) biblical texts according to Paul,[93] though Peter cites Psalm 16: 10, accompanied by a special exegetical reasoning:

> ' "*For thou wilt not abandon my soul to death, nor let thy loyal servant suffer corruption.*" Let me tell you plainly, my friends, that the patriarch David died and was buried, and his tomb is here to this very day. It is clear therefore that he spoke as a prophet, who knew that God had sworn to him that one of his own direct descendants should sit on his throne; and when he said he was not abandoned to death, and his flesh never suffered corruption, he spoke with fore-knowledge of the resurrection of the Messiah.'[94]

Peter further argues, from Psalm 110: 1, 'Sit at my right hand', that the Messiah's ascension to heaven was also foretold, as was his celestial existence until the time of 'universal restoration'.[95]

It is remarkable that the only element of the Synoptic tradition to appear unchanged in Acts is the definition of the Messianic proclamation as an offence against the state. Denouncing Paul and Silas, the Jews of Thessalonica say of them:

> 'The men who have made trouble all over the world have now come here . . . They all flout the emperor's laws, and assert that there is a rival king, Jesus.'[96]

The Fourth Gospel

Of all the New Testament writings it is the Gospel of John that signals the most advanced interpretation of the Messiahship of Jesus. It is impossible not to notice that apart from the passion story, the Fourth Gospel's presentation bears no resemblance at all to the Synoptics.

John, whose work was composed to prove that 'Jesus is the Christ',[97] impresses on his readers that he was recognized as such from the very outset of his ministry. As early as chapter 1, Andrew informs his brother Simon Peter:

> 'We have found the Messiah!'[98]

Nathanael, too, confesses him to be 'the king of Israel', and a little later, a friendly crowd attempts to hail him as king, whilst the authorities try to demonstrate that he cannot be the Messiah. Already during his lifetime his followers are threatened with expulsion from the synagogues.[99]

However, the most important difference between John and the Synoptists is that he introduces a formal statement by Jesus to the effect that he was the Messiah. It is implied in the prayer pronounced in the presence of the apostles:

> 'This is eternal life: to know thee who alone art truly God, and Jesus Christ whom thou hast sent.'[100]

But in the dialogue between the Samaritan woman and Jesus, it is explicit:

> 'I know that the Messiah (that is Christ) is coming. When he comes he will tell us everything.' Jesus said, 'I am he, I who am speaking to you now.'[101]

Yet, notwithstanding its considerable extension and broadening of the Messianic field, the Fourth Gospel still stops short of asserting that Jesus declared in public that he was the Christ.

This survey of New Testament Christology remains perplexing throughout. The firmness of early Christian emphasis on Jesus' Messianic status is matched by the reluctance of Synoptic tradition to ascribe to him any unambiguous public, or even private, declaration in this domain. Hence the dilemma, which is seldom faced squarely: if Jesus thought of himself as the Christ, why was he so reticent about it? If he did not consider himself as such, why did his immediate followers insist on the opposite?

Apart from such radicals as Bultmann, who denies that the Synoptic Gospels saw in Jesus the 'promised Messiah',[102] the large majority of New Testament scholars, including a number of non-Christians – this is not a denominational issue – champion the view that Jesus had a 'Messianic consciousness', but since his notion of 'the Christ' differed from the popular one, he chose not to touch on the question.[103]

III. NEW TESTAMENT MESSIANISM IN THE LIGHT OF ANCIENT JUDAISM

As the key to the Gospel mystery appears not to lie in the New Testament alone, it remains to be seen whether Jesus' self-awareness may be clarified by supplementing the Gospel evidence with contemporary Jewish ideas.

For a religious teacher like Jesus, addressing not an esoteric minority but Israel at large, appeal to a concept such as 'the Messiah' would have been meaningful and worthwhile only if his notion of it corresponded in substance at least to that of his listeners: otherwise his use of a Messianic terminology would merely have hindered a meeting of minds.

To judge by the absence from the main Synoptic tradition of any allusion to himself as the Priest Messiah, this cannot have been Jesus' conception of his role.[104] Neither is it permissible to conclude, from texts indicating that he thought of himself in prophetic terms, that he recognized himself as the Prophet Messiah. For such an idea to be intelligible, a much clearer formulation would have been needed than that presented by the evangelists. Again, the concept of a pre-existing heavenly Messiah revealed on earth[105] provides no solution by itself because, as has been shown, this figure was also to be the King Messiah. Finally, the Messiah slain at the end of days in battle against the armies of Gog is no more appropriate than either of the others.[106]

It seems, in fact, from the preceding examination of Jewish prayer and Bible interpretation that the only kind of Messianism Jesus' audience would have understood, and the only kind that might have possessed applicability in the world and context of the Gospels, is that of the Davidic King Messiah. Yet if an ounce of credibility is to be attached to the witness of the Synoptics, there appears to be no point of contact between this and Jesus' life and aspirations. He is not portrayed as a contender for the royal throne of David, or as intending to take over the leadership of the Jews against Rome. Indeed, if the Gospels have any coherent meaning at all, his comment on Peter's confession and the answers to the high priest and Pilate are only to be understood as a denial of Messiahship.

But does not this radically negative conclusion lead to an even more perplexing dilemma? For if Jesus rejected the Messianic title, why did it nevertheless 'stick'? Why did both his immediate and more remote followers persist in acknowledging and describing him as 'the Messiah son of David'? Even more incomprehensible, why did the Gentile Church, to which neither the Semitic 'Messiah' nor its literal Greek rendering, *Christos*, meant anything at all, not allow it to fall into oblivion? A number of tentative suggestions come to mind.

(1) Taking into consideration the spirit of first-century AD Palestine, with its eschatological, political and revolutionary ferment, it is quite conceivable that Jesus' denial of Messianic aspirations failed to be accepted by his friends as well as his foes.[107] His Galilean partisans continued to hope, even after the crushing blow of his death on the cross, that sooner or later he would reveal himself and 'restore the kingdom of Israel'. Moreover, his Jerusalem prosecutors were bound to suspect that this Galilean, whose popular impact was now spreading in Judea itself, was impelled by motives of subversion.

(2) The primitive Church transferred the whole ideology to the historically unverifiable 'post-Easter' interval because no Messianic (political) end was achieved during his lifetime. Jesus the Messiah is he who is seated in heaven on God's right hand[108] and who will be revealed as universal judge and king on his triumphal return at the Parousia. In this two-stage Messianic doctrine with its sequence of darkness and light, humiliation and exaltation, the otherwise perplexing element of suffering and death was accommodated without major difficulty.

(3) Although the christological notion reshaped in this way must have struck Jews as extraordinary and, as far as can be judged, unattractive, it proved useful within the closed circle of early Christians. Their Messianic speculation, partly following this new line, and partly adhering to Jewish models in vogue in

the latter part of the first century AD (the heavenly Messiah, the pre-existent Messiah, etc.), soon resulted in a remote, complex, but for internal use satisfactory, theological synthesis.

(4) The transmission of the title 'Christ' to the Gentile Church, and its survival in Hellenistic Christianity, are, as has been said, astonishing, because for it to mean anything, apostles and preachers were obliged to instruct prospective believers in the principles of Jewish Messianism and adapt it to the new realities. This may not have been too difficult at the beginning of the Gentile mission, when many, perhaps the majority, of converts to faith in Jesus were recruited from Gentile proselytes attached to Jewish synagogues of the Dispersion, who thus had already received a certain grounding in Judaism. But after its break with the mother religion, the Church was bound to wonder, as it expanded, whether such efforts were worth while. That it decided in favour of retaining the Messianic idea is chiefly due, it seems, to its psychological and polemical value in the Jewish-Christian debate.

In the conscious mind of first-century Gentile believers in Jesus – and in the subconscious of the Church throughout the ages – the most alarming element of the Christian story was the incomprehensible fiasco of an essentially Jewish religious movement among the Jewish people themselves. How could the man from Rome, Athens, Ephesus or Alexandria, to whom the Gospel of a Galilean Master was preached by his Jewish disciples in an alien, half-intelligible technical jargon, develop a secure faith in their message when those to whom it was originally given, people familiar with all these moving but outlandish matters, refused *en bloc* to be impressed. Was there something wrong with the Gospel itself?

The Christian controversialist appears to have followed an established pattern. The Gospel was perfect, but something was fundamentally wrong with the Jews. Their obstinacy in rejecting the Messiah, the greatest of God's promises to Israel, was explained as the culmination of age-old wickedness and as the principal reason for the irrevocable transference of their privileges to the Gentiles.

Soon after the crucifixion, the Christian Hellenist, Stephen, is seen inveighing against an unsympathetic Jerusalem congregation:

'You always fight against the holy spirit. Like fathers, like sons. Was there ever a prophet whom your fathers did not persecute? They killed those who foretold the coming of the Righteous One; and now you have betrayed him and murdered him . . .'[109]

Paul, as early as the First Letter to the Thessalonians, uses even more heated language:

You (Thessalonians) have been treated by your countrymen as they (the Christians of Judea) are treated by the Jews, who killed the lord Jesus and the prophets and drove us out, the Jews who are heedless of God's will and enemies of their fellow-men . . .[110]

Finally John composes a similar speech and places it in the mouth of Jesus himself in an address to the Jews in Jerusalem:

'Your father is the devil and you choose to carry out your father's desires. He was a murderer from the beginning . . .'[111]

In short, the success of the Messianic idea probably owed more to polemical convenience than to theological usefulness.

Excursus I: Jesus, son of David

A few comments on Jesus' Davidic title, traced in the genealogical tables of Matthew and Luke, are apposite as an appendix to the chapter on the Messiah.

The secondary, and consequently historically insignificant, nature of these genealogies is no longer denied by responsible New Testament scholars, but there is at least one primary Gospel episode in which Jesus is addressed as 'son of David', namely the occasion on which, during the fateful journey towards Jerusalem, apparently in Jericho, a blind beggar – or perhaps two blind beggars – shouted to catch his attention in the middle of a noisy crowd:

'Son of David, Jesus, have pity on me!'[112]

As the Davidic title is dropped in all three Gospels once Jesus hears him and replies – from then on he is simply called 'lord'[113] – its initial use seems to have served only as *captatio benevolentiae*.

The paraphrase of Psalm 118: 25, 'Hosanna *to the son of David*', given by Matthew 21: 9 and 15, can hardly be authentic, however: not only are the italicized words missing from the Synoptic parallels,[114] but even graver, they would be meaningless in Hebrew or Aramaic. (*Hosanna* signifies 'save, please!' and the best rendering of the prayer, assuming that the gloss was originally in Aramaic, would be the following: 'Save, please, the son of David!')[115] The random use of the title 'son of David' seems therefore to have no particular historical bearing. On the other hand, the phrase may have acted as a useful support in the early Christian argument concerning the Messiahship of Jesus.

Although the question in itself is not far-fetched, and the possibility of genealogical knowledge in the first century AD cannot be *a priori* excluded,[116] because of the intense dogmatic, apologetical and polemical tendencies of the relevant New Testament documents it would be useless to try to ascertain whether the family of Jesus actually claimed affiliation to the tribe of Judah and the royal clan of David. Nevertheless, it should be remarked that derivation, real or spurious, from Judah was an important weapon in the political arsenal. During the fight for the paramount leadership of world Jewry around AD 200 both the Galilean patriarch and the Babylonian exilarch asserted such a claim, the second with apparently more justification than the first.[117] By contrast, the repression of the Davidic house by the victorious Romans after AD 70 is recorded by early church historians. The martyrdom suffered by certain Palestinian Christian leaders, reputed to have been Jesus' blood relations, was attributed to anti-Davidic imperial decrees; but this explanation would seem to be dogmatic rather than historically reliable.[118]

Excursus II: the metaphorical use of 'to anoint'

The present chapter might be thought incomplete if no mention is made of the possible non-technical use of the notion 'to anoint'. As is well known, this ceremonial rite was employed in the Old Testament at the conferment of certain superior offices, principally those of high priest, king, and occasionally prophet. Developing from this liturgical background, the term acquired, possibly already at the biblical stage, and definitely in the post-biblical usage, a non-ritualistic meaning, 'to appoint', or 'to elevate to a dignity'. The change is firmly attested in the Targums, where the Hebrew *mashah* (to anoint) is fairly regularly rendered, not by the identical Aramaic *meshah*, but by the verb *rabbe*, literally, 'to make great'. In Exodus 28: 41, 'You will anoint them (Aaron and his sons)', is translated, 'You will appoint them'. 'To anoint a king over them' is paraphrased in Judges 9: 8 as 'to establish a king over them'. Likewise, 'The spirit of the Lord God is upon me because the Lord has anointed me' is reinterpreted in the Targum of Isaiah 61: 1 as, 'The spirit of prophecy from the Lord is upon me, therefore he has appointed me'.

It should further be noted that the Hebrew phrase, 'to call a person by name', of Exodus 31: 2 is variously Aramaicized in the Targums as, 'to appoint by name' (*Onkelos*), 'to establish and call by name' (*Neofiti*), or 'to appoint and call' (*Neofiti margin*). In other words, the same Aramaic verbs are employed to render both the plain idea of nomination and the ritualistic metaphor of anointment. That this interpretative technique was not merely instinctive, but conscious, is manifest from the early rabbinic commentary on Numbers 18: 8:

> Anointing means installation in office.[119]

It is no doubt in this sense that the designation in Isaiah 45: 1 of the Persian king Cyrus as the Lord's Messiah was understood.

He was a ruler, not physically anointed with oil, but chosen, appointed and installed by the God of Israel.

Is it possible that the recognition of Jesus as the Messiah evolved from his own idiosyncratic recourse to the verb, 'to anoint'? As a charismatic, he was certainly aware of a divine vocation and need not have objected to the title, the appointed one. But this is no more than a linguistic possibility: the figurative employment of Messiah is not supported on the historico-literary level by any actual evidence in the Greek New Testament.

7. Jesus the *son of man*

Shortly before his death, Paul Winter remarked stoically that the literature on the *son of man*[1] was becoming more and more impenetrable with no two people agreeing on anything. At about the same time, A. J. B. Higgins, in an article bearing the typical title, 'Is the Son of Man Problem Insoluble?' suggested that the answer 'for all we know already exists among the widely divergent ones familiar to workers in this field'.[2] Soluble or not, the problem is held by most interpreters of the New Testament to be of crucial significance. 'Of all the Christological titles', writes F. Hahn, 'that of the Son of man has been the most thoroughly investigated. The reason for this is that it has been hoped, by means of this predicate of dignity, *to penetrate most deeply to the preaching of Jesus Himself* . . . The consideration of the title of the Son of man is an appropriate starting point for an investigation of *the oldest Christological traditions*.'[3]

The undeniable fact is that one stands here at a cross-road of paradoxes. In the Synoptic Gospels the *son of man* title is used frequently – it occurs over sixty times – and it still figures relatively often in the Fourth Gospel. But outside the Gospels it appears once in Acts 7: 56, and twice in Revelation 1: 13 and 14: 14. In other words, this presumed christological formula is given nowhere in Paul or the other epistles, i.e. in the explicitly theological compositions of the New Testament.

The second paradoxical feature is that the title is never used by others in the Synoptics but is placed exclusively on the lips of Jesus. By contrast to its common vocative employment in Ezekiel, where God regularly addresses the prophet as *son of man*, it never serves this capacity in the New Testament. In addition, the full expression, *the son of man*, is found only once as a title outside the Synoptics. In a mystic vision immediately before his execution, Stephen confesses in Acts 7: 56:

> 'I can see the *son of man* standing at God's right hand!'

But neither this text, which is probably inspired by Jesus' answer to the high priest,[4] nor the two examples in Revelation, which are lifted directly from Daniel 7, can stand on their own as independent evidence and diminish the solid testimony of the Synoptists.

The third paradox lies in the curious lack of impact made by the expression on the contemporaries of Jesus. Far from being treated as a mystery, the most problematic of all New Testament problems, there is no record in either Matthew, Mark or Luke of any query concerning its meaning or objection to its use. Among friends and adversaries it arouses neither enthusiasm nor hostility. In fact, the words written by Julius Wellhausen over seventy years ago are still valid:

> Jesus uses (the expression) not esoterically at all, not merely in front of his disciples, yet no one finds it strange and requires an explanation. All let it pass without being astonished, even the quarrelsome Pharisees . . . who were not accustomed to accept something unintelligible.[5]

The one discordant note is struck by a single, confused and confusing passage of the Fourth Gospel which, even apart from general chronological considerations in regard to the date of John, shows itself to be irrelevant to the historico-linguistic issue. In John 12: 32 Jesus is made to declare:

> 'I shall draw all men to myself, when I am lifted up from the earth.'

The bystanders see in these words an allusion to his death, and as though thinking aloud, express their puzzlement in the following terms:

'Our Law teaches us that the Messiah continues for ever. What do you mean by saying that the *son of man* must be lifted up? What *son of man* is this?'[6]

The second question is nevertheless not to be construed as showing the people's incomprehension of an obscure title. It is a comment which makes sense only if, in the first place, the original wording of John 12: 32 was 'when the *son of man* is lifted up', instead of 'I am lifted up'. Next, their acceptance of Jesus' role as Messiah must be supposed. And finally, the verb, 'to be lifted up', must be understood to mean death by crucifixion, and not in its more usual sense of exaltation and glory.[7] If these three provisos are accepted, matters become intelligible. The *son of man* is a self-designation and the doubt voiced by the questioners arises from the coupling of the mutually exclusive notions: Christhood and death by execution.

To sum up, it is not only permissible but essential to tackle the *son of man* problem in its Synoptic presentation as an unambiguous and unprovocative phrase always used by Jesus alone. But the preliminary step, as always in this field, must be a careful analysis of its use outside the Gospels.

I. THE *SON OF MAN* IN JEWISH WRITINGS

There is general negative agreement on the linguistic aspect of the puzzle. The evangelical Greek composite, 'the son of the man', is not a genuine Hellenic idiom, so it must be a translation-Greek rendering of a Semitic original. This Semitic original is unlikely to be Hebrew because neither biblical nor post-biblical language employs the definite article before *son of man*.[8] The one remaining alternative is the Aramaic tongue, i.e. the vernacular speech in common use in Palestine in the first century AD. Scholarly research must therefore begin with Aramaic literature, for if the 'son of man' sayings originated with Aramaic speakers, their authentic meaning must be discoverable in that language.[9]

Here there is accord among scholars on two points and wide disagreement on two others. It is now accepted by every expert that the phrase was in general use as a noun ('a man', 'the man') at all stages of the Palestinian Aramaic dialect, and as a substitute for the indefinite pronoun ('one', 'someone'). There is by contrast dissent concerning the circumlocutional use of the expression, i.e. the application of the idiom to the speaker himself, and its attachment to an eschatological or Messianic figure deriving in some way from Daniel 7: 13. It is these two controversial issues that are to be considered here.[10]

(a) Son of man – *a circumlocution*

A number of writers have postulated during the past eighty years that the expression, *son of man*, could serve a speaker as an indirect reference to himself, as, that is to say, a substitute for the personal pronoun 'I'.[11] This theory is founded on the model of what is believed to be an Aramaic synonym of the *son of man*, namely 'that man' (*hahu gabra*). For the sake of the uninformed, it should be pointed out that the phrase 'that man' is not always a circumlocution, and even when it is, does not invariably mean 'I'. It is often to be understood literally. Moreover, when it is employed as a circumlocution, it sometimes relates to the first person singular, and sometimes to the second: 'that man' can be 'I' or 'you'. Consequently, the interpreter must first determine whether it is intended plainly or figuratively, and if he concludes that it is a circumlocution, he must rely on the context to establish its precise meaning.

Thus, for instance, he will find that it can only be used as a substitute within the context of direct speech, in dialogue or monologue. Furthermore, the topic of the conversation must belong to a few well-defined patterns. The speaker may wish to refrain from immodest emphasis on himself:

> A certain man came to Rabbi Yose ben Halafta and said to him: It has been revealed to *that man* (=me) in a dream . . .[12]

Again, very frequently the unpleasant, frightening or fateful nature of a statement calls for a circumlocution. Sickness and death, in particular, are subjects never to be associated directly with oneself:

Jacob asked Esau: Do you want money or a burial place? Esau replied: Does *that man* (=Do I) want a burial place? Give me the money and keep the burial place for yourself![13]

Another situation demanding camouflage is one in which the speaker mentions a topic unpalatable to someone else present. Here 'that man' will replace 'you'.

May the spirit of *that man* (=your spirit) perish![14]

Were it not for the fact that I have never anathematized anyone, I would do so to *that man* (=you).[15]

Can *bar nash(a)*, *(the) son of man*, be said to have been used in a manner similar to *hahu gabra*, 'that man'? The claim has been made but backed by no evidence. It is not surprising therefore that the parallel is rejected by scholars who hold that 'such a use . . . is nowhere to be found in Aramaic sources'.[16] That this is a mistake has been shown in my earlier essay, only the salient points of which need to be reproduced here.[17]

Most of the examples so far discovered consist of sayings that imply something detrimental or embarrassing to the speaker. For instance, a question is put to his master, Rabbi Yohanan, by the disenchanted Babylonian *émigré*, Rab Kahana, who found mid-third-century AD Galilean life not to his liking.

If *bar nash* is despised by his mother, but honoured by another of his father's wives, where should he go? Yohanan replied: He should go where he is honoured. Thereupon Kahana left. Then Rabbi Yohanan was told: Kahana has gone to Babylon. He exclaimed: What! Has he gone without asking leave? They said to him: The story he told you was his request for leave.[18]

In Kahana's parable, the mother is the land of Israel, the other wife, Babylon, and the *son of man*, Kahana himself. Apart from the elderly, unsuspecting Yohanan, no one missed the real meaning: 'Since you, Palestinians, do not respect me enough, I am going home.' If the sentence is subjected to a purely logical analysis, it can be argued that *bar nash* has here a generic meaning ('any man') that includes the speaker as well.[19] Yet, as everyone knows, verbal communication is governed as much by the laws of psychology and sociology as by those of logic. An equivocal turn of phrase may be chosen deliberately as a path of escape in case the speaker is pressed by his interlocutor, but he may nevertheless be intending to say nothing ambivalent. It is quite rational to paraphrase Kahana's words to mean that any man unappreciated in one place is entitled to move to another; but reasonable though this may be, it would distort their true significance. Kahana was not concerned about other people, but only about himself. The original purpose of the circumlocution is to provide a *double entente*. In the present account, this is achieved perfectly.

Another story concerning the late-second-century AD Galilean patriarch, Judah the Prince, provides an illustration of indirect reference to the supreme taboo, death, and to the supreme bliss, the speaker's glorious resurrection.

> It is related that Rabbi (Judah) was buried wrapped in a single sheet, for he said: It is not as *bar nasha* goes that he will come again. But the rabbis say: As *bar nash* goes, so will he come again.[20]

To grasp the exact sense of Judah's remark, it should be borne in mind that the teaching of 'the rabbis' insists on the total continuity of this life and the world to come. The risen body was expected to be identical with the body before death, including, it seems, the garments in which it was buried. Judah, renowned for his humility, corrected and transformed the proverbial saying expressed by the rabbis. He was interpreted correctly, and although rich, his body was laid in the grave with no display of wealth.

The use of *son of man* is more formal here than in the Kahana episode. The replacement of *bar nash* (*a son of man*) by the determined *bar nasha* (*the son of man*) appears to have been made expressly to show that it refers to a single, definite character, Judah himself.

Two sayings of Simeon ben Yohai, a Galilean teacher of the first half of the second century AD, offer what appears to be the strongest evidence in favour of the circumlocutional use of *son of man*. Both survive in several recensions in, as it were, a Synoptic transmission, and this factor proves most helpful in determining their precise significance.

> Rabbi Simeon ben Yohai said: 'If I had stood on Mount Sinai when the Torah was given to Israel, I would have asked the Merciful One to create two mouths for *bar nasha*, one for the study of the Torah and one for the provision of all his needs.'
>
> He said again: 'If the world can scarce endure because of the denunciations uttered by one mouth, how much worse would it be if there were two!'[21]

A preliminary remark seems necessary. The passage quoted represents not one *logion*, but two: (1) 'Rabbi Simeon ben Yohai said' and (2) 'He said again'. The only connecting link is the idea of two mouths. Nothing suggests that the second saying followed immediately on the first, and even less that it was meant as an interpretative gloss attached to the Sinai vision.

Considered, therefore, as an independent sentence, Simeon's prayer on Sinai was on behalf, either of everyone, or of every Israelite, or of himself, Simeon ben Yohai.

Of the three alternatives, the first was chosen by E. Sjöberg, mainly on the grounds that in the second *logion* Simeon cannot have been alluding to himself. As a staunch opponent of Rome, he could hardly have been envisaging himself as a potential informer.[22] Yet why should Simeon, the greatest xenophobe of his age, quoted as having said, 'The noblest of the Gentiles deserves death',[23] have prayed for two mouths for every man? He certainly did not expect all mankind to recite the Torah. Also, if such a meaning had been intended, one would expect to find, not *the son of man*, but 'every *son of man*' or 'every *son of man* and *son of man*'.[24]

The second alternative, every Israelite, seems to be stylistically equally inappropriate. After all, why 'every *son of man*' rather than literally 'every Israelite'?

The third possibility, that *bar nasha* refers here to Simeon ben

Yohai himself, is nevertheless not based solely on a process of elimination. It is supported also by the textual evidence that, in a second recension surviving in Aramaic, 'the *son of man*' is replaced by 'this *son of man*'.[25] It can therefore be definitely established that when he prayed for the unique gift of a second mouth for secular use so that he could devote the first entirely to the recitation of Scripture, Simeon ben Yohai spontaneously expressed himself in a humble third person.

Simeon's second *son of man* dictum, which has also been handed down in several recensions,[26] is incorporated into the account of his departure from the cave where he, and possibly his son, apparently hid for thirteen years after the end of the second Jewish War.

> At the end of those thirteen years, he said: 'I will go forward and see what is happening in the world . . .' He sat down at the entrance to the cave. There he saw a fowler trying to catch birds by spreading his net. He heard a heavenly voice saying (in Latin!), *Dimissio!* (release) and the bird escaped. He then said: 'Not even a bird perishes without the will of heaven. How much less *bar nasha*.'[27]

It is worth noting that the crucial last sentence not only contrasts bird and man in general. By setting 'a bird' side by side with 'the *son of man*' it appears to be emphasizing that a particular person is meant, not some random representative of the human race. In the circumstances, this person cannot be other than the speaker himself.

The parallel in the Midrash Rabbah reads:

> Not even a bird is caught without the will of heaven. How much less the soul of *bar nasha*. So he (Simeon) went forth and found that matters had calmed.[28]

Again, Simeon's immediate exit from the hiding-place indicates that 'the *son of man*' whose soul would not perish unless Heaven willed was meant to allude to none other than the speaker. Furthermore, the interpreter's deduction is confirmed also by manuscript evidence substituting 'my soul' for 'the soul of the *son of man*'.[29]

These examples demonstrate that in Galilean Aramaic the *son of man* occurs as a circumlocutional reference to the self. Like the parallel idiom, 'that man', it is employed in a context where humiliation or death are mentioned, but there are also instances in which the avoidance of the first person is motivated by reserve and modesty. On the other hand, whereas 'that man' can designate either 'I' or 'you', all the *son of man* sayings so far analysed refer back to the speaker.

An important point to note is that chronologically the *bar nasha* circumlocution appears from the second century AD onwards, and that geographically, it is restricted to Galilee. It has never been verified in the Aramaic speech of Babylonian Jews. Nothing suggests that the idiom was a second-century innovation and no valid argument can be raised against its being in use in the previous century also. The small number of parallels so far assembled do not necessarily indicate that the style was un-common; their rarity may be due to the fact that in the extant Aramaic literature the kind of idiomatic setting requiring this circumlocution is in short supply.[30]

In sum, and with apologies to the non-linguist for these un-avoidable, but it is hoped not incomprehensible technicalities, if the internal logic of the situation is obeyed and it is admitted that Aramaic usage plays an essential part in the interpretation of the New Testament style, 'the son of the man' (*ho huios tou anthrōpou*), two conclusions, one positive, the other negative, must be integrated into any acceptable theory. In Galilean Aramaic, i.e. the language of Jesus and his first followers, *son of man* was at least occasionally employed as a circumlocution. By contrast, no trace survives of its titular use, from which it must be inferred that there is no case to be made for an eschatological or Messianic office-holder generally known as 'the *son of man*'.

Nevertheless, in a matter such as this, language is not the only factor to be considered, and before asserting positively that no such style existed, the problem of the exegesis of Daniel 7: 13 must be taken into account.

(b) *The* son of man *and Daniel 7 : 13*

Chapter 7 of the Book of Daniel consists of an Aramaic account of a dream seen by Daniel and its interpretation by a supernatural witness. The dream begins with a vision of four fearsome beasts, one succeeding the other. Then suddenly the scene changes and one that is 'ancient of days' takes his seat on a throne of fiery flames surrounded by a vast throng of attendants. Books are next opened, and the last of the beasts is condemned to death and executed; the other three are given a brief respite. But it is the end of the dream that is of particular interest here.

> I was looking in a night vision and, behold,
> one like a *son of man* was coming with the clouds of heaven
> and went as far as the Ancient of Days and was brought
>   near him.
> Sovereignty, glory and kingship were given him,
> and all the peoples, nations and languages were to serve him.
> His sovereignty was to be an eternal sovereignty never to
>   cease,
> and his kingship imperishable. [31]

The rest of the chapter provides, in the form of a heavenly exegesis, the key to this climax, the enthronement of the man-like figure. The four beasts, it is explained, symbolize four kingdoms, the last of which will oppress 'the saints of the Most High'. They will however be vindicated by the Ancient of Days and everlasting kingship will be conferred on 'the people of the saints of the Most High'. [32]

There is clearly no doubt that in the mind of the biblical narrator this phrase, 'one like a *son of man*', refers collectively to 'the saints of the Most High', those whom the fourth beast ill-treated on earth: the Israelites persecuted by Antiochus Epiphanes (175–163 BC). Whether the image of the human figure raised up to heaven depends on earlier mythological or semi-mythical conceptions, and whether, detached from this context, 'the saints of the Most High' are to be identified as angels, is basically irrelevant.

In the actual Daniel narrative no knowledge of such a conjectural prehistory is shown or presumed.

Yet some commentators with an interest centred mainly on the New Testament insist on the mystical value of the term, 'like'. The author of a major work writes: 'How do we have to understand the statement that the appearance of this marvellous supraterrestrial being is "like a man"? The word "like" (a human being) of the vision hints not only at the similarity to men but even more at a mysterious dissimilarity. It is not a man who is appearing but one like a man.'[33] In fact, the Aramaic or Hebrew preposition, 'like', is stylistically common in the description of a dream. In this very same chapter, three of the four beasts are 'like' a lion, 'like' a bear, 'like' a leopard, and the garment and hair of the Ancient of Days are 'like' snow and 'like' wool. And if it were argued that in the case of the three beasts the prefixed 'like' is an oblique allusion to their unusual features (e.g. the lion has eagle's wings), it could well be pointed out that, curiously, the 'one like a *son of man*' possesses no abnormal traits.

In short, the hero of the Daniel narrative is a human being elevated above the wicked beasts and granted everlasting dominion over all things, a symbolical representation, according to the interpretative conclusion, of the eschatological triumph of the historical Israel. So, at the risk of being repetitive, it must be made clear once and for all that, in the mind of the author of Daniel 7, 'one like a *son of man*' is not an individual. Furthermore, as a collective term employed in the setting of descriptive narrative, it is not conducive to circumlocutional use. Nor does it entail, or even suggest, a titular style applicable to a single person.

Is it possible, however, that such a title was coined in the process of the exegetical development of Daniel 7: 13? A few relics of early Jewish interpretation of this biblical passage are extant and may well provide the pieces missing from this puzzle.

Exegesis of Daniel 7: 13 in antiquity
Ancient Greek translations of the verse contribute nothing new to the original Aramaic significance. 'One like a *son of man*' is

rendered literally by both the Septuagint and Theodotion. The lack of all paraphrastic attempts on the part of the Greek translators indicates that for them the sense of the original text was clear and acceptable. Their only disagreement – echoed in the Gospels – concerns whether he is to come 'with' (as in Aramaic) or 'upon' the clouds.

The rabbis are more illuminating. In the earliest comment available, that of Rabbi Akiba (died in AD 135), the mention of 'thrones' in Daniel 7: 9 is said to indicate that there will be two of them, one occupied by God, the other by 'David', the royal Messiah. This exegesis, identifying by inference 'one like a *son of man*' with the Christ, appears to have had some success despite the violent objections of Akiba's colleagues.[34]

A century or so later Rabbi Joshua ben Levi is reported to have reconciled the apparent contradiction between Daniel 7: 13 ('coming with the clouds') and Zechariah 9: 9 ('humble and mounted on an ass') by claiming that the glorious or lowly manifestation of the Messiah would depend on the virtue or sinfulness of Israel in the last days.[35]

Finally, Daniel 7: 13 serves as scriptural basis for two feats of exegesis in regard to the much sought-after name of the Messiah. Both appear in late compositions, though the date of their attestation does not necessarily equal that of their origin.

A commentary on Genesis identifies the King Messiah as *Anani*, the last scion of the family of David mentioned in 1 Chronicles 3: 24, by interpreting his name from Daniel 7: 13, *Anani*='clouds' ('*anane*): i.e. Cloud-Man.[36] The same explanation is incorporated into the Targum of 1 Chronicles 3: 24:

Anani is the King Messiah who is to be revealed.[37]

The second *tour de force* is that of the Babylonian Rabbi Nahman bar Jacob of the early fourth century AD, who obtained the obscure Messianic title, *bar niphle* ('son of the Fallen One' in Aramaic=the 'son of David') from Amos's allusion to the raising up of the fallen tent of David.[38] His Galilean interlocutor, Rabbi Isaac the Smith, was not impressed, no doubt because for him *niphle* was not an Aramaic but a Greek word meaning 'cloud' (*nephele*). It is in fact likely that in Galilee, where Jews were to some degree Hellenized, Daniel 7: 13 was the source of the half-Aramaic, half-Greek Messianic title, *bar nephele*, 'son of the cloud'.

Sporadic though the evidence may be, it seems reasonable to deduce that mainstream Jewish interpretative tradition recognized Daniel 7: 9-14 from the early second century AD at least, but almost certainly even earlier, as a Messianic text depicting the coming of the new, glorious, and exalted David. No trace survives of any preceding humiliation of 'the people of the saints of the Most High'; indeed, the concept of a humble Messiah is thought to be incompatible with the Daniel vision.[39]

Such a Messianic interpretation is founded, as far as can be detected, on the mention of the additional throne, and probably on the conferment of an everlasting crown on the human figure. It does not depend on the expression 'one like a *son of man*' at all. The phrase is no more employed as a title here than it is in any other text.[40] Indeed, the derivation from Daniel 7: 13 of such Messianic names as *Anani* or *bar nephele* proves that *son of man* was never understood as a title.[41]

Eschatological speculation prompted by Daniel 7: 13

1. 4 Ezra

Chapter 13 of the Fourth Book of Ezra is also concerned with a dream. The pseudonymous author saw 'as it were the form of a man' rising from the sea and flying 'with the clouds of heaven'. A multitude of men assembled to fight him, but he annihilated them with his mouth. God then explains the meaning of the vision. The 'man' is the preserved, hidden, heavenly Messiah, the son of God. In other words, the dream is modelled on Daniel 7; its flying hero, the pre-existent royal Messiah, is Daniel's 'one like a son of man'.

Can this text be used as an argument in favour of the titular use of *son of man*? Decidedly not. 4 Ezra 13 confirms and antedates the rabbinic exegesis of Daniel 7: 13, but it still does not employ *son of man* as a title.[42] It should also be noted that everything datable in 4 Ezra is definitely later than AD 70, and is conditioned by the destruction of the Temple. Its evidence is consequently of more relevance to an understanding of the origins of Christianity than to Jesus and his time.

11. *1 Enoch*

As the Ethiopic Book of Enoch has often been described as the most important witness to the titular use of *son of man*, it is appropriate that its study should conclude the present survey.

In this work of extreme complexity, in which textual and exegetical problems are matched by those of composition and dating, the *son of man* figure appears sixteen times in descriptive prose in the Book of Parables (chapters 37–71), the second of its five sections; or to be more precise, between chapters 46 and 71.[43] The other four sections do not refer to it at all.

The language problems are frightening. For one thing, three different Ethiopic phrases are all translated into English as *son of man*.[44] Two conflicting scholarly explanations are advanced for this curious feature. According to one, the variations are entirely due to a careless Ethiopian translator, who rendered one and the same Greek formula in three different ways;[45] according to the other, they correspond to three different Aramaic expressions underlying the Greek.[46] Moreover, although thirteen of the sixteen examples are preceded by 'this' or 'that' *son of man*, it is asserted, though without convincing proof, that this may simply be the Ethiopic style of rendering the Greek definite article in '*the*' *son of man*.[47]

In short, the nature of the Ethiopic usage, and *a fortiori* the identity of the lost Greek equivalents of the three phrases, not to mention the conjectural Aramaic original (or originals) of one (or three) Greek expression(s) from which the three Ethiopic terms derive, remain, to say the least, problematic. Yet in the context of the present study none of this matters very much because, according to the latest and most reliable expert opinion, from the philological point of view the Ethiopic Enoch has in any case practically nothing to contribute to the *son of man* problem.[48]

In regard to the meaning of the *son of man* parable itself, the dependence of 1 Enoch 46 on Daniel 7 is obvious.

> And there I saw one who had a head of days,
> And his head was white like wool.
> And with him was another being whose countenance had the
>   appearance of a man . . .
> And I asked the angel . . . concerning that *son of man* . . .
>   And he answered and said unto me:
> This is the *son of man* who hath righteousness . . .
> And this *son of man* whom thou hast seen . . .
> Shall loosen the reins of the strong
> And break the teeth of the sinners.[49]

It will be seen that, whether or not the Ethiopic demonstratives are able to render the definite article, 'that' or 'this *son of man*' in the present passage alludes to the being described in the beginning as having 'the appearance of a man'. In effect, 'the *son of man*' is not an independent entity in any of these passages, but always requires added definition.

The next text, in which 'that *son of man*' – also portrayed as God's 'Messiah' – is said to have been named 'before the stars and heaven were made', is the earliest testimony extant to the rabbinic teaching that the name of the Christ was created before the world itself was formed.[50]

In chapter 62: 5–14, 'that *son of man*'[51] appears in full Messianic splendour, seated on his throne of glory. After his long, hidden pre-existence, he is now 'revealed to the elect' and venerated by the rulers of the earth as their judge. The wicked will be carried from his presence,[52] but the righteous will abide with God and 'that *son of man*' for all eternity.

The concluding part of the third parable merely reiterates the main points: the name of 'that *son of man*' is revealed and as universal judge he will banish evil for ever.[53]

In the last two chapters of the second section of 1 Enoch, Enoch's own relationship to 'that *son of man*' is disclosed. Until his ascension to heaven to 'that *son of man* and the Lord of the spirits',[54] there is duality. But on his arrival on high, he is greeted with the following words:

> 'Thou art the *son of man* who art born unto righteousness . . . and the righteousness of the Head of Days forsakes thee not.'[55]

Unless one is prepared to rewrite the whole passage, as R. H. Charles did, no other inference is logical except to identify the heavenly Enoch with the *son of man*=the Messiah.[56] More concretely – if such a word may be used here – the name of the Messiah, i.e. the Messiah not yet 'real' but awaiting the predestined moment of his birth, is henceforth incarnate in the heavenly body of Enoch, and sitting next to God, acts as his chief assistant.[57]

This survey of *son of man* passages in Enoch further confirms the Messianic connotations of Daniel 7 in post-biblical Jewish religious thought, as well as the exclusively glorious features by which it is distinguished, with no admixture of humiliation or suffering. Moreover, 1 Enoch contributes to it certain esoterical ramifications. But contrary to a large body of opinion,[58] analysis of the relevant texts, taken severally and together, never points to the titular use of *son of man*. Phrases such as 'the Anointed' or 'the Lord of the spirits' are sufficient in themselves, they are titles. This can never be said of *son of man*, which always needs to be explained either by referring to the original vision, or to some other determining clause: for example, 'the *son of man* born unto righteousness'.[59] Without such qualification it is neither clear, nor distinctive enough to act as an autonomous title.[60]

Moreover, since Enoch's *son of man* never talks, this work exhibits no structural similarity to the Gospel usage of the term, for there the phrase is always part of direct speech. The esotericism of this apocalypse admittedly has links with several New Testament themes, but for all the philological and exegetical reasons given, it is unable to throw light on the constant and specifically divergent idiom employed by the writers of the Synoptic Gospels.

One final warning: the correct dating of the Book of the Parables is a pertinent issue. In 1912, R. H. Charles assigned it to the

beginning of the first century BC;[61] in 1946, E. Sjöberg preferred
the turn of the eras.[62] Since the Qumran discoveries, however,
the whole matter appears differently. Section I of Enoch (chapters
1–36) is fragmentarily represented by five Aramaic manuscripts
in Cave 4, section III (chapters 72–82) by four, section IV (chapters
83–90) by five, and section V (chapters 91–107) by one manuscript.
Section II (chapters 37–71), however – the *son of man* book – is
missing completely. Is this purely accidental? Possibly. Yet the
scholar who knows most about these still unpublished documents
does not think so. In his opinion, the Parables are 'the work of a
Jew or a Jewish Christian of the first or the second century AD',[63]
and he now places the composition of the book in the second half
of the third century.[64] A post-AD 70 dating would find corrobora-
tive support in the late attestation of such concepts as the pre-
existence, concealment and revelation of the Messiah.[65] In
consequence, it would be methodologically most unwise to rely
on Enoch in an attempt to reach back to Jesus, although it would
be perfectly admissible to do so in an examination of the evolving
early Christian theology.

As a recapitulation, *son of man* in Jewish Aramaic appears
frequently as a synonym for 'man', and as a substitute for the
indefinite pronoun; more seldom, as a circumlocution by which
the speaker refers to himself.

The biblical Aramaic idiom, 'one like a *son of man*', in Daniel
7: 13, though not individual and Messianic in its origin, acquired
in the course of time a definite Messianic association. However,
none of the interpretative sources employ it as a title, or place it
on the lips of a speaker as a self-designation.

The clear avoidance of the titular use, even when the subject is
a precisely defined person, cannot be attributed to hazard, and
the only rational explanation that springs to mind is that *bar
nasha* was found unsuitable for titular usage because it was too
commonplace, and possibly because of its occasionally pejorative
meaning.[66] As a roundabout confirmation, it might be added that
when the unequivocal and strikingly peculiar Gospel idiom, 'the
son of the man', was rendered into Christian Aramaic, the trans-

lators opted for unusual and tautologous formations, judging the vulgar *son of man* unfit for the expression of an idea as meaningful as the phrase by which Jesus habitually alluded to himself.

Before turning to the New Testament, it may not be useless to ensure that no misunderstanding remains. Since 'the *son of man*' is not a Greek phrase, but Aramaic, if it is to make sense at all it must be Aramaic sense. It would be a caricature of scholarship first to admit these premisses, then to decide, on unhistorical and unlinguistic grounds, what the New Testament expression means, and finally to assert that this must also be the import of the Aramaic idiom: and a fig for the absence of any evidence of such use in the extant corpus of Aramaic literature!

II. THE *SON OF MAN* IN THE SYNOPTIC GOSPELS

Rudolf Bultmann, whose name is a landmark in the study of the problem considered here, classifies Gospel references to the *son of man* under three headings: those dealing (a) with his earthly activity; (b) with his death and resurrection; and (c) with his future return.[67] Of these categories, only the last relies on very old traditions. The others he believes to be inauthentic. H. Conzelmann 'out-Bultmanns' Bultmann by declaring all the *son of man* utterances foreign to Jesus.[68] This fashionable German scepticism is nevertheless not unanimous among New Testament experts, and a writer as perspicacious as C. K. Barrett, though admitting that some *son of man* sayings are secondary, recognizes the idea as 'a connecting thread which holds together Jesus' work in the present and in the future'.[69] However disparate, these views have two points in common in that they presume both the existence of a Jewish *son of man* 'concept' and the occurrence of a corresponding 'title'.[70] But if the preceding pages prove anything, it is that neither of these claims may be taken for granted. Furthermore, it is suggested here that another method of classification of *son of man* sayings is more suitable, based not on purely subjective exegetical criteria, but on others that are objective and formal.

As the large majority of scholars agree in distinguishing a connection between the *son of man* phrase and Daniel 7: 13, it is proposed that the Synoptic use of it be examined from the vantage-point of the absence or presence of such a relationship.

Mark, Matthew and Luke contain sixty-six *son of man* passages. In thirty-seven of these there appears to be no link with the Old Testament text; six, however, cite Daniel 7: 13 explicitly, and twenty-one allude to it indirectly – to the coming, or the glory, or the kingship of the *son of man*, or to the clouds transporting him. If triple and double parallels are counted as one saying – a more significant way of reckoning – the statistical table opposite is obtained.

Two striking peculiarities emerge from this table. Firstly, only two passages quote Daniel expressly (less than 10 per cent of the total sample), against twenty examples with no noticeable apocalyptic relevance (nearly 60 per cent of the total). Moreover, ten of the thirteen Marcan instances belong to the latter category, whilst the joint Matthew-Luke material is split roughly in the middle. Secondly, fifteen of the examples have no Synoptic parallel but are peculiar to Matthew or Luke and are likely to be later additions. If they are discounted, the final total of the *logia* appearing in at least two Gospels looks even odder:

No reference to Daniel: 16 (8 in a triple and 8 in a double attestation)
Direct reference: 2 (both in a triple attestation)
Indirect reference: 5 (1 in a triple, 4 in a double attestation)

Here is a real unbalance. In the oldest Gospel the *son of man* passages are mainly non-Danielic; in the Matthew-Luke category there are five neutral examples against four indirect Daniel quotations; and in the specific Matthean and Lucan supplements, the indirect references to Daniel increase substantially – eleven as against Mark's one and Matthew-Luke's four. These figures must mean something.

No reference to Daniel   Direct reference   Indirect reference

Mark 13:26 = Matt. 24:30 = Luke 21:27   Mark 8:38 = Matt. 16:27 = Luke 9:26
Mark 14:62 = Matt. 26:64 = Luke 22:69†

Mark 2:10 = Matt. 9: 6 = Luke 5:24
Mark 2:28 = Matt. 12: 8 = Luke 6: 5
Mark *8:27 = Matt. 16:13* = Luke 9:18*
Mark *8:31 = Matt. 16:21 = Luke 9:22*
Mark 9: 9 = Matt. 17: 9
Mark 9:12 = Matt. 17:12
Mark 9:31 = Matt. 17:22 = Luke 9:44
Mark 10:33 = Matt. 22:18 = Luke 18:31
Mark *10:45 = Matt. 20:28* = Luke 22:27*
Mark 14:21 = Matt. 26:24 = Luke 22:22
Mark 14:41 = Matt. 26:45

Matt. 5:11 = *Luke 6:22*
Matt. 8:20 = Luke 9:58
Matt. 11:19 = Luke 7:34
Matt. 12:32 = *Luke 12:10*
Matt. 12:40 = Luke 11:30
Matt. 26:22

Matt. 19:28 = Luke 22:30
Matt. 24:27 = Luke 17:24
Matt. 24:37 = Luke 17:26
Matt. 24:44 = Luke 12:40

Matt. 10:23
Matt. 13:37
Matt. 13:41
Matt. 16:28
Matt. 24:30
Matt. 25:31

Luke 19:10
Luke 22:48
Luke 24: 7

Luke 12: 8
Luke 17:22
Luke 17:30
Luke 18: 8
Luke 21:36

* Only the references in italics contain the actual phrase, *son of man*.
† Luke's altered reading could, strictly speaking, be qualified as an indirect citation of Daniel 7:13.

Son of man *sayings unconnected with Daniel* 7 : 13

Mark 2: 10 (Matthew 9: 6; Luke 5: 24)

In the controversy surrounding the healing of the paralytic, Jesus asserts that to heal the consequences of sin and to forgive sin itself is one and the same. He could therefore preface his command, 'Stand up, take your bed, and walk', with the equivalent statement:

> 'To convince you that the *son of man* has the right on earth to forgive sins, *I* say to you . . .'

Here, *son of man* points either to man in general or to the speaker, and both interpretations are attested in the Gospels themselves. Matthew 9: 8 relates that the bystanders praised God for having given such power to 'men', whereas Mark 2: 12, 'Never before have we seen the like', implies that the words were associated with the person of Jesus alone. As has been shown, an equivocal circumlocution of this sort is perfectly in place in Aramaic. A direct claim, 'I have the authority to forgive sins on earth', would have sounded immodest.

Mark 2: 28 (Matthew 12: 8; Luke 6: 5)

> 'The Sabbath was made for man, not man for the Sabbath; so the *son of man* is lord even of the Sabbath' (*RSV*).

This again may indicate a general statement to the effect that God made man lord of all creation, including the Sabbath. A similar understanding of the Sabbath underlies the rabbinic rule that, if there is a choice, it is more important to safeguard human life than to observe the Sabbath laws. Expounding the significance of Exodus 31: 13, 'You shall observe my Sabbaths', an old commentary cites the following interpretations from second-century AD teachers:

> The Sabbath was given to you, not you to the Sabbath.[71]

Again, Rabbi Akiba taught:

> If punishment for murder has precedence over Temple
> worship, which in turn has precedence over the Sabbath,
> how much more the safeguarding of life must have precedence
> over the Sabbath.[72]

The first saying from Mekhilta echoes the essence of the Gospel
logion; the second recalls its justification in Matthew 12: 1–6, where
Sabbath laws are grouped together with cultic observances. If
priests may profane the Sabbath without blame in the Temple
service, even more so may the ordinary man when he is in need.

The separate existence of a proverb, 'The *son of man* is lord of
the Sabbath', cannot be proved positively, but if it was used, its
meaning was generic. Be this as it may, in the context of the
Gospels, and especially in Mark's formulation, a circumlocutional
reference to the speaker affords the best sense.

Matthew 16: 13 (Mark 8: 27; Luke 9: 18)
Jesus asked his disciples:

> 'Who do men say that the *son of man* is?' ('that I am?' in
> Mark and Luke)

The variant in Mark and Luke and in some Matthean manuscripts, as well as the question, 'And you, who do you say *I* am?'
in Matthew 16: 15, leave the meaning of *son of man* in no doubt.
The only real issue is to determine whether Matthew's expression
is original and the 'I' form in the other Synoptics its Greek
'translation', or inversely, whether Matthew's *son of man* is a
secondary Aramaism. Since however the contrast between 'men'
(*bene nash*) and 'the *son of man*' (*bar nasha*) sounds convincingly
idiomatic, it has a good chance of being primitive.

The remaining eight *son of man* sayings independent of Daniel
7: 13, as they appear in Mark, paralleled by Matthew and Luke
or by Matthew alone, are spoken by Jesus in connection with his
betrayal, suffering, death and resurrection. As has been argued
earlier, it is most probable that in their original form these *logia*
mentioned only his imminent martyrdom, without reference to

any immediate vindication.[73] Consequently, the use of a circumlocution in such a context is to be expected rather than a direct prediction of the speaker's violent death.

Several of these sayings are doubtless no more than duplicates, though the need to repeat them may lie in the bewildering nature of their content and its shocking impact. Nonetheless, the Gospel account of the apostles' behaviour during Jesus' ordeal would suggest that they must have thought he was exaggerating and that the crisis in Jerusalem took them unawares.[74]

Among the instances from the common stock of Matthew-Luke, two concern his fate. The first, Matthew 12: 40=Luke 11: 30, alludes to the *son of man* lying in the bowels of the earth for three days and three nights.[75] The second, Luke 6: 22=Matthew 5: 11, foretells the persecution of the disciples 'because of the *son of man*' (='because of *me*' in Matthew). On three further occasions, Jesus makes statements concerning his homeless existence,[76] and concerning the derogatory criticism which would be levelled against him.[77] Finally, in Luke 19: 10, 'The *son of man* has come to seek and save what is lost', he speaks from a position of reserve.

In a preliminary assessment of these twenty sayings, it should be emphasized that they are sound from both the linguistic and the contextual point of view. They echo a peculiar speech-form that is genuinely Aramaic, and fit so well into the Gospels that, if the interpretations advanced here are accepted, there is no reasonable doubt why Jesus should not have uttered them. In fact, if only half these sayings are authentic, it would still be justifiable to infer that the *son of man* circumlocution belonged to the stylistic idiosyncrasies of Jesus himself.

Son of man *sayings directly connected with Daniel 7: 13*

The two Synoptic passages quoting Daniel 7: 13 literally belong to the type of doctrinal elaboration characterized, not as straightforward teaching, but as sectarian and dogmatic speculation backed by technical proof from Scripture.

Mark 13: 26 (Matthew 24: 30; Luke 21: 27)

The theme of the eschatological discourse presented by all three Synoptists is that at the end of days Jesus' disciples must read the signs aright and not follow after false prophets and pseudo-Messiahs arriving in his name. It reflects, as has already been explained, the politico-religious upheaval of the years immediately prior to the outbreak of the first Jewish War.[78] The traditional portents are described, the darkening of the sun and the moon and the falling of the stars from the skies. Then the *son of man* will come with (or on) the clouds, invested with power and glory. The evangelist's intention is to affirm that after his earthly career, Jesus, like the figure of Daniel's vision, will be seen in all his Messianic heavenly prestige, conferred on him by God through his resurrection and ascension.

Can such a use of the *son of man* idiom be judged historically genuine and attributable to Jesus? The contrast with its employment as a self-designation, outlined in the previous section, is not sufficient reason to deny the authenticity of this other usage. After all, the present text can also be understood as a circumlocution for 'I'. On the other hand, the necessary prerequisite of a full Messianic consciousness on the part of the speaker – so contrary to all that has been established in chapter 6 – and the general tenor, content and climax of the discourse itself, militate against the possibility of its genuineness. Indeed, these speak against the historicity of the composition as a whole. It was after his death, when Jesus had been proclaimed the exalted Messiah, that the portrayal of his glorious manifestation could be successfully effected with the help of Daniel 7: 13. It is difficult therefore not to conclude that Mark 13: 26 and its parallels are the product of Christianity rather than of Jesus.[79]

After Jesus', at best equivocal, answer ('It is as you say') to the high priest's solemn adjuration whether or not he is the Messiah, tradition adds a corrective to counterbalance the disturbing impression caused by his initial reply:

Mark 14:62	Matthew 26:64	Luke 22:69
'And you will see the *son of man* seated at the right hand of the Power and coming with the clouds of heaven.'	'From now on, you will see the *son of man* seated at the right hand of God and coming on the clouds of heaven.'	'But from now on, the *son of man* will be seated at the right hand of Almighty God.'

This saying, which is shortened in Luke, combines the idea of Messianic enthronement announced in Psalm 110: 1,[80] and the final manifestation of the glorified Christ as described by Daniel 7: 13. Here again, as in the eschatological discourse, Daniel serves as a biblical basis for the Parousia motive.[81]

The formal association of 'the *son of man*' in the Synoptics with Daniel 7: 13 appears to be derivative and can scarcely be ascribed to Jesus himself. Nevertheless, it is most remarkable that even at this stage its use as a form of self-designation still survives. The final dilemma which the historian is asked to solve is whether direct reference to Daniel 7: 13 results from an attempt to render explicit the underlying significance of innuendoes genuinely uttered by Jesus, or whether indirect references are secondary developments from the formal quotations just investigated.

Son of man *sayings indirectly connected with Daniel 7 : 13*

The only saying of this class to appear in all three Synoptists is Mark 8: 38 (Matt. 16: 27; Luke 9: 26):

'For whoever is ashamed of *me* and of my words in this adulterous and sinful generation, of him will the *son of man* also be ashamed, when he comes in the glory of his Father with the holy angels' (*RSV*).

It has been cogently argued that this *logion* has evolved from a more distinctively Semitic original represented by Luke 12: 8:[82]

'Everyone who acknowledges *me* before men, the *son of man* will acknowledge before the angels of God.'

If this is correct, it would follow that the implicit reference to Daniel 7: 13 was added as a chronological pointer: Jesus will reject the unfaithful at the moment of his return.

Among the remaining indirect associations with Daniel 7: 13, six appear in the eschatological discourse and are consequently dependent on the belief in a second coming or Parousia, which arose after Jesus' death.[83] Matthew, in particular, the only evangelist actually to use the term Parousia,[84] dwells heavily on this feature. He several times inserts the motif of the coming *son of man* into sayings which originally had no such connotation,[85] and interpolates eschatological parables among genuine ones.[86]

In the last phase of its evolution, the *son of man* formula is intimately bound to a context of time, the moment in which Jesus is to be finally revealed; yet formally, it still remains a self-designation.

'Before you have gone through all the towns of Israel the *son of man* will have come.'[87]

'But when the son of man comes, will he find faith on earth?'[88]

In the demonstrable absence of any axiomatic, pre-existent Jewish concept of 'the *son of man*', it is to be concluded that the indirect references in the Synoptic Gospels to 'the *son of man* coming with the clouds', in the company of the angels, are timid, early 'post-crucifixion' hints at the exaltation and imminent glorious revelation of the Messiah.

It has recently been conjectured that the Parousia image of the coming Judge was preceded by an interpretation of Jesus' resurrection as the ascension of the *son of man* portrayed in Daniel 7: 13.[89] Be this as it may, in the only certain form of the Synoptic tradition, the one actually extant, the Daniel symbol always serves to describe an earthward journey on the clouds in place of the original upward trip.[90]

To sum up, there is no evidence whatever, either inside or outside the Gospels, to imply, let alone demonstrate, that 'the *son of man*' was used as a title. There is, in addition, no valid argument to prove that any of the Gospel passages directly or indirectly referring to Daniel 7: 13 may be traced back to Jesus. The only possible, indeed probable, genuine utterances are sayings independent of Daniel 7 in which, in accordance with Aramaic usage, the speaker refers to himself as the *son of man* out of awe, reserve, or humility. It is this neutral speech-form that the apocalyptically-minded Galilean disciples of Jesus appear to have 'eschatologized' by means of a midrash based on Daniel 7: 13.

Contemporary New Testament scholarship has expended much effort, erudition and ink, to agree in the end on almost nothing except that the *son of man* is a vitally important title. That the conclusion arrived at in the present study differs so radically from this is due to the different questions it asks. For if a problem is approached wrongly, wrong answers are bound to multiply. In this respect the irony of Paul Winter, in his review of Norman Perrin's *Rediscovering the Teaching of Jesus*, makes amusing reading:

> If Perrin's interpretation of the Son of Man sayings in the Synoptic Gospels is correct – and it is supported by Vermes's . . . study of the linguistic use of 'bar-nash(a)' in Jewish Aramaic – then the place of origin of the myth is not to be sought in Iran, or in Judea or even in Ugarit, but in the German universities.[91]

Excursus I: the cloud, a means of heavenly transport

It has been argued that the 'one like a *son of man*' coming with the clouds in Daniel 7: 13 is a person journeying upwards.[92] The idea seems to have been common. It was on a cloud that Moses was lifted up to God and finally translated to heaven.

> Moses ascended in the cloud, was hidden by the cloud, and was sanctified by the cloud.[93]

When Moses was to ascend, a cloud descended and lay before him . . . And the cloud covered Moses and carried him up.[94]

The same upward movement is attested in the New Testament's ascension story:

As they watched, he was lifted up, and a cloud removed him from their sight.[95]

Likewise, the Christian faithful, dead and living, are to travel on clouds to meet Christ in the air according to 1 Thessalonians 4: 16. A similar idea of individual heavenly transport is contained in the Palestinian Targums on Exodus 19: 4 where it is explained that God will carry the children of Israel, not on 'eagle's wings', but on 'clouds', or 'small clouds', or 'in the clouds of my Presence'.[96]

Although Daniel 7: 13 could have provided an excellent scriptural basis for the construction of the Christian belief in the resurrection of Jesus, and even more so for his ascension, there is no evidence of its direct use in any other context but that of an earthward journey at the Parousia. Here the Gospels anticipate the doctrine expressed in rabbinic literature concerning the revelation and coming of the Messiah previously concealed in heaven.[97] Allegedly, the most striking parallel is provided by the printed text of the Fragmentary Targum on Exodus 12: 42 describing the arrival, on the final Passover night, of Moses and the King Messiah 'led on the top of the cloud'. But the phrase is very clumsy and the alternative reading of Targum Neofiti, which does away with the cloud altogether, appears to be far superior: the Messiah (the good shepherd) will 'lead at the head of the flock'.[98]

Some New Testament passages, it is true, speak not only of an ascent or descent, but a return journey of Christ.

'This Jesus, who has been taken away from you up to heaven (on a cloud), will come in the same way as you have seen him go.'[99]

The Fourth Gospel envisages Jesus' appearance on earth as a descent from heaven, and his journey in the opposite direction as an ascent.

'No one ever went up into heaven except the one who came down from heaven, the *son of man*.'[100]

'What if you see the *son of man* ascending to the place where he was before?'[101]

Thus from the single upward excursion of the Danielic dream, Christianity developed a threefold theological sequence: (1) a downward journey (Incarnation); (2) an upward journey (Resurrection-Ascension); (3) a second downward journey (Parousia).

Excursus II: debate on the circumlocutional use of *son of man*

My earlier study of the use of *son of man* in Jewish Aramaic, delivered as a lecture at an Oxford New Testament Conference in September 1965 and printed in 1967 as a special appendix to the third edition of Matthew Black's book, *An Aramaic Approach to the Gospels and Acts*, has two principal conclusions. It denies the existence of the titular use and proves with examples the circumlocutional employment of *bar nasha*. The two parts of the argument being independent, it should have been realized that criticism levelled against one of them does not automatically dispose of the other. It should have also been obvious that the onus of proof that 'the *son of man*' is a title lies squarely on the shoulders of the theologians.

This last point has generally been missed, partly because demonstration of the non-titular character of *son of man* in Daniel, 1 Enoch and 4 Ezra was postponed for further discussion[102] and had temporarily to be taken on trust, but partly also because there was at that time a need to react quickly to my academically 'unorthodox' theses. Several books and papers were at a final stage of redaction or already with the printers when the news of my *bar nasha* attack broke, and as a large number of advance off-prints were in circulation from 1966 onward, a new line of defence had to be improvised in haste.

One factor that took me completely by surprise was to discover that Matthew Black, after having persuaded me to allow my article to appear in his book, had decided to append to it his criticism. 'Clear and convincing' though he declared it to be, this did not prevent him from reiterating, without advancing new proofs, a nearly twenty-year-old thesis concerning 'eschatological over-tones' in Jesus' employment of the phrase in reference to himself.[103]

F. H. Borsch, whose book *The Son of Man in Myth and History* appeared in 1967, reluctantly admitted after a glance at an advance off-print that the Aramaic expression is used 'possibly also (but only possibly) . . . as a first person circumlocution', though he found that none of my examples constitute 'unambiguous illustrations'.[104]

The first writer to advance reasoned criticism was Joachim Jeremias,[105] who saw the basic flaw in my argument to be the assimilation of the idiom 'that man' (*hahu gabra*) with 'the *son of man*'. Jeremias believes that whereas 'that man' is an exclusive phrase meaning 'I' and no one else, *son of man* is a generic term, though it may also include the speaker. Part of this objection has already been dealt with apropos of the *double entente* inherent to circumlocutional speech.[106] As for the claim that the expression, 'that man', is unequivocal, it does not tally with the facts. Because of its intrinsic ambiguity, it is on the contrary sometimes necessary to analyse the context very carefully before deciding whether it means 'I' or 'you'. For instance, Vespasian whilst still Nero's general is reported to have been greeted by Yohanan ben Zakkai with '*Vive Domine Imperator!*'; to which the future emperor replied, 'Were the King to hear this, he would kill *that man*'.[107] Now 'that man' could indicate Yohanan (='you'), whom Nero would put to death for acclaiming a rival emperor. But it could equally refer to Vespasian ('I'), who might be denounced as a pretender.[108]

The position adopted by J. A. Fitzmyer is curious. On the one hand, he accepts my principal conclusions in full;[109] but on the other, he submits that these valid features of my argument derive from documents irrelevant to the study of the New Testament. In his view, no writings later than Aramaic texts from the first century AD are admissible as philological terms of comparison: so no rabbinic literature, please!

In an ideal situation, with a plethora of Aramaic sources to turn to dating from the first century AD and representing the appropriate vocabulary, style and linguistic structure, such a limitation would be justified. For example, if we possessed Aramaic gospels written at about the same time as the New Testament and in the same dialect, we could then forget about the writings of the rabbis codified a century or two later. Such, however, is not our good fortune. Besides, an Aramaic source predating the Gospels may be less pertinent than one posterior to it. Who can tell whether a Galilean Aramaic phrase uttered in AD 150 may not be closer to the language underlying the New Testament than Qumran Aramaic written in 100 BC?[110]

The second objection made by Fitzmyer is that all my examples except one Qumran quotation are unsuitable, not only because of their dating in general, but because from the form in which nash ('man') is attested there it is evident that the phrase is a more recent development: in earlier sources it is spelt 'enash or 'enosh. His conclusion is that 'the lack of the initial aleph . . . is a sign of the lateness of the phrase'.[111] But if he were to follow his own rule, he would find himself with a problem on his hands. For instance, obliged to explain the New Testament form of the name Lazar(us) from contemporary or earlier sources, he would discover that first-century AD witnesses – a bill of divorce from Murabba'at and a Jerusalem ossuary epigraph – write it as Eleazar with an aleph at the beginning.[112] Now the form Lazar derives from Eleazar by omission of the initial aleph in the same way as nash is a shortened version of 'enash. But as is well known, this dropping of the opening guttural is a peculiarity of the Galilean Aramaic dialect, and characteristically the Palestinian – i.e. Galilean – Talmud often truncates the names of Eleazar and Eliezer to read Lazar or Liezer.[113] Similarly, in the Galilean necropolis of Beth She'arim, Greek-Jewish inscriptions attest the abbreviated form *Lazar* and even *Laze*.[114] Thus, far from detracting from the validity of evidence concerning the Galilean dialect spoken as we believe by Jesus, and forming the Aramaic basis of the Gospel tradition, the *aleph*-less spelling of *nash* rather enhances it.

It should perhaps be put on record that the first leading New Testament scholar to rethink his whole approach to the *son of man* problem in the light of the new Aramaic data was that youthful and indefatigable octogenarian, C. H. Dodd.[115]

8. Jesus the *son of God*

It is a fact that Jesus is often called *son of God* in the New Testament. It is equally a fact that even non-Christian readers of the Gospels influenced willy-nilly by church dogma are liable to identify as a matter of course the title *son of God* with the notion of divinity. Within Christianity and without, accepted as an article of faith or rejected, the assumption is that when the evangelists apply this term to Jesus they are acknowledging him as equal to God. In other words, the tendency, conscious or otherwise, is to inject into the first Christian writings, and beyond them into a tradition sprung from Jewish soil, the most un-Jewish doctrine of the Council of Nicea: 'Jesus Christ, the only-begotten Son of God . . . God of God . . . being of one substance with the Father.'

To assess this final and most influential christological title, the usual exegetical, historical and chronological questions must be formulated and answered. Can it be shown from extant New Testament evidence that Jesus himself claimed divine sonship? Did his immediate Jewish-Galilean disciples accept and affirm it? Or did the style come into being among the second generation followers, either in Palestinian or in Hellenistic Judeo-Christianity? Finally, what was its original meaning and did it undergo any substantial transformation when it passed from Jewish to the Gentile-Hellenic world?

Starting with the first question, if the theory is accepted that Jesus rejected the title of 'Messiah the *son of God*' on the occasion of Peter's confession, and the high priest's question,[1] there is not a sign in the Synoptic Gospels of his having arrogated to himself this exalted relationship. Writers who desire to maintain that he thought himself 'the son of God in a pre-eminent sense'[2] are compelled to rely on what is clearly the ultimate phase of the title's development, the substitution of 'the Son' for *son of God*,[3] and to pretend that it is historically authentic. But apart from a few conservatives, all the more open-minded New Testament interpreters, irrespective of Christian denominational loyalties, stop short of such an assertion.

To name but a few examples of more recent scholarly opinion, B. M. F. van Iersel admits that Jesus never alluded to himself as *son of God*,[4] and C. K. Barrett declares without hesitation that the doctrine of sonship played no part in the public proclamation of Jesus.[5] H. Conzelmann, after remarking that the title never figures in a narration, but always in confessions, concludes from his attentive examination that all the examples are unhistorical and that 'according to the texts we have, Jesus did not use the title'.[6]

New Testament experts distinguish, following Bultmann, two stages in the evolution of the *son of God* concept. The first is ascribed to the Palestinian community, where the ancient oriental formula of royal divine adoption, 'You are my son', is applied to Jesus *qua* King Messiah.[7] The second stage is represented by the preaching of the Gentile Hellenistic Church. Here, the Jewish meaning of *son of God* suffered an essential metamorphosis so that it came to indicate, not Jesus' office, but his nature, this latter being conceived by analogy to the half-divine, half-human offspring of the deities of classical mythology renowned for their prowess and redemptive acts.

Ferdinand Hahn sees the amalgamation of the Messianic and Hellenistic elements of the *son of God* idea as taking place in three stages. It is first used in the 'post-Easter' Palestinian community as the fitting title of a Messiah whose earthly career had ended and who was now adopted by God and enthroned in heaven. As a next development, Hellenistic Judeo-Christianity, turning from Jesus' heavenly existence to his life on earth, saw him as a supernaturally endowed miracle-worker and exorcist whose conception in the womb of a virgin was due to God's direct intervention. And lastly, Jesus' divine sonship was recognized principally as the result of an apotheosis, a deification, that also implied pre-existence and an, as it were, physical filiation due to the part attributed to God in his peculiar mode of conception.[8]

With a view to exploring further the implications of the term, *son of God*, and to throwing new light on its original meaning, it is proposed now to look for parallels in Judaism – biblical and post-biblical – and in the Greco-Roman world, and to follow this enquiry with an exposition of the Gospel evidence. As a supplement, Jesus' habit of addressing or discussing God as 'my Father' will be considered. A final excursus will treat of the issue of the virgin birth.

I. THE NOTION *SON OF GOD* IN THE INTER-TESTAMENTAL WORLD

1. *The Old Testament heritage*

The expression, *son of God*, or when God speaks, 'my son', has been the subject of such frequent and intensive examination that the briefest sketch of the facts agreed on will suffice.[9]

The Bible mentions three types of *sons of God*: (a) heavenly or angelic beings;[10] (b) Israelites or the people of Israel as such;[11] and (c) kings of Israel. There is no correspondence between the first two categories and the New Testament usage; orthodox Christianity never conceived Jesus to be an angel and the son relationship accorded to any Jew would not give him the distinction intended by the Gospels. Scholarly attention has therefore been confined to the appellation, 'my son', addressed by God to David and the Israelite ruler in general.

'I will be his father, and he shall be my son.'[12]

I will tell of the decree of the Lord:
He said to me, 'You are my son,
    today I have begotten you.'[13]

He will say to me, 'Thou art my father . . .'
And I will name him my first-born,
    highest among the kings of the earth.[14]

This royal sonship of God would account, it is argued, for the transference of the title at the end of time to the King Messiah. In fact, it is commonly held that the three passages just quoted, and in particular that from Psalm 2, played a central and decisive part in the formation of post-biblical Jewish Messianic thought.

2. *Post-biblical Judaism*

Among the usages noted by scholars, two deserve special attention in that they develop tendencies begun in the Old Testament. Whereas every Jew was called *son of God*, the title came to be given preferably to the just man, and in a very special sense to the most righteous of all just men, the Messiah son of David.

(a) *The just man*

Concluding his exhortation on social responsibility, the author of Ecclesiasticus, Jesus ben Sira, admonishes his readers to care for others:

> Be a father to the fatherless,
> and as a husband to widows,
> and God shall call you *son*,
> and shall have mercy on you,
> and deliver you from the pit.[15]

In a not dissimilar tone, the writer of the Wisdom of Solomon records the wicked as saying apropos of the just man:

> Let us test the truth of his words, let us see what will happen to him in the end; for if the just man is *God's son*, God will stretch out a hand to him and save him from the clutches of his enemies.[16]

In the Book of Jubilees, Israelites with circumcised hearts and filled with the holy spirit are addressed by God:

> 'I will be their Father and they shall be my *sons*. And they all shall be called *sons of* the living *God*, and every angel and every spirit shall know . . . that these are my *sons*, and

that I am their Father in uprightness and righteousness, and that I love them.'[17]

Depicting the days of the Messiah, the poet responsible for Psalm 17 of Solomon equates goodness with being a *son of God*.

> And he shall gather together a holy people, whom he shall lead
>   in righteousness . . .
> And he shall not suffer unrighteousness to lodge any more
>   in their midst,
> Nor shall there dwell with them any man that knoweth
>   wickedness,
> For he shall know them, that they are all *sons of* their *God*.[18]

It should, however, not be assumed from these examples that the metaphor, *son of God*, was commonly employed in inter-Testamental Judaism. For instance, there is no sign of it in the literature from the Dead Sea published so far. Angelic beings are referred to there as 'sons of heaven',[19] and the members of the community as 'sons of his (or 'thy', i.e. God's) truth'[20] or 'sons of his (or 'thy') loving-kindness',[21] but not simply as *sons of God*.

The moralizing overtone in vogue in the Apocrypha and Pseudepigrapha – *son of God*=just man – appears also in Philo and rabbinic literature, with special reference to those who remain faithful to the divine commandments. Commenting on Deuteronomy 13: 19 in conjunction with 14: 1, 'If you obey the voice of the Lord . . . , keeping all his commandments . . . and doing what is right in the sight of the Lord your God, . . . You are the *sons of* . . . *God* . . .' (*RSV*), Philo interprets God as declaring:

> This promise of mine is confirmed by the Law, where it says that they who do 'what is pleasing' to nature and what is 'good' are *sons of God*.[22]

Akiba in turn proclaims:

> Beloved are the Israelites, for they are called *sons of God*. Out of an even greater love for them they are told that they

are called *sons of God*; as it is written, You are the *sons of the Lord your God* (Deut. 14: 1).[23]

The mid-third-century AD teacher, Rabbi Lazar (Eleazar ben Pedath), sets out the old doctrine in full detail in the Palestinian Talmud.

When the Israelites do the will of the Holy One, blessed be he, they are called *sons*; but when they do not do his will, they are not called *sons*.[24]

It might be tempting to deduce from these sayings that the more punctilious a Jew showed himself to be in his religious observances, the closer he came to being a *son of God*, flawless obedience leading to perfect sonship, but logical though such reasoning may sound, it is unsupported by concrete evidence.[25]

(b) *The Messiah*

As has been repeatedly noted, the Bible from time to time alludes to the Israelite king as *son of God*. Moreover, although the texts in question, in particular Psalm 2: 7 and 2 Samuel 7: 14, originally applied to a reigning monarch, they were later transferred to the Davidic ruler of the future, the Messiah. Yet, for reasons peculiar to rabbinic thinking, there was a general tendency to avoid employing the phrase, *son of God*, divorced from an actual scriptural quotation, as an independent christological title.

Gustaf Dalman, who was the first to underline the facts, explained this neglect as being only in part due to Jewish opposition to the Christian interpretation of Psalm 2. The main reason, he thought, was rabbinic unwillingness to use such a basically equivocal expression as *son of God*. This would account for the Psalm having had little significance even in earlier times for Jewish Messianism, in which *son of God* was not a current title.[26] Restating Dalman's view, E. Lohse argued as recently as 1967 that the description of the Messiah as 'my son' in 1 Enoch 105: 2 is not authentic but an Ethiopic interpolation absent from the Greek Enoch, and that the parallel 'my son' terminology in

4 Ezra[27] is not to be taken literally, but as deriving from an original Hebrew/Greek 'my servant'.[28]

Available Qumran documents have not substantially affected the issue, although they appear to point to a central position of the *son of God* concept in the Messianic nomenclature of the Dead Sea sect. They include two crucial passages, the more important of which figures in a Commentary on the Last Days, part of a florilegium discovered in Qumran Cave 4. Here, excerpts from 2 Samuel 7: 11–14 are followed closely by an unfortunately mutilated exegesis of Psalm 2.

> *2 Samuel 7*
> The Lord declares to you that he will build you a house. I will raise up your seed after you and I will establish the throne of his kingdom [for ever]. I [will be] his father and he shall be *my son*.
> He is the Branch of David who shall arise with the Interpreter of the Law [to rule] in Zion [at the end] of time . . .
>
> *Psalm 2*
> [Why] do the nations [rage] and the peoples meditate [vanity]?
> [The kings of the earth] rise up, [and the] princes take counsel together
> against the Lord and against [his Messiah].
> Interpreted, this saying concerns [the kings of the nations] who shall [rage against] the elect of Israel in the last days . . .[29]

The second and more controversial text comes from the Messianic Rule. According to the *editio princeps*, the manuscript gives the following reading.

> This is the order of the session of the men of renown, called to the assembly of the common council when [God] shall beget the Messiah.[30]

Clearly, the phrase as it stands – 'when [God] shall beget the Messiah' – is meaningless unless the begetting of the Messiah was an established metaphor for the public appointment of

Israel's royal saviour. But no evidence exists that would bear this out; in fact, apart from its prototype – 'You are my son, today I have begotten you' – in Psalm 2: 7 (*RSV*), the Qumran expression is a unique example. In the circumstances, therefore, it is reasonable to question the correctness of the decipherment or the copy itself. Having seen the fragment in 1952, shortly after its arrival in the Palestine Archaeological Museum, I can testify that even then it was scarcely legible. Its condition will not have improved with the passing of time. Characteristically, the editor of the text himself substitutes 'God shall *lead*' (YWLYK), for 'God shall *beget*' (YWLYD). Different reconstructions have since been proposed, generally resulting in a meaning irrelevant to the *son of God* problem.[31] In short, the passage is too problematic in itself to serve as basis for further deductive argument.

Thus, unless an as yet unpublished *son of God* fragment from Cave 4, the existence of which is rumoured in scholarly circles, produces something substantially new,[32] all that may be said of the Scrolls in this connection is that they indicate that the epithet, *son of God*, can accompany the title, 'Messiah', but any claim to an equality or interchangeability of the two exceeds the evidence.

3. *The Hellenistic world*

Two noteworthy usages of the *son of God* concept in Hellenistic literature are stressed by New Testament interpreters. The first is part of the nomenclature of the Ptolemaic king of Egypt portrayed as the son of the sun-god Helios, and also of the emperor of Rome, who from Augustus onwards bears the title, 'son of god' (*theou huios, divi filius*).[33] The second use is connected with the 'divine man' notion deriving from classical legend and underlying the imperial cult. However, although the two Greek expressions, 'divine man' (*theios anêr*), and 'son of god' (*huios theou*), are almost synonymous, their joint occurrence seems to be rare and accidental. Consequently, even though some of the charismatic figures of Hellenism may be described as 'gods' and 'sons of Zeus',[34] the utilization of this Greek concept in the domain of the New Testament is bound to prove awkward and difficult.

All in all, it would appear that a first-century AD Palestinian Jew, hearing the phrase *son of God*, would have thought first of all of an angelic or celestial being; and secondly, when the human connection was clear, of a just and saintly man. The divine sonship of the Messiah was expected to be within a royal context. In a Hellenistic milieu – and there alone – the epithet would allegedly have called to mind a miracle-worker.

II. *SON OF GOD* IN THE NEW TESTAMENT

1. *The Synoptic Gospels and Acts*

Two types of sayings are relevant to the study of *son of God* in the Gospels and Acts: those in which Jesus is understood to have identified himself as *son of God*, and those in which others address or describe him as such.

(a) *Self-identification*

Discounting the trinitarian formula appended to the Gospel of Matthew 28: 19 – 'in the name of the Father and the Son and the Holy Spirit' – as representative of the latest stage of the doctrinal evolution and consequently out of place in a historical investigation of Jesus and his age, only two texts have been transmitted in which Jesus expresses his position *vis-à-vis* God in terms of a father-son relationship.[35]

> *Mark 13: 32 (Matthew 24: 36)*
> 'About that day or that hour no one knows, not even the angels in heaven, not even *the son*; only the Father.'

Although the *logion* is part of the eschatological discourse ascribed earlier to a layer of tradition posterior to Jesus,[36] it has been Vincent Taylor's contention that the admission of ignorance of 'that hour' on the part of Jesus militates in favour of the genuineness of this verse at least.[37] Yet, as C. K. Barrett has aptly remarked, the employment by Gospel tradition of the highest honorific title, '*the* son', is likely to have been introduced precisely in order to counterbalance the disturbing impression left by the saying as a whole.[38]

> *Matthew 11: 27 (Luke 10: 22)*
> 'All things have been delivered to me by my Father; and no one knows *the son* except the Father, and no one knows the Father except *the son* and any one to whom *the son* chooses to reveal him' (*RSV*).

In removing this hymn from the lips of Jesus and accrediting it instead to the primitive Church, contemporary exegetical scepticism joins forces for once with common sense; for no unbiased interpreter can fail to notice how discrepant these words are in both tone and content from the normal sayings of Jesus.[39]

Thus, on the basis of his surviving teaching, it turns out that it is impossible to prove, and unwise to suppose, that Jesus defined himself as *the son of God*. It should nevertheless be added immediately that the absence of an explicit identification of himself as *the son* does not impinge *ipso facto* on the authenticity of the mode of addressing God as 'Father', with its concomitant notion of sonship.[40]

(b) *Description or address*
  i. *Son of God*=Messiah
In a first group of sayings the description of Jesus as *son of God* is almost automatically associated with the Messianic concept.

> 'You are the Messiah, *the son of* the living God.'[41]

> 'Are you the Messiah, *the son of the Blessed One?*'[42]

In these passages, to which may be added the title, 'the Gospel of Jesus Christ, *the son of God*', prefixed to Mark in a number of old manuscripts, the phrase simply expressed the symbolism inherent in Psalm 2: 7: 'You are *my son*, today I have begotten you.'[43] No significance should in consequence be ascribed to it beyond that of divine appointment and adoption.[44]

In effect, therefore, the addition of *son of God* to 'Messiah' in the two main Gospel texts seems to be secondary and attributable to the stylistic needs of a Messianic confession of faith. It must follow that if, as has been concluded in the previous chapter,[45] Jesus declined the status of Messiah, he must also have rejected the title, 'Messiah *son of God*'.

Finally, the expression figures twice in the annunciation narrative of Luke's Gospel.

> 'You will conceive . . . and bear a son . . . He will be great and will be called *the son of the Most High*; and the Lord God will give to him the throne of his father David . . .'[46]

> 'The holy spirit will come upon you, and the power of the Most High will overshadow you; therefore the child to be born will be called holy, the *son of God*.'[47]

The first passage clearly shows the synonymity of *son of God* and 'Messiah son of David', whilst the second hints already at a sonship resulting from a miraculous conception. Yet it is remarkable that in both quotations Jesus is described as being 'called' *son of God*. Such a terminology must have been deeply rooted in primitive tradition; even Paul was influenced by it, asserting not that Jesus 'was' the *son of God*, but that he was 'declared' to be *son of God*.[48] It was only at a later phase of the virgin birth story that 'being *son of God*' was substituted for 'being called *son of God*'.[49]

ii. *Son of God*=miracle-worker

In a second and larger collection of Gospel passages,[50] the *son of God* notion is closely associated with the superhuman power and authority recognized in Jesus by demons, men, and the heavenly Voice.

Son of God *used by demons*

The two contexts in which such a usage is attested are the stories of exorcism and the legendary dialogue between Satan and Jesus in the temptation episode. In the first the sick person's words are attributed to the devils possessing him.

> The unclean spirits too, when they saw him, would fall at his feet and cry aloud, 'You are the *son of God!*'[51]

> Devils also came out of many of them, shouting, 'You are the *son of God.*'[52]

The demon called *Legion* is said to have implored Jesus (in the name of God!) to leave him in peace.

> 'What do you want with me, Jesus, *son* of the Most High God? In God's name, do not torment me.'[53]

Almost identical is the complaint of the two possessed men from the country of the Gadarenes in Transjordan.

> 'You *son of God*, what do you want with us? Have you come here to torment us before our time?'[54]

These texts reveal an association between the title, *son of God*, and the charismatic exorcist, a person able to dominate and purge unclean spirits. From this basic idea of a *son of God* it was easy to go on to invest him with wider miraculous powers.

It is in effect this larger image that is projected in the story of the temptation of Jesus in the wilderness. Satan is shown asking the *son of God* to perform useless wonders, miraculous tricks, simply to prove that he can do them.

> The tempter approached him and said, 'If you are the *son of God*, tell these stones to become bread.'[55]

> The devil then took him to the holy city and set him on the parapet of the Temple. 'If you are the *son of God*,' he said, 'throw yourself down!'[56]

Son of God *used by men*

One rather curious feature of the Synoptic Gospels is that although Jesus was venerated as *son of God*, this title, as distinguished from 'Messiah *son of God*', is almost totally ignored by his disciples.

The only exception is Matthew, who appends it to the account
of Jesus' walking on the waters of the Lake of Gennesaret.

> The men in the boat fell at his feet, exclaiming, 'Truly you
> are the *son of God*.'[57]

There is one other instance in which it is used as a compliment,
this time by the centurion, the official witness of the death of
Jesus on the cross:

> 'Truly this man was a *son of God*.'[58]

It has frequently been noted that, spoken by a Gentile, *son of God*
is employed here in a sense meaningful to non-Jews. Inspired by
the miraculous events surrounding the crucifixion, it foreshadowed
the conversion of the Roman empire.[59] Yet, if Mark and Matthew
deliberately chose this Greek formula, how can it be explained
that Luke, the Gentile evangelist, substitutes for it, 'Certainly
this man was innocent'?[60]

The theory of a Hellenistic terminology is further undermined
by the parallel story of the execution of the miracle-worker
Honi/Onias, where the Hebrew sources refer to him as 'son of
the house (of God)', whilst Josephus, writing in Greek, describes
him as a 'just man and dear to God'.[61] It would seem, therefore,
that the phrase *son of God* has definitely Semitic associations.

Finally, Matthew alone among the evangelists places the title
son of God in the mouth of Jesus' enemies. As he dies, the on-
lookers challenge him to prove his miraculous powers by freeing
himself from the gibbet:

> 'If you are the *son of God*, come down from the cross.'[62]

Similarly, the main culprits in the tragedy – the chief priests,
lawyers and elders – mockingly declare that here is a splendid
opportunity to test Jesus' pretensions to a special relationship
with God.

> 'He saved others; he cannot save himself. . . . Let him come
> down now from the cross, and we will believe in him. . . .
> for he said, "I am the *son of God*." '[63]

Son of God *used by the heavenly Voice*

In two Gospel sections of central importance, the baptism and the transfiguration narratives, Jesus is referred to as 'my *son*' by a mysterious heavenly Voice, reckoned to be that of God, addressing either Jesus' friends, or Jesus himself.[64] The first alternative is attested by Matthew, according to whom the Voice declares in the scene of the baptism:

'This is *my* beloved *son*, with whom I am well pleased.'[65]

Commentators fail to agree on the beneficiary of this revelation. Was it John the Baptist? The majority argue, on the basis of the Marcan and Lucan parallels and from the content of the preceding verse – Jesus saw the heavens opening – that Jesus alone heard the Voice; in which case Matthew's recension falls into line with the formula presented by the two other Synoptists:

'Thou art *my* beloved *son*; with thee I am well pleased.'[66]

It is nevertheless possible to raise serious doubts concerning the authenticity of the second-person style. In addition to Matthew's baptism narrative, all three Synoptic versions of the Transfiguration give the commendation – presumed to have been heard by apostolic witnesses - in the third person.[67] Moreover, the Jewish notion of the *bath kol*, i.e. loud Voice speaking from heaven, also suggests that the original form of the story was that of a public or semi-public announcement. By substituting, 'Thou art *my* beloved *son*', for 'This is *my* beloved *son*', Mark – and Luke in his wake – skilfully uses the episode to explain Jesus' nascent awareness of a supernatural vocation.[68]

Although the passages employing *son of God* in the sense of miracle-worker form the numerically largest group in the Synoptic material, and must consequently have played a significant part in the development of Christian tradition, they – or at least the confessions by Satan and the Roman centurion – are considered to be of recent, i.e. of Jewish- or Gentile-Hellenistic, origin.[69] In fact, many commentators see, as does Rudolf Bultmann, a New Testament adaptation of the Greek 'divine man' concept in the sonship of Jesus.[70] However, even those who reject Bultmann's thesis on account of the essentially polytheistic connotations of the Hellenistic 'divine man' and its inapplicability to a monotheistic framework,[71] show little willingness to assign an early date to the usage. In one of the latest attempts to combine Jewish and Greek elements, E. Schweizer gives the following assessment in connection with the temptation legend:

> The question asked by Satan presupposes a tradition in which the *son of God* reveals himself primarily through his miracles. Since the title had no pre-Christian link with a miracle-worker, it must have derived from Mark 1: 11 par. (i.e. the story of the Baptism of Jesus).[72]

In short, average academic opinion of today would hold that the Messianic application of the *son of God* title was the original one in Judeo-Christianity; its association with a miracle-worker is secondary, and was possibly due to the impact of a parallel but wholly separate linguistic usage current in Hellenistic circles.

The only trouble with this well-articulated argument is that it is put together without the benefit of the evidence of a group of Jewish texts, not merely pertinent, but essential, to the correct approach to the issue, texts in which are incorporated demonic confessions, exorcism, the heavenly Voice and the designation, 'my son'.

III. SUPPLEMENTARY EVIDENCE

As has been said in regard to Jewish charismatics,[73] it was a firmly held rabbinic conviction that saints and teachers were commended in public by a heavenly Voice. Furthermore, when such a commendation is directly accredited to God, the person in whose favour it is made is alluded to as 'my *son*'.[74] It may be recalled that according to Rab the following comment was heard day after day during the life of Hanina ben Dosa:

> The whole universe is sustained on account of *my son* Hanina; but *my son* Hanina is satisfied with one kab of carob from one Sabbath eve to another.[75]

According to this tradition, the frugal Hanina was the person to whom all his contemporaries owed their survival. It is as mankind's benefactor that the heavenly Voice calls him *my son*.

In a different context, the famous second-century AD Rabbi Meir is described by God – despite the fact that he had studied with the generally detested heretic scholar, Elisha ben Abuyya – as 'Meir *my son*', whose words are judged worthy of being borrowed and repeated by the Holy One himself.[76]

The next point to be noted is that there is an association in Jewish thinking between the heavenly Voice and demons. The primary purpose of this type of divine communication was, as has been seen, to act as a substitute for prophecy, but it was taken for granted that in addition to those to whom it spoke directly, it could also be heard by spiritual beings, devils included.

> Do they know? How's that? They hear (God's Voice) from behind a curtain, like the ministering angels.[77]

This view is not only expressed in general terms but *in concreto* as well. Several famous first- and second-century AD rabbis are said to have been spared by Satan only because he had been warned about them in advance. Three anecdotes come to mind, the first two of which concern the greatest legal authorities of the second century AD, and the third, Hanina ben Dosa.

> Rabbi Meir used to scorn sinners.[78] One day, Satan appeared to him as a woman on the farther bank of a river. As there was no ferry there, he tried to cross by holding to a rope-bridge. When he was half-way across, Satan allowed him to pass saying: 'Had there been no commendation from heaven, "Take heed of Rabbi Meir and his teaching!" I would have valued your blood at two pence.'[79]

> Rabbi Akiba used to scorn sinners. One day, Satan appeared to him as a woman at the top of a palm-tree. He took hold of the palm-tree and began to climb. Half-way up, Satan allowed him to pass, saying: 'Had there been no commendation from heaven, "Take heed of Rabbi Akiba and his teaching!" I would have valued your blood at two pence.'[80]

These anecdotes, both told at the expense of venerated rabbis, are of special interest to the student of the New Testament because they show Satan to be unwilling to injure those commended by the heavenly Voice, even when they have exposed themselves to moral and physical peril through lust.

The beginning of the third episode conforms to pattern, but the story ends with the devil's defeat instead of the humiliation and confusion of the protagonist. Although it has already been told briefly, this rabbinic lesson and the comment which follows it deserve a second and more thorough examination.[81]

The original saying, part of a rule of conduct pertaining to seemly Pharisaic-rabbinic behaviour runs as follows:

> Do not go out alone at night, for it is taught: Let no one go out alone at night![82]

The first three of a total of six such prohibitions have sexual connotations. No respectable man is to walk around anointed with perfume for he may be taken for a homosexual. He is not to be seen unchaperoned after sunset. He is not to start a conversation with a woman. But the recommendation not to appear alone in the streets at night was not just a common-sense measure inspired by *petit bourgeois* morality; beneath the social taboo lurked the age-old superstitious fear that it was during the hours of darkness that the demons emerged from their lairs.

Into this unconditional rule never to go out at night, the Babylonian Talmud text, Pesaḥim 112b, introduces a change reducing the ban to two nights a week.

> Not on Wednesday nights nor on Sabbath nights, for Agrath daughter of Mahlath and eighteen myriads of destroying angels are on the prowl, and each of them is empowered to strike.

That Agrath, the queen of the demons at the head of a vast army of evil spirits, strikes only twice a week and not every night, is said in this legend to be due to an intervention of Hanina ben Dosa.

> In former times she was seen daily. Once she met Rabbi Hanina ben Dosa, and said to him: 'Had there been no

commendation from heaven, "Take heed of Hanina and his teaching!" I would have harmed you.' He said to her: 'If I am so highly esteemed in heaven, I decree that you shall never again pass through an inhabited place.' She said to him: 'Please allow me in for a limited time.' He then left to her Sabbath nights and Wednesday nights.

Unlike Meir and Akiba who were seduced by Satan's shapely appearance, Hanina, although infringing the code of Pharisaic etiquette, was not humiliated but asserted his own superiority instead.

Taken together, the various elements of the Hanina tale coalesce to form a picture closely resembling that included in the Gospels. Like Jesus, he is commended by the heavenly Voice and proclaimed *son of God*. And as in the case of Jesus, this commendation is heard by the demons who, in consequence, know, fear and obey him.

Thus, if the Hanina parallel is given the attention it deserves, it may be argued that the greatest, and no doubt earliest, part of the Synoptic evidence concerning the divine sonship of Jesus corresponds exactly to the image of the Galilean miracle-working Hasid. The Hellenistic *son of God*/'divine man' then appears not as an original element in the Gospel tradition, but as one superimposed on a solidly established Palestinian Jewish belief and terminology. There is, in other words, no reason to contest the possibility, and even the great probability, that already during his life Jesus was spoken of and addressed by admiring believers as *son of God*.

To the legitimate question whether he could also have considered *himself* a *son of God*, the answer must be that he could, even taking into account that none of the surviving *son* sayings in the Gospels may be genuine. In ancient Hasidic circles, as will be seen, this kind of style was by no means unthinkable. Honi, for example, in the famous prayer reproduced in the Mishnah,[83] addresses God:

> Lord of the universe, thy sons have turned to me because I am as a *son of the house* before thee.[84]

The phrase, 'son of the house', can admittedly refer to a household servant, a slave enjoying his master's special confidence and favour.[85] But this is not the way in which the expression was understood, for even Honi's chief Pharisee critic, Simeon ben Shetah, compares the holy man's intimacy with God to that of a son with his father.[86]

It is in this sense that Jesus could have spoken of himself as *son of God*. Moreover, a special filial consciousness is manifest in the frequent and emphatic mention of God as his Father, an awareness firmly reflected in the New Testament usage.

IV. ABBA: FATHER!

The apparent idiosyncrasy of Jesus in referring to God as 'my Father' has been the subject of many learned discussions.[87] It is universally assumed that he addressed God in Aramaic, and that his habitual form of invocation, *Abba*, survives not only in the Gospel of Mark, with the Greek explanatory gloss, 'Father',[88] but also in prayers used in the Pauline churches:

> To prove that you are sons, God has sent into our hearts the spirit of *his son*, crying '*Abba!* Father!'[89]

> The spirit you have received is not a spirit of slavery . . . but a spirit that makes us sons, enabling us to cry, '*Abba!* Father!'[90]

Furthermore, not only is it argued that *Abba* is to 'be regarded with certainty as a mark of Jesus' manner of speech'; it is also said to be 'unthinkable in the prayer language of contemporary Judaism'.[91] Another claim made is that in characterizing God as 'Father', Jesus reveals that he is aware of his exclusive and incommunicable sonship.[92]

Do these positive and summary theological assertions take sufficient notice of the facts of Jewish history?

For instance, whereas the customary style of post-biblical prayer is 'Lord of the universe', one of the distinguishing features of ancient Hasidic piety is its habit of alluding to God precisely as 'Father'.

The ancient Hasidim spent an hour (in recollection before praying) in order to direct their hearts towards their Father in heaven.[93]

Again, the following anecdote is told of the Hasid, Hanan, grandson of Honi the Circle-Drawer and first cousin of Abba Hilkiah, the charismatic rain-makers.[94]

When the world was in need of rain, the rabbis used to send school-children to him, who seized the train of his cloak and said to him, *Abba, Abba*, give us rain! He said to God: Lord of the universe, render a service to those who cannot distinguish between the *Abba* who gives rain and the *Abba* who does not.[95]

Although the text is probably slightly distorted, the central point, as far as the present study is concerned, appears to be that for the charismatic, as for Jesus, God is *Abba*. It gives, incidentally, an interesting corroboration of the significance implicit in Jesus' words in Matthew 23: 9 (*RSV*):

'Call no man your father on earth, for you have one Father, who is in heaven.'

What he meant was, 'Do not give to your *Abba* on earth, your religious teacher, the respect and love you owe only to your *Abba* in heaven.' Inversely, as the context shows, it is also an admonition to the religious teacher not to divert to himself the honour and reverence primarily due to God.[96]

If the reasoning followed in these pages is correct, the earliest use of *son of God* in relation to Jesus derives from his activities as a miracle-worker and exorcist, and from his own consciousness of an immediate and intimate contact with the heavenly Father.

In the next stage of development, Jesus recognized as the Messiah is acknowledged *son of God* by adoption, a popular and much cherished formula inspired by Galilean religious and political fervour. As a further step towards deification, the concept of a Messianic pre-existence[97] is associated with that of eternal sonship. Paul, advancing this view, recognizes in the birth of Jesus of Nazareth the coming into the world of the eternal *son* sent by the Father.

> When the time had fully come, God sent forth *his son*, born of woman . . . that we might receive adoption as sons.[98]

The Fourth Gospel testifies to the same association of ideas in a formula such as that of Martha:

> 'I now believe that you are the Messiah, the *son of God* who was to come into the world.'[99]

But the prologue of John goes much further. There the *son of God* is not a miracle-working Hasid, or a son by adoption. He is *son of God* by nature, he who manifested on earth the splendour of the Godhead, the eternal *Logos* or Word familiar to Philo of Alexandria and Jewish Hellenism, the chief instrument of creation and revelation.

> In the beginning was the *Logos*, and the *Logos* was with God and the *Logos* was God . . . And the *Logos* became flesh and dwelt among us and we saw his glory, the glory as it were of a *Father's* only *son*, full of grace and truth. . . . No one has ever seen God; *God's* only *son* who is in the Father's bosom, he has explained him.[100]

Thus, in the final amalgam represented by the dogma of the Incarnation, these concepts are all brought together: the *son* by adoption, the pre-existent Messiah-*Logos* and the son born of a virgin through divine intervention.

A final word must be said about the bridging of the gulf between *son of God* and God.

None of the Synoptic Gospels try to do this. Indeed, it is no exaggeration to contend that the identification of a contemporary historical figure with God would have been inconceivable to a first-century AD Palestinian Jew. It could certainly not have been expressed in public, in the presence of men conditioned by centuries of biblical monotheistic religion. Paul, the Jew from

Tarsus at home in the Greco-Roman world, shies away from it. Even the theologizing author of the Fourth Gospel, writing a couple of generations later, shows understandable diffidence. One well-known contemporary, by no means radical, New Testament scholar is of the opinion that when 'God' is occasionally used apropos of Jesus in some of the epistles of the New Testament, this usage never exceeds the notion of exalted Lord and revelation incarnate.[101]

It was not until Gentiles began to preach the Jewish Gospel to the Hellenized peoples of the Roman empire that the hesitation disappeared and the linguistic brake was lifted. Paul, and that true Hellenist, the author of the Letter to the Hebrews, were satisfied with phrases such as the 'image of God', and the 'effulgence of God's splendour and the stamp of God's very being'.[102] They would without doubt have recoiled from language such as that used by the Syrian Ignatius of Antioch in the first decade of the second century AD, who found no difficulty in alluding to Jesus as 'our God', and as 'the God who bestowed such wisdom upon you'.[103]

Whether Jesus himself would have reacted with stupefaction, anger or grief, can never be known. One thing, however, is sure. When Christianity later set out to define the meaning of *son of God* in its Creed, the paraphrase it produced – 'God of God, Light of Light, true God of true God, consubstantial with the Father' – drew its inspiration, not from the pure language and teaching of the Galilean Jesus, nor even from Paul the Diaspora Jew, but from a Gentile-Christian interpretation of the Gospel adapted to the mind of the totally alien world of pagan Hellenism.

Excursus: *son of God* and virgin birth

Whereas in Palestinian and Hellenistic Judeo-Christianity the colourful narrative of the birth of Jesus in Matthew 1–2 and

Luke 1–2 was read as evidence of his Messiahship and proof of his Davidic lineage, in the Gentile Christian world it was understood to prove the divine nature of the son born miraculously to a virgin.[104]

As far as the evolution of the tradition is concerned, Mark, the least doctrinally developed of the Gospels, has no infancy story at all. At the other extreme, John the Divine needs none. In between, Matthew and Luke treat it merely as a preface to the main story, and as neither of these two, nor the rest of the New Testament, ever allude to it again, it may be safely assumed that it is a secondary accretion.

Apart from sharing the common basic aim of letting it be known that the child born to Mary was the promised Messiah, the seed of David surnamed 'God is with us' (Emmanuel) or *son of God*,[105] the two stories are no more than vaguely similar as far as details – even essential details – are concerned, and reflect different inspirations.

According to Matthew, Mary and the man to whom she is betrothed live (apparently) in Bethlehem. Mary finds herself unexpectedly pregnant, and Joseph is reassured by an angel in a dream that the conception is the work of the spirit of God.[106]

In Luke, Mary and Joseph are citizens of Nazareth. She is visited by an angel and told of her impending pregnancy, effected by the holy spirit or the power of God. Joseph's reaction remains unrecorded. That Jesus is born in Bethlehem in Judea is ascribed to a providentially contrived historical accident, i.e. the census allegedly ordered by Augustus, the Roman emperor.[107]

Both evangelists are, as it seems, adamant in denying Joseph any part in the affair, Matthew emphasizing his astonishment, and Luke, Mary's virginity.[108]

The conflict between the story and its purpose is obvious: on the one hand, the divinely conceived child of a virgin mother, and on the other, the wish to prove Jesus' legitimate Davidic descent as set out in the genealogical table. For it is clear that if Joseph had nothing to do with Mary's pregnancy, the intention prompting the reproduction of the table is nullified, since Joseph's royal Davidic blood would not have been passed on to Jesus.

Even more perplexing, Matthew's table of ancestry differs from Luke's, not insignificantly, but to such an extent that the two lists are mutually irreconcilable. Taking into account the child's virgin conceptions, what can have been the point of such involved calculations?[109]

If, by contrast, Joseph's paternity is presumed – 'the only possible conclusion, if the genealogy was to have any meaning'[110] – what sense is to be made of the solidly established virgin birth tradition? For in the same way that there was no point in faking Jesus' resurrection since it was in any case not expected, so no biblical reason existed for inventing a virgin birth since it was not, and never had been, believed in biblical or inter-Testamental Judaism that the Messiah would be born in such a way.

Perhaps a fresh examination of the data may throw new light on these problems.

I. JESUS, SON OF JOSEPH

To consider first the case for natural paternity, one (negative) argument in favour of it is that Mark makes no mention of an alternative. In addition, Matthew and Luke allude in their main story to the 'father of Jesus' as though having forgotten the supernatural agency described in their infancy stories.

Secondly, the logic of the genealogies demands that Joseph was the father of Jesus. To make place for the dogma of the virgin birth, this logic had to be tampered with by the compilers of the Gospels of Matthew and Luke. Thus Luke's redactor inserts into the table an as it were saving clause:

> When Jesus began his work he was about thirty years old, the son, *as people thought*, of Joseph, son of Heli, son of Matthat, etc.[111]

The implication is that the supposition was erroneous. But if so, why did Luke, and the tradition responsible for the genealogical table before him, waste their time compiling a sequence of irrelevant ancestors in order to trace Jesus' lineage back to 'Adam, the son of God'?

In Matthew, the emendation of the original reading is less successful and has resulted in a number of textual variants. If the formalized style of the genealogy had remained constant, it would have ended:

> Matthan begot Jacob, and Jacob begot Joseph, and (Joseph begot) Jesus who is called the Messiah.

Instead, the large majority of the best manuscripts of Matthew 1: 15–16 read:

> Matthan begot Jacob, and Jacob begot Joseph, the husband of Mary, of whom was begotten (or born) Jesus who is called the Messiah (AT).

As a continuation of the preceding list of births and independent of the subsequent new story, the verse would still most likely imply that Joseph was the father of Jesus. He is plainly described as the husband of Mary, and the substitution of the passive, 'was begotten/born', for the active 'begot',[112] introduces at best a small degree of equivocation and an imperfect adjustment to the following virgin birth narrative.

Another group of Greek and Old Latin texts preserve the original 'begot', but replace the epithet, 'the husband of Mary', with a formula allowing for the idea of supernatural impregnation. Nonetheless, the reviser betrays himself by applying to the mother the active verb, 'to beget', contrary to the established genealogical terminology which attaches it to males alone.

> Matthan begot Jacob, and Jacob begot Joseph, to whom was betrothed Mary, a virgin, who begot Jesus, who is called the Messiah (AT).

The earliest surviving Semitic version of Matthew, the Old Syriac Gospel found in a monastery on Mount Sinai, is based on a text emended in this way; nevertheless it manages to reassert that Joseph was the father of Jesus.

> Matthan begot Jacob, and Jacob begot Joseph. Joseph, to whom was betrothed Mary, the virgin, begot Jesus who is called the Messiah (AT).

A final argument directly in favour of the paternity of Joseph is that the Ebionites, the Palestinian Judeo-Christians whom the Gentile Church declared heretics, accepted Jesus as the Messiah, but maintained that his conception was a natural one and that he was his parents' real son.[113]

Thus, supporting the hypothesis that Jesus was Joseph's son are: (1) Mark's silence concerning an alternative paternity; (2) the logic of the genealogies, brought into even stronger relief by the textual manipulations visible in both Luke and Matthew; and (3) the testimony of a branch of Judeo-Christianity divorced from the main Church at a very early stage, whilst apparently the story of the virgin birth was still under debate.

It is tempting to account for the origin of such a belief by ascribing it to an exegetical legend current among Greek-speaking Christians, namely that Isaiah 7: 14, 'Behold the virgin (*parthenos*) shall conceive and bear a son', is to be understood in the sense of a miraculous pregnancy. This temptation should be resisted, for there is no valid reason to suppose that the substantially conflicting genealogies followed, rather than preceded, the birth narratives. The citation of Isaiah 7 is in fact more satisfactorily explained as an endeavour to justify scripturally an otherwise inexplicable tradition, rather than as its source. Also, although it is conceivable in the case of Matthew, the argument would leave intact the problem of Luke, for this evangelist makes no use of the prophecy of Isaiah.

Finally, it should be repeated that even if birth legends are associated with many of the heroes of ancient Judaism, no notion of actual virgin birth, as it is normally understood, ever makes its appearance in Jewish religious speculation. The wives of the patriarchs – Sarah, Rebecca, Leah, Rachel, as well as Hannah, the mother of Samuel – were sterile women whose wombs, 'closed by God', were later 'opened'. But such divine intervention was never interpreted as divine impregnation.[114]

Again, it seems that an entirely different approach is called for if the problem of Jesus' origin is ever to be properly understood. For example, in the world of the New Testament did the word 'virgin' have the narrow and exclusive connotation customarily attached to it today?

2. JESUS, SON OF A VIRGIN

(a) *The meaning of 'virgin'*

In both the Greek and Hebrew parlance of the Jews, the term 'virgin' was used elastically. It was certainly not confined to denoting men and women without experience of sexual intercourse. The Greek word could explicitly or implicitly include this meaning, or the main stress could fall on the youth of a girl or boy, and generally, though not necessarily, on their unmarried state.[115] As a matter of fact, Greek (and Latin) inscriptions found in the Jewish catacombs of Rome reveal that the word 'virgin' could apply, even after years of matrimony, to either a wife or a husband, probably implying that the marriage in question was his or her first one. A certain Argentia is described as having lived with her *virgin* husband for nine years; the wife of Germanus lived with her *virgin* husband for three years and three days. There is also mention of Irene, *virgin* wife of Clodius.[116]

A similar imprecision is manifest in the Greek version of Genesis, where the Greek for virgin (*parthenos*) renders three different Hebrew words: *bethulah*=virgin, *na'arah*=girl, and *'almah*=young woman.[117]

In Hebrew, biblical and rabbinic, the term *bethulah* can indicate *virgo intacta*. The Pentateuch describes Rebecca as 'a very pretty girl, a *virgin* whom no man has known'. The rabbis also explain that a virgin is a woman 'who has never had sexual intercourse'.[118]

Nevertheless, another well-established usage of *bethulah* associates virginity, not with absence of sexual experience, but with an inability to conceive: a virgin is a girl who has not yet attained puberty. This sort of 'virginity' ends, not with intercourse, but menstruation. Asking 'Who is a virgin?' the two earliest rabbinic codes, the Mishnah and the Tosephta, answer:

Whoever has never seen blood even though she is married.[119]

The Tosephta, reflecting the teaching of the late-first-century AD Rabbi Eliezer ben Hyrcanus, adds:

> I call a virgin whoever has never seen blood, even though she is married and has had children, until she has seen the first show.[120]

The Palestinian Talmud goes even further:

> Who is a virgin? According to the Mishnah, whoever has never seen blood even though she is married. – She is said to be a virgin in respect of menstruation but not a virgin in respect of the token of virginity. Sometimes she is a virgin in the latter respect, but not a virgin in respect of menstruation.[121]

(b) *Marriage prior to puberty*

It was possible, the evidence shows, for a girl to marry and cohabit with her husband before reaching puberty. In fact, it appears to have happened often enough to give rise to a dispute between the two leading rabbinic schools of the first century AD on the subject of whether a bloodstain on the wedding-night of a minor (i.e. a virgin in respect of menstruation) should be attributed to the rupture of the hymen or to her first period. The more rigorous House of Shammai settled for the first alternative for the first four nights only; the House of Hillel decided similarly but 'until the healing of the wound'.[122]

Another consequence of such a state of affairs was that a girl could conceive whilst still a 'virgin' in respect of menstruation, i.e. at the moment of her first ovulation. She could thus become a 'virgin mother'. Indeed, in the event of her becoming pregnant a second time before menstruating, she could be, as Eliezer ben Hyrcanus argues, the 'virgin mother' of several children!

Moreover, in an age when physiological knowledge was rudimentary and the supreme blessing of fertility was attributed quite naturally to God, the reaction to such an unusual occurrence as pregnancy prior to the onset of puberty would have been to regard

it as a particularly miraculous intervention of Heaven. In parenthesis, the consummation of marriage by minors was frowned on
by those who considered procreation as the sole purpose of
matrimony. For this reason, the Essenes who accepted marriage
forbad cohabitation until after the girl had menstruated three
times and thus proved herself ready for, and capable of, conception.[123]

3. VIRGIN BIRTH IN PHILO

One last source must be examined, the work of Philo of Alexandria,
contemporaneous with the lifetime of Jesus and antedating by
several generations the composition of the infancy Gospels. The
Jewish philosopher seems acquainted with the rabbinic concept
of virginity=inability to conceive, since he constructs around it a
complex allegorical interpretation of the birth of Isaac.

For Philo, the infertility of a woman who had passed the age
of child-bearing was comparable to virginity. Thus it was when
she had advanced 'from womanhood to virginity' that Sarah, with
whom, according to Genesis 18: 11 (*RSV*), 'it had ceased to be
. . . after the manner of women', conceived the son of promise,
Isaac.[124] Philo then allegorizes Isaac. Taking his inspiration from
the meaning of his name, Isaac=laughter, and identifying the
child as *son of God*, he describes him as 'the Isaac who is the
laughter of the heart, son of God'.[125] In another passage he refers
even more explicitly to God's paternity:

> Abraham . . rejoices and laughs because he is to beget
> Isaac, Happiness; and Sarah, who is Virtue, laughs also . . .
> Let Virtue always rejoice, for when Happiness has been born
> she says proudly, 'The Lord has made laughter for me . . .'
> (Gen. 21: 6). Therefore, initiates, open your ears and accept
> most holy teachings: 'laughter' is 'joy', and 'has made' equals
> 'to beget'. So that which is said is similar to this: 'The Lord
> begot Isaac.'[126]

It would be unscholarly to pretend that it is possible with the aid of the rabbinic ideas on virginity outlined in these pages and Philo's speculation on the conception of Isaac, the *son of God*, by Sarah the virgin, to solve definitively the problems that arise from the Infancy Gospels of Matthew and Luke. It nevertheless helps to see something of the material out of which they are likely to have been built.

That the genealogies had a prehistory is disclosed by the state of the New Testament text itself, but although there is no similar textual indication of a reworking of the birth stories, the wording in which they survive is, when scrutinized closely, curious and equivocal. According to Matthew, Joseph regards Mary's pregnancy as grounds for divorce, but when he is reassured in a dream, he takes his wife, though refraining from sexual contact with her until after the child's birth, an ascetic rule mentioned by Josephus in connection with the marrying Essenes:[127]

He knew her not until she had borne a son.[128]

In the Lucan version, by contrast, when told by an angel that she would conceive and bear the future Messiah, Mary asks:

'How can this be, for I know no man?'[129]

On the lips of a girl described as betrothed – which in ancient Jewish law normally implied that she was a minor[130] awaiting the right biological moment to change to the status of wife – these words might be paraphrased: 'How can this be, for I have not yet begun to menstruate? Should I nevertheless marry in spite of seeming not yet ready?' To which the angel replies with the information that her cousin, who had passed the menopause and was technically 'virgin' once more, had also conceived, the implication being that the one achievement was not more unthinkable than the other:

'Your kinswoman Elizabeth in her old age has also conceived a son; and this is the sixth month with her who was called barren. For with God nothing will be impossible.'[131]

In the end, the only reasonable conclusion appears to be that if the earliest interpreters of the primitive tradition had wished to do so, they could have read into the story of Jesus and his virgin mother a meaning that would have brought his origin into line with the legendary births of such heroes as Isaac, Jacob and Samuel, whose fathers, though credited with responsibility for their conception, were provided with offspring by means of a divine intervention whereby their wives' incapacity was healed.

That primitive Christianity turned from this alternative of faith in divine mediation to the totally novel belief in an act of divine impregnation, with as its consequence the birth of a God-man, belongs of course to the psychology of religion rather than to its history.

Postscript

> I am more than ever certain that a great place belongs to (Jesus) in Israel's history of faith . . . There is a something in Israel's history of faith which is only to be understood from Israel . . .*

What has been the main finding of this exploration of the historical and linguistic elements of which the Gospels are composed?

Without doubt, it is that whereas none of the claims and aspirations of Jesus can be said definitely to associate him with the role of Messiah, not to speak of that of *son of man*, the strange creation of the modern myth-makers, everything combines, when approached from the viewpoint of a study of first-century AD Galilee, or of charismatic Judaism, or of his titles and their development, to place him in the venerable company of the Devout, the ancient Hasidim. Indeed, if the present research has any value at all, it is in this conclusion that it is most likely to reside, since it means that any new enquiry may accept as its point of departure the safe assumption that Jesus did not belong among the Pharisees, Essenes, Zealots or Gnostics, but was one of the holy miracle-workers of Galilee.

The discovery of resemblances between the work and words of Jesus and those of the Hasidim, Honi and Hanina ben Dosa, is however by no means intended to imply that he was simply one of them and nothing more. Although no systematic attempt is made here to distinguish Jesus' authentic teaching – this is an enormous task that will, it is hoped, be undertaken on another occasion – it is nevertheless still possible to say, even in the

*Martin Buber, *Two Types of Faith* (Harper Torchbooks, New York, 1961), p. 13.

absence of such an investigation, that no objective and enlightened student of the Gospels can help but be struck by the incomparable superiority of Jesus. As Joseph Klausner wrote in the final paragraph of his famous book, *Jesus of Nazareth*, published in its original Hebrew edition exactly fifty years ago:

> In his ethical code there is a sublimity, distinctiveness and originality in form unparalleled in any other Hebrew ethical code; neither is there any parallel to the remarkable art of his parables.

Second to none in profundity of insight and grandeur of character, he is in particular an unsurpassed master of the art of laying bare the inmost core of spiritual truth and of bringing every issue back to the essence of religion, the existential relationship of man and man, and man and God.

It should be added that in one respect more than any other he differed from both his contemporaries and even his prophetic predecessors. The prophets spoke on behalf of the honest poor, and defended the widows and the fatherless, those oppressed and exploited by the wicked, rich and powerful. Jesus went further. In addition to proclaiming these blessed, he actually took his stand among the pariahs of his world, those despised by the respectable. Sinners were his table-companions and the ostracised tax-collectors and prostitutes his friends.

The uncovering of Jesus' real background and true Jewishness is, in other words, meant to be no more than an endeavour to clear away misunderstandings which for so long have been responsible for an unreal image of Jesus, a first step in what appears to be the direction of the real man. For it has emerged in these pages that from the beginning his followers have had the greatest difficulty in accepting his expressed opinions regarding himself. Whereas he explicitly avoided the title 'Messiah', he was very soon invested with it, and in the Christian mind has since become inseparable from it. By contrast, although he approved the designation 'prophet', this was one of the first of his appellations to be discarded by the Church, one that has never since been readopted. The result has been that, unable or unwilling to establish and admit the historical meaning of words recorded by the evangelists, orthodox Christianity has opted for a doctrinal structure erected on the basis of an arbitrary interpretation of the Gospel sayings, a structure which must by nature be vulnerable to reasoned criticism. This explains why Christian New Testament scholars of today display an agnostic tendency in regard to the historical authenticity of most of these words. Indeed, they even go so far as to reject the possibility of knowing anything historical about Jesus himself.

Certainly, unless by some fortunate chance new evidence is unfolded in the future, not a great deal can be said of him at this distance of time that can be historically authenticated. Nevertheless, this much at least can be asserted with some fair measure of conviction. The positive and constant testimony of the earliest Gospel tradition, considered against its natural background of first-century Galilean charismatic religion, leads not to a Jesus as unrecognizable within the framework of Judaism as by the standard of his own verifiable words and intentions, but to another figure: Jesus the just man, the *zaddik*, Jesus the helper and healer, Jesus the teacher and leader, venerated by his intimates and less committed admirers alike as prophet, lord and *son of God*.

Abbreviations

Ab.	*Aboth (Sayings of the Fathers)*
Acts	*Acts of the Apostles*
Ann. of Leeds Univ. Or. Soc.	*Annual of Leeds University Oriental Society*
Ant.	*Antiquitates Judaicae (Jewish Antiquities)* by Flavius Josephus
Apol.	*Apologia* by Philo
ARNa	*Aboth de-Rabbi Nathan: First recension (Sayings of the Fathers according to R. Nathan)*
AZ	*'Abodah Zarah (Idolatry)*
b	*Babylonian Talmud* (prefixed to the title of a tractate, e.g. *bAZ*)
2 Bar.	*Second Book or Syriac Apocalypse of Baruch*
BB	*Baba Bathra (Last Gate)*
Ber.	*Berakhoth (Benedictions)*
BJ	*Bellum Judaicum (Jewish War)* by Flavius Josephus
BK	*Baba Ḳamma (First Gate)*
BM	*Baba Meẓi'a (Middle Gate)*
CBQ	*Catholic Biblical Quarterly*
CDC	*Cairo Damascus Covenant (Damascus Rule)*
1, 2 Chr.	*Chronicles (First and Second Books of)*
Col.	*Colossians (Letter to the)*
1, 2 Cor.	*Corinthians (First and Second Letters to the)*
Dan.	*Daniel*
Dem.	*Demai (Doubtful Things)*
Deut.	*Deuteronomy*
Deut. R.	*Deuteronomy Rabbah (Great Midrash on Deut.)*
DJD	*Discoveries in the Judaean Desert*
DSSE	*The Dead Sea Scrolls in English* by G. Vermes (Penguin, Harmondsworth and Baltimore, Md., 1968)
Eccles.	*Ecclesiastes*
Eccles. R.	*Ecclesiastes Rabbah (Great Midrash on Eccles.)*
Ecclus.	*Ecclesiasticus*

Ed.	'Eduyoth (Testimonies)
1 En.	Enoch (First Book of)
Erub.	'Erubin (Blending)
Exod.	Exodus
Exod. R.	Exodus Rabbah (Great Midrash on Exod.)
4 Ezra	Ezra (Fourth Book of)
Flor.	Florilegium
Fragm. Targ.	Fragmentary Targum
Gal.	Galatians (Letter to the)
Gen.	Genesis
Gen. Ap.	Genesis Apocryphon
Gen. R.	Genesis Rabbah (Great Midrash on Gen.)
Hag.	Hagigah (Festival Offering)
Heb.	Hebrews (Letter to the)
Hist. Nat.	Historia Naturalis by Pliny the Elder
History	The History of the Jewish People in the Age of Jesus Christ: 175 BC–AD 135 by E. Schürer, revised and edited by G. Vermes and F. Millar. Literary editor: P. Vermes. Organizing editor: M. Black. Vol. I (T. & T. Clark, Edinburgh, 1973)
Hod.	Hodayoth (Hymns)
Hor.	Horayoth (Decisions)
Hos.	Hosea
HTR	Harvard Theological Review
Hul.	Hullin (Profane Things)
IEJ	Israel Exploration Journal
Isa.	Isaiah
Jas.	James (Letter of)
JBL	Journal of Biblical Literature
Jer.	Jeremiah
Jew. Enc.	Jewish Encyclopaedia
JJS	Journal of Jewish Studies
John	John (Gospel according to)
Journ. Hist. St.	Journal of Historical Studies
JTS	Journal of Theological Studies
Jub.	Jubilees (Book of)
Kel.	Kelim (Vessels)
Ket.	Ketuboth (Marriage Documents)
1, 2 Kgs.	Kings (First and Second Books of)
Kid.	Kiddushin (Betrothals)
Kil.	Kila'im (Diverse Seeds)
LAB	Liber Antiquitatum Biblicarum of Pseudo-Philo
Lam.	Lamentations
Lam. R.	Lamentations Rabbah (Great Midrash on Lam.)
Lev.	Leviticus
Luke	Luke (Gospel according to)

m	Mishnah (prefixed to the title of a tractate, e.g. m*Ber.*)
1 Macc.	Maccabees (*First Book of the*)
Mal.	Malachi
Mark	Mark (*Gospel according to*)
Matt.	Matthew (*Gospel according to*)
Meg.	Megillah (*Scroll of Esther*)
Meil.	Meʻilah (*Trespassing*)
Mekh.	Mekhilta (*Tractates*)
Mic.	Micah
Milḥ.	Milḥamah (*War Rule*)
MK	Moʻed Ḳaṭan (*Mid-Festival*)
MSh.	Maʻaser Sheni (*Second Tithe*)
Ned.	Nedarim (*Vows*)
Nid.	Niddah (*Female Uncleanness*)
NT	Novum Testamentum
NTS	New Testament Studies
Num.	Numbers
Pea	Peʼah (*Corner*)
Pes.	Pesaḥim (*Passover Lambs*)
PR	Pesiḳta Rabbathi (*Great Sections*)
PRK	Pesiḳta de-Rab Kahana (*Rab Kahana's Sections*)
Prov.	Proverbs
Ps.	Psalms
Ps.-Jonathan	Pseudo-Jonathan (*Targum*)
Ps. Sol.	Psalms of Solomon
1, 2Q, etc.	Qumran (First, Second, etc., Cave of)
RB	Revue Biblique
Rev.	Revelation (*Book of*)
Rom.	Romans (*Letter to the*)
RQ	Revue de Qumrân
1, 2 Sam.	Samuel (*First and Second Books of*)
Sanh.	Sanhedrin (*Tribunal*)
Scripture and Tradition	Scripture and Tradition in Judaism. Haggadic Studies by G. Vermes (Brill, Leiden, 1961)
Ser.	Serekh (*Community Rule*)
Ser[a]	Serekh[a] (*Messianic Rule*)
Ser[b]	Serekh[b] (*Blessings*)
Shab.	Shabbath (*Sabbath*)
Sheb.	Shebiʻith (*Seventh Year*)
Shek.	Sheḳalim (*Shekels*)
Siphre on Num.	Siphre on Numbers
Song of S.	Song of Songs
Song of S. R.	Song of Songs Rabbah (*Great Midrash on the Song of S.*)
Sot.	Soṭah (*Unfaithful Woman*)

Suk.	*Sukkah* (*Tabernacle*)
t	*Tosephta* (prefixed to the title of a tractate e.g. *tBer.*)
Taan.	*Ta'anith* (*Fasting*)
Tanh. B.	*Tanḥuma* (*Midrash*) [ed. Buber]
Targ.	*Targum*
TDNT	*Theological Dictionary of the New Testament*, edited by G. Kittel and G. Friedrich (Eerdmans, Grand Rapids, Mich., 1963–)
Ter.	*Terumoth* (*Heave-Offerings*)
Test.	*Testimonia*
Test. of Levi	*Testament of Levi*
1 Thess.	*Thessalonians* (*First Letter to the*)
VT	*Vetus Testamentum*
Wisd.	*Wisdom*
y	*Jerusalem Talmud* (prefixed to the title of a tractate, e.g. *yBer.*)
Yad.	*Yadayim* (*Hands*)
Yeb.	*Yebamoth* (*Sisters-in-Law*)
Zech.	*Zechariah*
ZNW	*Zeitschrift für die neutestamentliche Wissenschaft*

Notes

Introduction

1. Needless to say, this overall judgement does not exclude the possibility of an occasional, or even more than occasional, inclusion in the Fourth Gospel of historically reliable data. Cf. C. H. Dodd, *Historical Tradition in the Fourth Gospel* (Cambridge University Press, Cambridge, 1963).

Chapter 1: Jesus the Jew

1. See below, p. 39.
2. Cf. below, pp. 213–15.
3. *Luke* 4: 22.
4. *Matt.* 13: 55.
5. *Mark* 6: 3; *Matt.* 13: 55–6.
6. *Luke* 3: 23.
7. *Luke* 14: 26; 18: 29; cf. *Mark* 10: 29; *Matt.* 19: 29.
8. *De vita contemplativa*, 13.
9. Cf. below, pp. 99–102.
10. *Mark* 6: 3.
11. *Matt.* 13: 55; *Mark* 6: 3 var.
12. *Mark* 6: 2–3.
13. D. Flusser, *Jesus* (Herder & Herder, New York, 1969), p. 20.
14. *yYeb.* 9b; *yKid.* 66a.
15. *bAZ* 50b.
16. If the term is employed simply as a metaphor in the Gospels, the combination of the saying with Jesus' family situation must be seen as secondary, and meaningful only in the Greek stage of storytelling, that is to say when the original phrase was no longer understood.
17. *Luke* 13: 32.
18. *Mark* 1: 32–4; *Matt.* 8: 16; *Luke* 4: 40–1.
19. *Mark* 1: 39. – *Matt.* 4: 23: '. . . curing whatever illness or infirmity there was among the people.'
20. *Mark* 5: 1–13; *Matt.* 8: 28–31; *Luke* 8: 26–32.
21. *Mark* 9: 15–27; *Matt.* 17: 14–18; *Luke* 9: 38–42.
22. *Mark* 1: 23–6; *Luke* 4: 33–5.
23. *Mark* 7: 24–30; *Matt.* 15: 21–8.
24. *Matt.* 9: 32–4; *Luke* 11: 14–15; *Matt.* 22–4.
25. *Mark* 6: 7–13; *Matt.* 10: 1, 7–11, 14; *Luke* 9: 1–6.

26. *Luke* 10: 17–20.   27. *Mark* 9: 38; *Luke* 9: 49–50.
28. Cf. below, pp. 63–5.
29. *Mark* 7: 29: 'The unclean spirit has gone out of your daughter.'
30. *Mark* 1: 25.   31. *Mark* 5: 8.
32. *Mark* 9: 25.
33. Cf. *Matt.* 12: 43–4; *Luke* 11: 24–6, and p. 63 below.
34. Cf. below, p. 209.   35. Cf. below, pp. 202–8.
36. *Matt.* 4: 3, 6.   37. *Mark* 1: 24; *Luke* 4: 34.
38. *Mark* 3: 11; *Matt.* 8: 29; *Luke* 4: 41.
39. *Mark* 5: 7; *Luke* 8: 28.
40. *Mark* 2: 1–12; *Matt.* 9: 2–8; *Luke* 5: 18–26.
41. *Mark* 1: 32–4; *Matt.* 8: 16; *Luke* 4: 40–1.
42. *Mark* 3: 10; *Matt.* 4: 15; *Luke* 6: 19.
43. *Mark* 6: 53–6; *Matt.* 14: 34–6.   44. *Mark* 6: 5; *Matt.* 13: 58.
45. *Mark* 10: 46–52; *Matt.* 20: 29–34; *Luke* 18: 35–43. – *Mark* 8: 22–6
    Matt. 9: 27–31.
46. *Mark* 1: 40–5; *Matt.* 8: 1–3; *Luke* 5: 12–13. – *Luke* 17: 11–19.
47. *Mark* 1. 30–1; *Matt.* 8: 14–15; *Luke* 4: 38–9.
48. *Mark* 5: 25–34; *Matt.* 9: 20–2; *Luke* 8: 43–8.
49. *Mark* 3: 1–5; *Matt.* 12: 9–13; *Luke* 6: 6–10.
50. *Mark* 7: 31–7; *Matt.* 15: 29–31.   51. *Matt.* 8: 5–13; *Luke* 7: 1–10.
52. *Luke* 13: 10–17.   53. *Luke* 14: 1–6.
54. *Mark* 6: 5.   55. *Luke* 13: 13.
56. *Mark* 1: 31; *Matt.* 8: 15; *Luke* 4: 39.
57. *Mark* 1: 41; *Matt.* 8: 3; *Luke* 5: 13.
58. *Matt.* 9: 29.
59. *Mark* 3: 10; *Luke* 6: 19. – *Mark* 6: 56; *Matt.* 14: 36.
60. *Mark* 5: 27; *Matt.* 9: 20; *Luke* 8: 44.
61. *Mark* 5: 30; *Luke* 8: 46.   62. *Mark* 7: 33–4.
63. *Mark* 8: 23–5. – For the medicinal use of saliva, see below, p. 65.
64. *Luke* 14: 4; 17: 14.
65. *Mark* 10: 52: 'Go; your faith has cured you.' Cf. *Matt.* 9: 29;
    Luke 8: 48.
66. *Matt.* 8: 13: 'Go home now; because of your faith, so let it be.'
67. *Mark* 3: 1–5; *Matt.* 12: 9–13; *Luke* 6: 6–10.
68. Cf. D. Flusser, *Jesus*, p. 49: 'Healing by word was always permitted
    on the sabbath . . . Jesus always conformed to these rules.' The latter
    claim is not strictly correct. In the story of the cripple woman cured
    on the Sabbath, there is a declaration of recovery as well as an act,
    the laying on of hands (*Luke* 13: 13–17). It is possible, however,
    that the rite was supplied by Luke to render more plausible the
    subsequent argument between Jesus and the president of the
    synagogue.
69. *Mark* 6:13; cf. *Jas.* 5: 14.   70. *Acts* 3: 6–7; 9: 34; cf. 5: 15–16.
71. *Mark* 5: 41; *Matt.* 9: 25; *Luke* 8:54.
72. *Luke* 7: 14.   73. Cf. below, pp. 80–1.

74. *Mark* 4: 39–41; *Matt.* 8: 26–7; *Luke* 8:24–5.
75. *Mark* 6: 35–44; *Matt.* 14: 15–21; *Luke* 9: 12–17; cf. also *Mark* 8: 1–10; *Matt.* 15: 32–9.
76. Cf. below, pp. 69–76.
77. *Mark* 6: 45–52; *Matt.* 14: 22–7, 31–3.
78. *Luke* 5: 11.   79. *Matt.* 17: 24–6.
80. Cf. *DSSE*, pp. 25–9.
81. *Matt.* 15: 24; cf. *Mark* 7: 27; *Matt.* 10: 6.
82. *Mark* 2: 15–17; *Matt.* 9: 10–13; *Luke* 5: 29–32.
83. *Mark* 1: 14; *Matt.* 4: 17; cf. *Luke* 4: 15.
84. *Mark* 4: 10–12; *Matt.* 13: 10–17; *Luke* 8: 9–10. – *Mark* 4: 33–4; *Matt.* 13: 34–5.
85. *Mark* 1: 39; *Matt.* 4: 23; *Luke* 4: 44. – *Matt.* 9: 35. – *Luke* 4: 15.
86. *Luke* 4: 16–27.
87. *Mark* 1: 22; *Matt.* 7: 29; *Luke* 4: 32.
88. *Mark* 1: 27; *Luke* 4: 36. Cf. T. A. Burkill, *Mysterious Revelation* (Cornell University Press, Ithaca and London, 1963), p. 35. – A good literary parallel is provided by *Eccles.* 8: 4: 'The king's word carries authority. Who can question what he does?'
89. Cf. C. E. B. Cranfield, *The Gospel according to St Mark* (Cambridge University Press, Cambridge, 1959), p. 74; E. Haenchen, *Der Weg Jesus* (Töpelmann, Berlin, 1966), pp. 86–7.
90. S. Sandmel, *We Jews and Jesus* (Gollancz, London, 1965, and Oxford University Press, New York), p. 137. For a less categorical statement, see D. E. Nineham, *The Gospel of St Mark* (Penguin, Harmondsworth, 1963), pp. 191–2.
91. *Mark* 7: 14–23; *Matt.* 15: 10–20.
92. *Matt.* 15: 17–19.
93. *Mark* 7: 18–19. – The last sentence is usually attributed, not to Jesus, but to the evangelist, who was intent on making the meaning of the *logion* clear to the Church. Cf. Cranfield, *St Mark*, p. 241.
94. *Acts* 10: 13–16.
95. Cf. J. Klausner, *Jesus of Nazareth* (Allen & Unwin, London, 1925), p. 123.
96. Cf. M. Black, *An Aramaic Approach to the Gospels and Acts* (Clarendon Press, Oxford, [3]1967), pp. 217–18.
97. Cf. A. Merx, *Die Evangelien des Markus und Lukas nach der Syrischen im Sinaikloster gefundenen Palimpsesthandschriften* (G. Reimer Berlin, 1905), pp. 73–4.
98. It is possible, though not as obvious as C. H. Dodd seems to imply, that such an explanation of the saying underlies Paul's words, 'I know and am persuaded in the Lord Jesus that nothing is unclean in itself' (*Rom.* 14: 14 (*RSV*)). Cf. *The Founder of Christianity* (Collins, London, 1971, and Macmillan, New York, 1970), p. 74.
99. *Mark* 1: 14; *Matt.* 4: 12; *Luke* 4: 14.
100. *Mark* 3: 13–19; *Matt.* 10: 1–4; *Luke* 6: 12–16.

101. *Mark* 10: 28–31; *Matt.* 19: 27–30; *Luke* 18: 28–30.
102. *Mark* 8: 14–21; *Matt.* 16: 5–12.
103. *Mark* 14: 50; *Matt.* 26: 56.   104. *Acts* 2: 1–41.
105. *Mark* 5: 24; *Luke* 8: 42.   106. *Luke* 7: 11.
107. *Mark* 2: 1, 13; 3: 20; 4: 1; 5: 21.
108. *Mark* 1: 45; *Luke* 5: 15.
109. *Mark* 3: 7–8; *Matt.* 4: 25; *Luke* 6: 19.
110. *Mark* 5: 17; *Matt.* 8: 34; *Luke* 8: 37.
111. *Luke* 9: 52.
112. *Mark* 10: 46; *Matt.* 20: 29; *Luke* 18: 35–6; 19: 1–3.
113. *Mark* 11: 18; cf. *Luke* 19: 48. – *Mark* 12: 37; cf. *Matt.* 23: 1; *Luke* 20: 45. – *Luke* 21: 38 alone asserts that the purpose of the crowd's daily visit to the sanctuary was to listen to Jesus.
114. *Mark* 11: 8 (*RSV*).   115. *Matt.* 21: 8–10.
116. *Luke* 19: 37–9.   117. *Mark* 2: 18–20.
118. *Mark* 6: 14, 16; *Matt.* 14: 1–2; *Luke* 7: 9. – *Mark* 8: 28.
119. *Mark* 11: 30–2; *Matt.* 21: 25–6; *Luke* 20: 4–6.
120. *Matt.* 3: 14.   121. *Matt.* 11: 2–3; *Luke* 7: 18–20.
122. *Isa.* 29: 18–19; 35: 5–6; 61: 1–2.
123. *Mal.* 4: 5 (Hebrew text: 3: 23). Mark inserts the Elijah *logion* into a different context and, although it also claims prophecy to have been fulfilled, it refrains from open identification.
124. *Matt.* 11: 7–15; *Luke* 7: 24–8.   125. *Matt.* 11: 3.
126. *Matt.* 11: 2.   127. *Matt.* 11: 6; *Luke* 7: 23.
128. *Mark* 9: 38–40; *Luke* 9: 49–50.   129. *John* 3: 26.
130. *Luke* 1: 44.   131. Cf. *Mark* 1: 2–4.
132. *Mark* 3: 21.
133. *Mark* 3: 31–5. – Without *Mark* 3: 21, the latter statement, awkward though it may be, can be understood purely metaphorically.
134. *John* 2: 1–5.   135. *John* 19: 25.
136. *Acts* 1: 14.
137. *Acts* 12: 17; 15: 13; 21: 18; *Gal.* 1: 19; Josephus, *Ant.* 20, 200.
138. *Mark* 6: 3.
139. *Mark* 6: 4; *Matt.* 13: 57; *Luke* 8: 24.
140. *Mark* 6: 6.   141. *Luke* 4: 28–30.
142. *Luke* 11: 27–8.
143. *Matt.* 10: 37 (*RSV*); *Luke* 14: 25.
144. *Mark* 3: 6; *Matt.* 12: 14; *Luke* 6: 7.
145. *Mark* 2: 16; *Luke* 5: 30; cf. *Acts* 23: 9.
146. Mention of chief priests and Pharisees in *Matt.* 21: 45 stands against chief priests, lawyers and elders in *Mark* 11: 27; 12: 12.
147. The Pharisees and Sadducees situated in Galilee in *Matt.* 16: 1 become Pharisees only in *Mark* 8: 11.
148. *Mark* 12: 18–27; *Matt.* 22: 23–33; *Luke* 20: 27–40.
149. *Mark* 12: 28–34; *Luke* 20: 39.

150. *Mark* 2: 16; *Matt.* 9: 11; *Luke* 5: 30. – *Mark* 7: 1; *Luke* 15: 1. – *Mark* 2: 24; *Matt.* 12: 2; *Luke* 6: 2.

151. *Mark* 2: 6; *Matt.* 9: 3. – *Mark* 3: 22; *Matt.* 12: 24; *Luke* 11: 15.

152. *mSanh.* 7: 5.   153. Cf. below, pp. 145–9 and 209.

154. For Jesus' avoidance of 'work' in the performance of such cures, see above, p. 25. According to *Luke* 13: 14ff. the president of the synagogue reprimands, not the healer, but the sick for seeking a cure on the Sabbath day. – For a definition of the Pharisees as 'a non-political group whose chief religious concerns were for the proper preservation of ritual purity . . . and for the observance of the dietary laws', see J. Neusner, *The Rabbinic Traditions about the Pharisees before 70* III (Brill, Leiden, 1971), pp. 304–5.

155. *Mark* 12: 13–17; *Matt.* 22: 16–22; *Luke* 20: 20–6.

156. For the geographical relevance of the question in Jerusalem, see below, p. 45.

157. *Mark* 11: 30; *Matt.* 21: 25; *Luke* 20: 4.

158. Galilee: *Mark* 3: 6; *Luke* 13: 31–3; cf. 23: 6–12; *Acts* 4: 27. Jerusalem: *Mark* 11: 18; *Luke* 19: 47. – *Mark* 11: 27; 12: 12; *Matt.* 21: 23, 46; *Luke* 20: 1, 19. – *Mark* 14: 1; *Matt.* 26: 3–4; *Luke* 22: 2. – *Mark* 14: 10; *Matt.* 26: 14; *Luke* 22: 4. – *Mark* 14: 43; *Matt.* 26: 47. – *Mark* 14: 53; *Matt.* 26: 57, 59; *Luke* 22: 66. – *Mark* 14: 63; *Matt.* 26: 65; *Luke* 22: 67. – *Mark* 15: 1; *Matt.* 27: 1; *Luke* 23: 66.

159. *On the Trial of Jesus* (de Gruyter, Berlin, 1961). None of the criticisms formulated against him, including that by D. R. Catchpole in *The Trial of Jesus* (Brill, Leiden, 1971), have seriously affected any of his main theses. – In a paper read in Cambridge before classical scholars on 29 July 1971, the Roman historian, F. G. B. Millar, argued that the concept of a *trial* of Jesus is a misnomer, for he was crucified as a result of an *informal* enquiry by Jewish community leaders followed by Pilate's equally informal examination. Cf. *The Times*, 30 July 1971, p. 3. – On the problem of Jesus and the revolutionary movements of his age, see below, pp. 49–50.

160. *Mark* 15: 1ff.; *Matt.* 27: 11ff.; *Luke* 23: 1ff.

161. Far from being a distinguishing feature of Jesus' thought, his outlook on the hereafter is more often expressed in terms of 'eternal life' than of 'revival of dead bodies'; but apart from the already mentioned discussion with the Sadducees in which Jesus echoes standard Pharisaic teaching, no other Gospel reference to resurrection can safely be traced back to him.

162. *Mark* 8: 31; *Matt.* 16: 21; *Luke* 9: 22. – *Mark* 9: 9; *Matt.* 17: 9. – *Mark* 9: 31; *Matt.* 17: 22–3; cf. *Luke* 9: 44. – *Mark* 10: 33–4; *Matt.* 20: 18–19; *Luke* 18: 32–3. – *Mark* 14: 28; *Matt.* 26: 32. – Saving events occurring 'on the third day' are listed in *Genesis Rabbah* 56: 1. They are attached to the story of the sacrifice of

Isaac (*Gen.* 22: 4) and include Jonah's escape from the belly of the big fish (*Jonah* 2: 1) and the resurrection of the dead (*Hos.* 6: 2).

163. *Mark* 8: 32–3; *Matt.* 16: 22–3. – *Mark* 9: 10. – *Mark* 9: 32. – *Matt.* 17: 23. – *Luke* 18: 34.
164. *Mark* 15: 46; *Matt.* 27: 59–60; *Luke* 23: 53.
165. *Mark* 16: 1–2; *Matt.* 28: 1–2; *Luke* 24: 1–2.
166. *Mark* 16: 3; *Matt.* 28: 2–5; *Luke* 24: 3–4.
167. *Matt.* 28: 5; *Luke* 24: 5.
168. *Mark* 16: 6; *Matt.* 28: 6; *Luke* 24: 6.
169. *Luke* 24: 6–9.
170. *Luke* 24: 9; *Matt.* 28: 8; *Mark* 16: 8.
171. *Matt.* 28: 8–9; *Luke* 24: 13–32; 24: 33–49; *Matt.* 28: 16–20. – Luke does not seem to know of a return to Galilee: cf. *Luke* 24: 50–3; *Acts* 1: 1–3.
172. *1 Cor.* 15: 5–7.
173. R. Bultmann, *History of the Synoptic Tradition* (Blackwell, Oxford, 1963, and Harper & Row, New York), pp. 287ff.
174. *Mark* 15: 47.   175. *Matt.* 27: 61.
176. *Luke* 23: 55.
177. *Matt.* 27: 62–6; 28: 2–4, 12–15.
178. *John* 20: 15.   179. *Luke* 24: 11.
180. *Luke* 24: 24; *John* 20: 1–9.   181. *1 Cor.* 15: 5–7.
182. *2 Kgs.* 2: 10, 15.
183. *Mark* 6: 14–16; *Matt.* 14: 1–2; *Luke* 9: 7–9. – *Mark* 8: 28; *Matt.* 16: 14; *Luke* 9: 19. – *Matt.* 16: 14. – *Mark* 8: 28; *Matt.* 16: 14; *Luke* 9: 19.
184. Cf. M. S. Enslin, *The Prophet from Nazareth* (McGraw-Hill, New York, 1961), p. 129; P. Winter, *On the Trial of Jesus*, p. 149.

Chapter 2: Jesus and Galilee

1. My guarded optimism concerning a possible recovery of the genuine features of Jesus is in sharp contrast with Rudolf Bultmann's historical agnosticism: 'I do indeed think', he writes, 'that we can now know almost nothing concerning the life and personality of Jesus, since the early Christian sources show no interest in either, are moreover fragmentary and often legendary' (*Jesus and the Word* (Fontana, London, 1962, and Scribner, New York, 1958), p. 14). The real question is this: how much history can be extracted from sources which are not primarily historical?
2. *Isa.* 9: 1 (*AT*).   3. *2 Kgs.* 17.
4. *1 Macc.* 5.
5. Josephus, *Ant.* 13, 318–19; *BJ* 1, 76.
6. *Ant.* 13, 319.
7. Contrary to the implication contained in *Luke* 2: 1–5, the census by

Quirinius is firmly dated by Josephus to the tenth year of Archelaus, i.e. thirty-seven years after the battle of Actium (31 BC); that is, AD 6. Cf. *Ant.* 17, 342; 18, 1–2, 26. The so-called Pilate inscription discovered in Caesarea in Israel has settled once and for all the old controversy whether the first governors of Judea (those between AD 6 and 41) were procurators or prefects. The text reads: [PO]NTIUS PILATUS [PRAEF]ECTUS IUDA[EA]E. Cf. Carla Brusa Gerra, *Scavi di Caesarea Maritima* ('L'Erma' di Bretschneider, Rome, 1966), pp. 217–20.

8. Josephus, *Vita* 235; *BJ* 3, 35; *mSheb.* 9: 2.

9. *Matt.* 9: 18. – Tiberias was ruled by a council of ten presided over by an *archon*. Cf. Josephus, *Vita* 69, 294–6, 134, 278.

10. *Ant.* 14, 91; *Vita* 232.

11. *Vita* 79. According to *BJ* 2, 570–1, Josephus appointed seventy persons as magistrates to deal under his own presidency with important matters and capital cases. This is slightly in contradiction with *Vita* 79 and with the opening sentence in the present passage. It seems more likely that the seventy administrators were existing leaders reappointed by Josephus.

12. *BJ* 3, 42. 13. *BJ* 3, 42–4.

14. *BJ* 2, 591–2; cf. *bShab.* 26a.

15. See M. Avi-Yonah, *Geschichte der Juden im Zeitalter des Talmud* (de Gruyter, Berlin, 1961), pp. 16–25, dealing with the social and economic situation of the second century AD.

16. *History of the Jews* I (Yoseloff, London and New York, 1967), p. 74.

17. Cf. Schürer – Vermes – Millar, *History* I, p. 381.

18. *BJ* 1, 203–4; *Ant.* 14, 158–9. 19. *BJ* 2, 56; *Ant.* 17, 271–2.

20. *BJ* 2, 118; *Ant.* 18, 4–10, 23. 21. *Ant.* 20, 102.

22. *BJ* 2, 433–48.

23. *BJ* 7, 253, 275, 320–401. He may be the Ben Yair whose name figures on a potsherd discovered recently in the ruins of the Zealot stronghold. Cf. Y. Yadin, *Masada* (Weidenfeld & Nicolson, London, 1966, and Random House, New York), p. 201.

24. *Luke* 13: 1. 25. *Ant.* 20, 120.

26. *BJ* 2, 585. 27. *BJ* 4, 558.

28. Cf. M. Hengel, *Die Zeloten* (Brill, Leiden, 1961), pp. 57–61.

29. *mYad.* 4: 8. 30. *BJ* 3, 41.

31. *mNed.* 5: 5; *bNed.* 48a. 32. *yKet.* 29b.

33. *Matt.* 6: 28–9; 13: 24–8.

34. On the Galilean administrative districts (*toparchies*), see M. Avi-Yonah, *The Holy Land from the Persian to the Arab Conquest (536 BC to AD 640): A Historical Geography* (Baker Book House, Grand Rapids, 1966), p. 97.

35. It appears, however, in *John* 6: 1, 23; 21: 1. The foundation of Tiberias was regarded with suspicion by the Galileans. Cf. *Ant.* 18, 36–8.

36. *Matt.* 9: 1.
37. 'Skirting the lake of Gennesar, and also bearing that name, lies a region whose natural properties and beauty are very remarkable. There is not a plant which its fertile soil refuses to produce . . . One might say that nature had taken pride in thus assembling, by a *tour de force*, the most discordant species in a single spot, and that, by a happy rivalry, each of the seasons wished to claim this region for her own. . . . For ten months without intermission (the country) supplies those kings of fruits, the grape and the fig; the rest mature on the trees the whole year round. Besides being favoured by its genial air, the country is watered by a highly fertilizing spring, called by the inhabitants Capharnaum': *BJ* 3, 516–21. There is a possible second mention in *Vita* 403 if the village of 'Cepharnocus' or 'Capharnomus' is identified as Capernaum.
38. *Matt.* 15: 24.
39. *Matt.* 7: 6; *Mark* 7: 27; *Matt.* 15: 26.
40. *Mark* 5: 18–19; *Luke* 8: 38–9.
41. *Matt.* 10: 5–6. That Jesus was prepared to cure the (probably Jewish) servant of the Roman centurion cannot be invoked to mitigate his anti-Gentilism. Perhaps the most striking feature of the story concerns his astonishment that a pagan could be so full of trust. Cf. *Matt.* 8: 5–13; *Luke* 7: 1–10.
42. *Acts* 10: 1–48.
43. M. S. Enslin, *The Prophet from Nazareth*, pp. 160–1.
44. *Matt.* 5: 44–8.
45. S. G. F. Brandon, *Jesus and the Zealots* (Manchester University Press, Manchester, 1967, and Scribner, New York).
46. *Ant.* 18, 117–18.
47. *Mark* 6: 17–29; *Matt.* 14: 3–12; *Luke* 3: 19–20. – Josephus's description, independent of, and conflicting with, that of the New Testament, is likely to be genuine.
48. *John* 11: 47–50.
49. *Gen. R.* 94: 9. Cf. D. Daube, *Collaboration with Tyranny in Rabbinic Law* (Oxford University Press, London, 1965).
50. *Ant.* 18, 63–4. For a full discussion, see *History* I, pp. 428–41.
51. The paragraph following the *Testimonium* (*Ant.* 18, 65) opens with the words: 'About this same time *another* outrage threw the Jews into an uproar . . .' Cf. P. Winter, 'Josephus on Jesus', *Journ. Hist. St.* 1 (1968), pp. 289–302.
52. *Mark* 3: 18; *Matt.* 10: 4; *Luke* 6: 15.
53. *Mark* 11: 9–10.   54. *Luke* 19: 37–8.
55. *Acts* 1: 6 (*RSV*).   56. Cf. below, p. 186.
57. Cf. J. T. Milik, *Discoveries in the Judaean Desert* II, *Les grottes de Murabba'at* (Clarendon Press, Oxford, 1961), pp. 159–61.
58. *bErub.* 53b.   59. *bErub.* 53a.
60. *bMeg.* 24b.

61. *Matt.* 26: 73 (*RSV*); *Mark* 14: 70.

62. *Luke* 16: 20–5.

63. Cf. M. Schwabe – B. Lifshitz, *Beth She'arim* II, *Greek Inscriptions* (Mosad Bialik, Jerusalem, 1967), nos. 93, 177. On Eleazar/Lazar, see below, pp. 190–1.

64. The masculine form of the imperative *kum* surviving in the oldest manuscripts, but replaced in other codices by the correct feminine form *kumi*, is best explained as a Galilean peculiarity. Cf. G. Dalman, *Grammatik des jüdisch-palästinischen Aramäisch* (J. C. Hinrichs, Leipzig, ²1905), p. 321, n. 1; p. 277, n. 2.

65. *Mark* 7: 34. J. A. Emerton, 'MARANATHA and EPHPHETHA', *JTS* 18 (1967), pp. 427–31, discusses both possibilities. However, even if it were true that the word is Hebrew, it would not mean that Jesus occasionally employed Hebrew as his vernacular language, but that the quasi-liturgical healing formula required the use of the sacred tongue. For the latest debate, see the articles by I. Rabinowitz and S. Morag in *Journal of Semitic Studies* 16 (1971), pp. 151–6, and 17 (1972), pp. 198–202.

66. *Mark* 15: 34–5; *Matt.* 27: 46–7. 67. *mNed.* 2: 4.

68. Cf. *yAZ* 11a; *ARNa*, 27 (ed. Schechter, p. 28b).

69. *bPes.* 112b; cf. *bBer.* 43b; see below, p. 76.

70. *bErub.* 53b, quoting *mAb.* 1: 5.

71. *Das galiläische 'Am-ha'Ares des zweiten Jahrhunderts* (Israel.-Theol. Lehranstalt, Vienna, 1906).

72. *bPes.* 49b. The first saying comes from an anonymous source; the second is handed down in the name of the late-first-century AD rabbi, Eliezer ben Hyrcanus.

73. In *John*, Jesus' country is Judea, and it is the Judeans, i.e. Jews, his own people, who failed to receive him, whereas the alien Galileans 'gave him a welcome, because they had seen all that he did at the festival in Jerusalem' (*John* 4: 45). Cf. W. A. Meeks, *The Prophet-King: Moses Traditions and the Johannine Christology* (Brill, Leiden, 1967), pp. 35–41.

74. *John* 7: 41.   75. *John* 7: 45–52.

76. *Mark* 3: 22; 7: 1.   77. *Vita* 189–98.

78. *tSanh.* 2: 6; *Midrash Tanna'im on Deut.* 26: 13 (ed. Hoffmann, p. 176), etc.

79. A. Finkel, *The Pharisees and the Teacher of Nazareth* (Brill, Leiden, 1964), p. 129. On the same page, note 3, the writer states: 'Shammai was a Galilean', and proves it by means of a reference to I. Abrahams, *Studies in Pharisaism and the Gospels* I (Cambridge University Press, Cambridge, 1924, and Ktav, New York, 1967 (reprint)), p. 15. But all that Abrahams expresses is a vague possibility: 'If it be the truth that Shammai (as Dr Büchler conjectures) was a Galilean . . .'

80. Cf. J. Neusner, *A Life of Rabban Yohanan ben Zakkai Ca. 1–80 C.E.* (Brill, Leiden, ²1970), p. 47.

81. *yShab.* 15d.
82. 'They are . . . extremely influential among the townsfolk; and all prayers and sacred rites of divine worship are performed according to their exposition. This is the great tribute that the inhabitants of the cities . . . have paid to the excellence of the Pharisees': *Ant.* 18, 15.
83. Cf. S. W. Baron, *A Social and Religious History of the Jews* I (Columbia University Press, London and New York, ²1952), p. 278.
84. *The History of the Jews in Palestine in the Period of the Mishnah and the Talmud* (in Hebrew) I (Hakibbutz Hameuchad, Jerusalem, ⁴1967), p. 319.

Chapter 3: Jesus and charismatic Judaism

1. *Luke* 13: 32.
2. *Mark* 2: 17.
3. *Gen.* 50: 2; *Exod.* 21: 19.'
4. Cf. *Exod.* 15: 26; *Deut.* 32: 39.
5. *2 Chr.* 16: 12.
6. Cf. *Lev.* 13–14; *Mark* 1: 44; *Matt.* 8: 4; *Luke* 5: 14; 17: 14. – *Lev.* 12. – *Lev.* 15.
7. *1 Kgs.* 17: 17–24.
8. *2 Kgs.* 4: 32–7.
9. *2 Kgs.* 5: 1–14.
10. *2 Kgs.* 20: 7; *Isa.* 38: 22.
11. *Ecclus.* 38: 1–15.
12. *Ecclus.* 38: 6–7.
13. *Ecclus.* 38: 13.
14. *Tobit* 6: 13–17; 8: 1–2.
15. *Tobit* 8: 3.
16. *1 En.* 7: 1; 8: 3ff. Cf. *LAB* 34: 5.
17. *1 En.* 10: 4–8.
18. *Jub.* 10: 10–14.
19. *Ant.* 8, 44–5.
20. *BJ* 2, 136.
21. Cf. 'The Etymology of Essenes', *RQ* 2 (1960), pp. 427–43; 'Essenes and Therapeutai', ibid. 3 (1962), pp. 495–504.
22. Philo, *De vita contemplativa* 2.
23. *Ant.* 8, 46–7. This famous Baaras root, growing in the area of Machaerus and thought to have possessed exorcistic properties, is described in detail by Josephus in *BJ* 7, 180–4. He concludes: 'It possesses one virtue for which it is prized; for the so-called demons – in other words, the spirits of wicked men which enter the living and kill them unless aid is forthcoming – are promptly expelled by this root, if merely applied to the patients' (*BJ* 7, 185).
24. *Ant.* 8, 48.
25. *Matt.* 12: 27; *Luke* 11: 19.
26. *Mark* 3: 22; *Matt.* 9: 34; 12: 24; *Luke* 11: 15, 18.
27. *Matt.* 7: 22; *Luke* 10: 20. – *Mark* 9: 38. Cf. also *tHul.* 2: 22–4 apropos of the intended healing of Rabbi Eleazar ben Dama by Jacob of Kefar Sama in the name of Jesus.
28. *Num.* 19: 1–10. The ashes of a ritually slaughtered red cow mixed in water provide the purificatory substance whereby uncleanness caused by contact with a corpse is removed.
29. *PRK* (ed. Buber), 40ab; *Tanh.* (ed. Buber), 4, 118–19

30. Ibid.
31. Cf. above, p. 23.
32. Cf. above, p. 25. See also *bShab.* 108b; *yShab.* 14d; *Deut. R.* 5: 15.
    Cf. L. Blau, *Das altjüdische Zauberwesen* (K. J. Trübner, Strasbourg,
    1898), p. 162.
33. In *Genesis* 20: 17 the patriarch plays the role of mediator, but the
    cure is brought about by God himself.
34. *Gen. Ap.* 20: 16–19. Cf. *DSSE*, p. 220; *Scripture and Tradition*,
    pp. 114–15.
35. Cf. above, pp. 22–4. The laying on of hands as a gesture of healing
    first appears in the Septuagint of *2 Kings* 5: 11. In the Hebrew
    text Naaman expresses hope that the prophet Elisha will 'wave' his
    hands over the leprous parts of his body, but the Greek translator
    renders the verb by 'to lay on'.
36. Cf. *Mark* 5: 23; *Matt.* 9: 18; *Mark* 6: 5.
37. *Mark* 1: 25; *Luke* 4: 35; *Mark* 9: 25; *Matt.* 17: 18; *Luke* 9: 42. –
    There are a few exceptions. In the episode of the healing of the
    deaf-mute physical contact and verbal command occur together
    (cf. *Mark* 7: 32–3). Again, if prayer as an element of cure is absent
    in the Gospels, it nevertheless appears in association with the laying
    on of hands at the blessing of the children in *Matthew* (*Matt.* 19: 13).
    Finally, there is the case of healing by word of mouth alone in the
    story of the man with the withered arm. Cf. above, p. 25.
38. *bMeil.* 17b.
39. Compare this to the miraculous deliverance of Peter from Agrippa's
    jail in *Acts* 12: 6–10.
40. Cf. *Mark* 5: 41.
41. Cf. *Praeparatio evangelica* IX. 29, 24–5, *Eusebius Werke* (ed. K.
    Mras) VIII (Akademie-Verlag, Berlin, 1954). Cf. Clement of
    Alexandria, *Stromata* I, 23: 154, 2–3. On Artapanus, see A.-M.
    Denis, *Introduction aux pseudépigraphes grecs d'Ancien Testament*
    (Brill, Leiden, 1970), pp. 255–7.
42. *1 Sam.* 16: 14–23.
43. *LAB* 60: 1–3.
44. 'Nunc molesta esse noli tamquam secunda creatura.'
45. 'Memorare tartari in quo ambulas.' – David's descendant, expected
    to triumph over Satan, is identified as the Messiah by M. Philo-
    nenko, 'Remarques sur un hymne essénien de caractère gnostique',
    Semitica 11 (1962), p. 52; but M. R. James, *The Biblical Antiquities
    of Philo* (S.P.C.K., London, 1917), interprets the allusion as referring
    to Solomon. See also L. H. Feldman's *Prolegomenon* to the reprint
    of the work (Ktav, New York, 1971), pp. CXXXIX–CXL.
46. Cf. J. T. Milik, 'Prière de Nabonide', *RB* 63 (1956), pp. 407–11;
    DSSE, p. 229. See also A. Dupont-Sommer, *The Essene Writings
    from Qumran* (Blackwell, Oxford, 1961, and Peter Smith, Gloucester,
    Mass.), pp. 321–5.

47. The manuscript includes a descriptive title followed by an auto-biographical account. Taken together, they are repetitive and thus facilitate the certain reconstruction of several gaps.

48. *Dan.* 2: 27; 4: 4; 5: 7, 11.   49. Op. cit., p. 322, n. 3.

50. Cf. *bPes.* 112b. See below, pp. 208–9.

51. *Mark* 2: 2–12; *Matt.* 9: 1–8; *Luke* 5: 17–26.   52. *bNed.* 41a.

53. The most important book on this topic is still A. Büchler, *Types of Jewish-Palestinian Piety from 70 B.C.E. to 70 C.E.* (Jews' College, London, 1922). Like most of the works of that celebrated scholar, it is a rich mine of information rather than a valid historico-critical assessment of the data. For a more recent treatment of the subject see G. B. Sarfatti, 'Pious Men, Men of Deeds and the Early Prophets', *Tarbiz* 26 (1956–7), pp. 126–53 (in Hebrew), and II–IV (English summary).

54. Cf. A. Büchler, op. cit., pp. 196–264.

55. Cf. *1 Kgs.* 17: 1.   56. *mTaan.* 3: 8.

57. *mTaan.* 3: 8.   58. *Ant.* 14, 22–4.

59. *mTaan.* 3: 8.   60. *bTaan.* 23a.

61. *Gen. R.* 13: 7. Some manuscripts mention only Honi without Elijah; cf. J. Theodor – C. Albeck, *Midrash Bereshit Rabba* I (Wahrmann, Jerusalem, ²1965), p. 117.

62. *bTaan.* 23ab.

63. *yTaan.* 64b; cf. A. Neubauer, *La géographie du Talmud* (Michel Lévy, Paris, 1868), p. 261.

64. For a full treatment of the relevant traditions, see my study entitled 'Hanina ben Dosa', *JJS* 23 (1972), pp. 28–50, and 24 (1973), pp. 51–64.

65. John Bowman's *The Gospel of Mark* (Brill, Leiden, 1965) is one of the rare recent publications with an index including several references to Hanina. As might be expected, D. Flusser devotes a somewhat larger space to him, but without examining the rabbinic sources in depth. Cf. *Jesus*, pp. 69–70, 93, 95.

66. *yBer.* 7c; cf. *bBer.* 34b.

67. *bBer.* 34b. On Arab, see M. Avi-Yonah, 'A List of Priestly Courses', *IEJ* 12 (1962), pp. 137–9; *The Holy Land . . . A Historical Geography*, p. 97.

68. Cf. below, pp. 74–5.   69. *Acts* 22: 3.

70. A. Büchler, *Types of Jewish-Palestinian Piety*, p. 87, and H. Danby, *The Mishnah* (Oxford University Press, London, 1933), p. 799, assert that Hanina flourished after AD 70. However, if J. Neusner's dating of Yohanan ben Zakkai's Galilean period to before AD 45 is accepted (cf. *A Life of Rabban Yohanan ben Zakkai*, p. 47), and the teacher-pupil relationship between him and Hanina assumed, the latter's birth might conjecturally be placed around AD 20. If so, he was a younger contemporary of the holy man from the neighbouring Nazareth.

71. *mBer.* 5: 1.

72. The terms used are unclear but must denote a dangerous snake.

73. *yBer.* 9a; *tBer.* 2: 20; *bBer.* 33a.   74. *bBer.* 33a.

75. *Mark* 16: 18 (*AT*); *Luke* 10: 19; cf. *Acts* 28: 3–5.

76. *bBer.* 34b.   77. Cf. *1 Kgs.* 18: 42.

78. *bBer.* 34b; *yBer.* 9d.

79. *Matt.* 8: 5–13; *Luke* 7: 1–10; *John* 4: 46–53

80. *Mark* 5: 30; *Luke* 8: 46.   81. *bBK* 50a; *bYeb.* 121b.

82. Cf. *bBer.* 43b.

83. *bPes.* 112b. One of the interesting features of this account is that the heavenly voice announcing Hanina's holiness is represented as being audible and intelligible to an evil spirit. For a Gospel parallel, see p. 24 above. Cf. also below, p. 207.

84. *bTaan.* 24b; *bYoma* 53b.   85. Cf. *1 Kgs.* 17: 1; 18: 45.

86. Cf. above, p. 72.

87. As a student of Rabbi Judah the Prince, he is said to have been a keen collector of Galilean traditions.

88. *bBer.* 61b. Other pertinent sayings are: 'Each day a heavenly voice came [from Mount Horeb] and said: The whole universe is sustained on account of my son, Hanina' (*bTaan.* 24b; *bBer.* 17b; *bHul.* 86a, saying reported by Rab). Rabbi Dimi, a fourth-century AD teacher presents Hanina as the prototype of the person on whose account all his contemporaries were favoured by God (*bHag.* 14a).

89. Cf. *Mark* 8: 28; *Matt.* 16: 14; *Luke* 9: 8, 19. See above, p. 41, and below, pp. 94–5.

90. *mAb.* 5: 10.   91. *bTaan.* 24b–25a.

92. Cf. *Exod.* 18: 21.

93. *Mekh.* (ed. Lauterbach) II, p. 183.

94. *Matt.* 6: 25–33.   95. *Mark* 10: 21.

96. *Matt.* 8: 20; *Luke* 9: 58.   97. *mAb.* 3: 9–10.

98. *mAb.* 3: 9.   99. *Prov.* 9: 10; *Ps.* 111: 10.

100. *mShek.* 5: 6.   101. *Matt.* 6: 1–4 (*RSV*).

102. *mSot.* 9:15; *tSot.* 15: 5; *ySot.* 24c; *bSot.* 49b.

103. For the traditional view, see Rashi on *bSot.* 49b; A. Geiger, *Urschrift und Übersetzungen der Bibel* (Hainauer, Breslau, 1857), p. 126; J. Levy, *Neuhebräisches Wörterbuch* III (Brockhaus, Leipzig, 1883), p. 197; L. Blau, *Zauberwesen*, p. 149, n. 5; K. Kohler, *Jew. Enc.* V, p. 227. Against the traditional view, see A. Büchler, op. cit., pp. 83–7; S. Safrai, 'The Teaching of Pietists in Mishnaic Literature', *JJS* 16 (1965), p. 16.

104. *Matt.* 11: 2; cf. *John* 7: 21, referring to *John* 5: 1–9.

105. *Luke* 24: 19 (*RSV*).

106. Cf. *Ant.* 18, 63. The same expression, 'marvellous deeds', appears in Josephus's account of the thaumaturgist Elisha: 'Through his prophetic power he performed astounding and marvellous deeds,

which were held as a glorious memory by the Hebrews' (*Ant.* 9, 182). See also *Luke* 5: 26.

107. Cf. *tHul.* 2: 22.

108. *Types of Jewish-Palestinian Piety*, p. 264.

109. Art. cit., *JJS* 16 (1965), pp. 19–20, 33.

110. *Jesus*, p. 56. In his recent study (*The Rabbinic Traditions about the Pharisees* III, p. 314), J. Neusner speaks of outsiders 'anachronistically and retroactively "Pharisaized", like Honi or possibly Hanina b. Dosa'.

111. Cf. above, p. 76. *bTaan.* 25a; *mBK* 7: 7. – Cf. *Lev.* 11: 29; *bBer.* 33a; cf. *bHul.* 127a.

112. *ARNa* 28 (ed. Schechter, p. 28b).

113. *mTer.* 8: 4; *yTer.* 45c; *yAZ* 41a.

114. *yBer.* 7c; *yDem.* 22a.

115. *mTaan.* 3: 8; *yTaan.* 67a; *bTaan.* 23a.

116. *bBM* 59b. It should be noted, nevertheless, that when the schools of Hillel and Shammai failed to reach agreement on dialectical grounds, the Hillelite opinion was proclaimed valid by a heavenly voice! Cf. *yBer.* 3b; *bBer.* 52a.

Chapter 4: *Jesus the prophet*

1. Cf., e.g., H. Conzelmann, *An Outline of the Theology of the New Testament* (SCM Press, London, 1969, and Harper & Row, New York), p. 85; O. Cullmann, *The Christology of the New Testament* (SCM Press, London, [2]1963, and Westminster Press, Philadelphia), p. 30; F. Hahn, *The Titles of Jesus in Christology* (Lutterworth Press, London, 1969), pp. 352–406; R. H. Fuller, *The Foundations of New Testament Christology* (Fontana, London, 1969, and Scribner, New York), pp. 127–9.

2. *Theologie des Neuen Testaments* (J. C. B. Mohr, Tübingen, [5]1965), pp. 35–6.

3. O. Cullmann, op. cit., p. 43.

4. V. Taylor, *The Names of Jesus* (Macmillan, London and Toronto, 1953), pp. 16–17.

5. *Mark* 8: 28; *Matt.* 16: 14; *Luke* 9: 19.

6. *Mark* 6: 15; *Luke* 9: 8.   7. *Matt.* 21: 11.

8. *Luke* 7: 16.   9. *Luke* 7: 39.

10. *Matt.* 21: 46. Cf. also *Mark* 11: 32; *Matt.* 14: 5; *Luke* 20: 6, concerning John the Baptist.

11. *Matt.* 26: 68.   12. *Mark* 14: 65.

13. *Luke* 22: 64.   14. *Luke* 24: 19 (*RSV*).

15. *Acts* 3: 22ff.; 7: 37. Cf. below, p. 97.

16. *Mark* 6: 4; *Matt.* 13: 57; *Luke* 4: 24.

17. *Luke* 13: 33.   18. *Mark* 6: 5; *Matt.* 13: 58.

19. Cf. *Ecclus.* 48: 1–14. Cf. G. B. Sarfatti, 'Pious Men, Men of Deeds and the Early Prophets', *Tarbiz* 26 (1956–7), pp. 144–5.

20. *Luke* 7: 11–17; *1 Kgs.* 17: 17–24; *2 Kgs.* 4: 18–38.

21. *Mark* 6: 31–44; *Matt.* 14: 13–21; *Luke* 9: 10–17; *Mark* 8: 1–10; *Matt.* 15: 32–9; *2 Kgs.* 4: 42–4.

22. *Luke* 4: 25–7; *1 Kgs.* 17: 9; *2 Kgs.* 5: 14. – An influence of the Elijah saga on Jesus' fast for forty days (*1 Kgs.* 19: 8; *Matt.* 4: 2) is doubtful. Cf. B. Gerhardsson, *The Testing of God's Son* (Gleerup, Lund, 1966), p. 43.

23. Cf. above, p. 75.

24. Cf. above, p. 76.   25. Cf. above, p. 76.

26. *1 Macc.* 9: 27.

27. *Contra Apionem* 1, 41; cf. 1, 29, 37, 40.

28. *mAb.* 1: 1.

29. *bMeg.* 3a. Rabbi Yohanan suggestedi n the third century AD that prophecy passed from the prophets to the simple and the babes (*bBB* 12a; cf. *Matt.* 11: 25). – The interpretative function of the primitive Christian order of 'prophets' resembles that of a public expositor of the difficult doctrine of a master in a Jewish school, known as an *Amora* or *Meturgeman*. Cf. *Jew. Enc.* I, p. 527.

30. *tSot.* 13: 3; *ySot.* 24b; *bSot.* 48b. On the interchangeability of 'holy spirit' and 'spirit of prophecy', see J. P. Schäfer, 'Die Termini "Heiliger Geist" und "Geist der Prophetie" in den Targumim', *VT* 20 (1970), pp. 304–14; *Die Vorstellung vom Heiligen Geist in der rabbinischen Literatur* (Kösel, Munich, 1972), pp. 21–6.

31. *tSot.* 13: 2.   32. Cf. above, p. 82.

33. Cf. *Mark* 1: 11; *Matt.* 3: 17; *Luke* 3: 22. Cf. *bMeg.* 3a.

34. See n. 37 below. Cf. *John* 11: 51.

35. *1 Macc.* 4: 46.   36. *1 Macc.* 14: 41.

37. *Ant.* 13, 300; cf. *tSot.* 13: 5.   38. *BJ* 2, 112–13.

39. *BJ* 3, 352–4.

40. *BJ* 3, 399–408. According to rabbinic literature, Yohanan ben Zakkai foretold to Vespasian his impending elevation to imperial office. Cf. *Scripture and Tradition*, pp. 34–5.

41. S. Schechter, *Some Aspects of Rabbinic Theology* (A. & C. Black, London, 1909), p. 7.

42. Cf. below, p. 98.

43. *Mal.* 3: 23 (=E.T. 4: 5); cf. *Mal.* 3: 1.

44. *Mal.* 3: 24 (=E.T. 4: 6).   45. *Ecclus.* 48: 10.

46. *mEd.* 8: 7.

47. *1 En.* 90: 31, 37. Elijah as a messianic precursor became an important part of rabbinic eschatology also: cf. L. Ginzberg, 'Elijah in Rabbinical Literature', *Jew. Enc.* V, pp. 122–7; J. Jeremias, *TDNT* II, pp. 928–41.

48. Cf. above, p. 41. See F. Hahn, *The Titles of Jesus in Christology*, p. 399, n. 156.

49. *Luke* 3: 15; *John* 1: 20; *Acts* 13: 25. See also the Judeo-Christian Pseudo-Clementine *Recognitiones* I, 60. Cf. G. Strecker, *Das Judenchristentum der Pseudoklementinen* (Akademie-Verlag, Berlin, 1958), pp. 241–2. – As has been pointed out (cf. above, pp. 32–3), the praises of John by Jesus are intermingled with veiled criticism, and concluded with the identification of the Baptist as Elijah already come, implying his status to be inferior to that of Jesus. Whether such a judgement is traceable to Jesus himself is, however, highly questionable, and has in effect been expressly questioned. Cf. F. Hahn, op. cit., p. 367.

50. *Deut.* 18: 15, 18–19. Cf. *Acts* 3: 22–3; 7: 37, and *4Q Test.* 5–8 (see J. M. Allegro, *Discoveries in the Judaean Desert* V (Clarendon Press, Oxford, 1968), p. 58; *DSSE*, pp. 247–8).

51. *1Q Ser.* 9: 11; *DSSE*, p. 87. Cf. *Scripture and Tradition*, p. 63 and n. 2.

52. Cf. J. M. Allegro, op. cit., pp. 57–8; *DSSE*, pp. 247–8.

53. Cf. *DSSE*, p. 50; *Scripture and Tradition*, p. 66.

54. *John* 1: 21.

55. *John* 6: 14; 7: 40. – In the Pseudo-Clementine *Recognitiones* I, 43, the Jews propose to discuss with the Apostles whether Jesus was the prophet promised by Moses, i.e. the eternal Christ in their belief. Cf. H. J. Schoeps, *Theologie und Geschichte des Judenchristentums* (J. C. B. Mohr, Tübingen, 1949), pp. 87–98.

56. *Acts* 3: 17–26; cf. 7: 37.

57. *Mark* 9: 2–8; *Matt.* 17: 1–9; *Luke* 9: 28–36.

58. *Deut. R.* 3: 10, 1.

59. *Palestinian Targums on Exod.* 12: 42. Cf. *Scripture and Tradition*, pp. 216–17; R. Le Déaut, *La nuit pascale* (Institut Biblique Pontifical, Rome, 1963), pp. 298–303.

60. *Acts* 3: 14; 7: 52; 22: 14.

61. Cf. *Mekh.* (ed. Lauterbach) I, pp. 115–16; *Targ. Song of S.* 4: 5; *Targ. Lam.* 2: 22; *Song of S. R.* 2: 9, 3. See Renée Bloch, 'Quelques aspects de la figure de Moïse dans la tradition rabbinique', *Moïse, l'homme de l'Alliance* (Desclée, Paris, 1955), pp. 156–61.

62. In addition to *Acts* 3: 22–3; 7: 37, see the Judeo-Christian *Preachings of Peter*, where 'true prophet' is 'the primary title for Jesus' (cf. O. Cullmann, *The Christology of the New Testament*, p. 39).

63. Cf. Josephus, *Ant.* 20, 167–8.
64. *Acts* 5: 36.

65. *Ant.* 20, 97.
66. *Ant.* 20, 169–70.

67. *Acts* 21: 38 (*RSV*).
68. *BJ* 6, 283–5.

69. *BJ* 6, 286.
70. Cf. *Mark* 13: 22; *Matt.* 24: 24.

71. *1 Sam.* 21: 5; *2 Sam.* 11: 11.

72. There is said to have been a compulsory abstinence before the Sinai revelation: 'Be ready by the third day; do not go near a woman!' (*Exod.* 19: 15; cf. 19: 10–15).

73. *Lev.* 15: 18–23.

74. Josephus excludes from Jerusalem all persons suffering from a
venereal disease, and from the Temple, every unclean male or
female Israelite (*BJ* 5,227). The Qumran Damascus Rule outlaws
intercourse 'in the city of the Sanctuary' (*CDC* 12: 1–2), a prohibition
bound to apply only to pilgrims.

75. *1Q Milh.* 7: 3–4; *DSSE*, p. 132.

76. *BJ* 2, 121. See also *Ant.* 18, 21, and Philo's tirade in *Apol.* 14–17:
'Women are selfish, excessively jealous, skilful in ensnaring the
morals of a spouse and seducing him by endless charms. Women
set out to flatter . . . If children are born, they then declare with
audacious arrogance what they were formerly content to insinuate
. . . and shamelessly employ violence to commit actions all of which
are contrary to the good of the common life. The husband, bound
by his wife's spells, or anxious for his children . . . is no more the
same towards the others, but unknown to himself he becomes a
different man, a slave instead of a freeman' (A. Dupont-Sommer,
The Essene Writings from Qumran, pp. 25–6).

77. *BJ* 2, 120; Philo, *Apol.* 3; Pliny, *Hist. Nat.* V, 15, 73.

78. Philo, *De vita contemplativa* 68; G. Vermes, 'Essenes and Therapeutai', *RQ* 3 (1962), pp. 495–502.

79. *Luke* 14: 26; 18: 29; cf. *Mark* 10: 29; *Matt.* 19: 29. In the Marcan
and Matthean recension, 'home' is synonymous with 'wife'. In
vernacular Aramaic 'one belonging to his house' is the owner's wife.

80. *bShab.* 87a.   81. *Siphre on Num.* 12: 1 (99).

82. *De vita Mosis* II, 68–9.   83. *bYeb.* 63b.

84. *mSot.* 9: 15; *bSot.* 49b, with variants. See A. Büchler, *Types of
Jewish-Palestinian Piety*, pp. 42–65.

Chapter 5: Jesus the lord

1. The only occasion on which Jesus is recorded as describing himself
as lord appears in the Fourth Gospel, where he declares to his
disciples: 'You call me teacher and lord; and you are right, for so I
am' (*John* 13: 13 (*RSV*)). The phrase is modelled on a commonplace
Aramaic sentence, 'My master, my lord' (*rabbi u-mari*). In the
Targum of 2 *Kings* 2: 12 the Hebrew 'my father' is rendered as
rabbi (referring to Elijah) and in 5: 13 as *mari* (my lord=Naaman).

2. See *The Names of Jesus*, pp. 38–51.

3. Op. cit., p. 41.   4. Ibid.

5. Ibid., p. 42.   6. Cf. *Luke* 24: 34.

7. *Mark* 16: 19–20.   8. *The Names of Jesus*, pp. 42–3.

9. Ibid., pp. 44–5.   10. Ibid., p. 47.

11. Cf. ibid., p. 49. For the parallels, see *Mark* 12: 9; *Matt.* 25: 9;
Luke 12: 36–7.

12. Op. cit., p. 50.   13. Ibid., p. 51.

14. Cf. W. Bousset, *Kyrios Christos – Geschichte des Christusglaubens von den Anfängen des Christentums bis Irenaeus* (Vandenhoeck & Ruprecht, Göttingen, ²1926), pp. 91–101; W. Foerster, *Lord* (A. & C. Black, London, 1958, and Harper, New York), pp. 13–35; *'Kyrios', TDNT* III (1965), pp. 1046–58; L. Cerfaux – J. Tondriau, *Le culte des souverains dans la civilisation Gréco-Romaine* (Casterman, Tournai, 1957), pp. 342–57. Cf. *Acts* 25: 26.

15. *1 Cor.* 1: 2 (*RSV*).

16. *Theologie des Neuen Testaments*, pp. 54–6.

17. *The Titles of Jesus in Christology* (1969).

18. *Mark* 7: 28; *Matt.* 8: 8; *Luke* 7: 6.

19. Op. cit., pp. 81–2. Cf. G. Bornkamm, *Tradition and Interpretation in Matthew* (SCM Press, London, 1963, and Westminster Press, Philadelphia), pp. 42–3.

20. See *Gen.* 23: 7, 12; 33: 3–4, etc.   21. *Matt.* 18: 26.

22. Op. cit., p. 86.

23. *1 Cor.* 7: 10; 9: 5, 14; *Gal.* 1: 19. – *John* 13: 13–14. Cf. op. cit., pp. 86–8.

24. *Matt.* 7: 21–2; *Luke* 13: 26–7. – *Matt.* 25: 11.

25. Op. cit., pp. 90–103.

26. Cf. *Acts* 2: 34–6; op. cit., p. 103.

27. Op. cit., p. 107.

28. *1 Cor.* 5: 5; *Mark* 1: 2ff.; *1 Cor.* 1: 2; *Acts* 2: 21; *Rom.* 10: 13.

29. *Matt.* 28: 20.

30. *Rom.* 10: 9 (*RSV*). Op. cit., pp. 108–9.

31. 'Ein Weg zur neutestamentlichen Christologie? Prüfung der Thesen Ferdinand Hahns', *Aufsätze zum Neuen Testament* (Kaiser, Munich, 1965), pp. 147–67, especially pp. 148, 152.

32. *Die Worte Jesu* (J. C. Hinrich, Leipzig, 1898, ²1930), pp. 146–50, 266–72. An English translation appeared in 1902 (T. & T. Clark, Edinburgh); cf. pp. 179–83, 324–31.

33. 'Maranatha und Kyrios Jesus', *ZNW* 53 (1962), pp. 125–44.

34. See *Commentarius in Psalmos* 2: 2.

35. Op. cit., pp. 130–2.   36. Ibid., pp. 134–5.

37. *Dan.* 2: 47; 5: 23. – 4: 16, 21. Cf. op. cit., pp. 134–6.

38. For the erroneous view that the earliest examples date to the third century AD, see below, p. 112, n. 42.

39. Op. cit., p. 137.

40. *Dan.* 2: 23: 'O thou God of my fathers!'

41. Op. cit., p. 143.

42. See, e.g., E. Schweizer, *Lordship and Discipleship* (SCM Press, London, 1960), p. 58; O. Cullmann, *The Christology of the New Testament*, pp. 201–2; F. Hahn, op. cit., p. 79 and n. 93.

43. N. Avigad – Y. Yadin, *A Genesis Apocryphon* (Magnes Press, Jerusalem, 1956); J. A. Fitzmyer, *The Genesis Apocryphon of Qumran*

Cave I (Pontifical Biblical Institute, Rome, 1965, ²1971). See *Scripture and Tradition*, pp. 98–126; *DSSE*, pp. 215–24.

44. *Gen. Ap.* 2: 4; 7: 7; 12: 17; 22: 16, 21. – 21: 2–3.

45. *Gen. Ap.* 20: 12–13.   46. *Gen. Ap.* 20: 15–16.

47. *Gen. Ap.* 20: 14, 15. – 22: 32. – 20: 12.

48. *Gen. R.* 13: 2.

49. See also A. Hurwitz, 'Adon Hakkol', *Tarbiz* 34 (1965), pp. 224–7.

50. *Ecclus.* 10: 7.

51. *Wisd.* 1: 1, 7, 9; 2: 13; 3: 8, 10, 14 (twice); 4: 13, 17, 18; 5: 7, 15, 16; 6: 3; 8: 20; 9: 1, 13, 18; 10: 16, 20; 11: 13; 12: 2; 16: 12, 26; 19: 9, 22. – It would be a reckless man who asserted that in these twenty-seven examples the Greek author never meant simply 'Lord' when writing 'Lord', but always intended the word to replace YHWH.

52. M. Schwabe – B. Lifshitz, *Beth She'arim* II, *The Greek Inscriptions* (Mosad Bialik, Jerusalem, 1967), no. 184, p. 54; cf. N. Avigad, *IEJ* 15 (1955), p. 234.

53. The Jewish linguistic custom appears also to have influenced the speech of Palestinian Greeks. It is known that the pagan deity *Marna(s)* ('Our Lord') was worshipped until AD 401 in the temple called *Marneion* at Gaza. Cf. S. A. Cook, *The Religion of Ancient Palestine in the Light of Archaeology* (Oxford University Press, London, 1930), pp. 180–6.

54. *Gen. Ap.* 2: 9, 13, 24; 20: 25; 22: 18.

55. *Gen. R.* 75: 5. According to Philo (*In Flaccum* 36–9), an Alexandrian idiot by the name of Carabas, clothed with royal insignia, was hailed *Marin*, the name for 'lord' among the Syrians. Cf. G. Dalman, *Grammatik des jüdisch-palästinischen Aramäisch*, p. 152, n. 3.

56. Op. cit. II, no. 130, p. 54; cf. B. Lifshitz, *RB* 68 (1961), pp. 117–18.

57. *bKid.* 31b.

58. Op. cit. II, no. 204, p. 91; cf. B. Lifshitz, *RB* 67 (1960), p. 61. A second-century AD Greek funereal inscription from Ephesus commemorates the name of a *Mar* Moussios, son of Jairus. Cf. J.-B. Frey, *Corpus Inscriptionum Iudaicarum* II (Pontificio Istituto di Archeologia Cristiana, Rome, 1952), no. 746, pp. 13–14.

59. See *bErub.* 53b; cf. *Gen. R.* 89: 5.

60. Cf. *bHul.* 139b.

61. *Die Worte Jesu*, pp. 267–8, 270–1; E.T., pp. 327, 331.

62. See F. Hahn, op. cit., pp. 74, 78–9.

63. Cf. W. Foerster, *Lord*, p. 107.

64. Cf. *bKet.* 23a. – The Babylonian exilarchs, or civil heads of the Jewish community, also bore the same title (Mar Ukba, Mar Ukban, Mar Kahana, Mar Zutra).

65. E.g. Rabbi Gamaliel, Rabbi Anianus, Ribbi [*sic*] Yose; see *Beth She'arim* II, no. 174, p. 72 (cf. *IEJ* 4 (1954), p. 104); no. 175, p. 72 (cf. *IEJ* 5 (1955), pp. 221–2); no. 41, p. 13 (cf. *Corpus Inscriptionum*

Iudaicarum II, no. 1052). *Rib* appears twice without a pronominal suffix: *Beth She'arim* II, nos. 45, 202, pp. 14, 90.

66. On *Maranatha*, see J. A. Emerton, 'Maranatha and Ephphatha', *JTS* 18 (1967), p. 427.

67. Op. cit., pp. 108–9.

68. Cf. *yBer.* 9c; *yPea* 21b; *yShek.* 49b.

69. *ySanh.* 23d.

70. *Gen. R.* 94: 9. Note by contrast the similar story of a teacher who decides to take a three-day holiday and fails to go to school. Unlike Elijah, he receives a straight question: 'Why did *you* stay away?' Cf. *bKet.* 111b.

71. *bSanh.* 98a. The stylistic similarity between this question (*le'emath athe mar*) and the New Testament's *maranatha*, as well as the eschatological colouring of both, are well worth noting.

72. *bBer.* 27b.   73. *bBer.* 28b.

74. *bBK* 60b.   75. *bBer.* 27b.

76. Cf. above, p. 116.   77. See above, p. 72.

78. In his humility, the miracle-worker wished to remain inconspicuous, and everything is described in such a way that if, despite the precautions taken, the rain was still attributed to their prayers, it should look as though it had really been produced by his wife, and not by Abba Hilkiah.

79. *bTaan.* 23ab.

80. There are variations in the number of examples in the manuscripts. The context indicates that the pronoun 'our' in 'our teachers' is redundant throughout.

81. *1 Kgs.* 18: 13 (*RSV*).   82. *2 Kgs.* 8: 12 (*RSV*).

83. For a valuable brief textual survey, see G. D. Kilpatrick, '*Kurios* in the Gospels', *L'évangile hier et aujourd'hui* (F. Leenhardt Jubilee Volume) (Delachaux et Niestlé, Neuchâtel, 1968), pp. 65–70.

84. *Mark* 7: 28 (*RSV*); cf. *Matt.* 15: 21–8.

85. (*RSV*). Cf. *Matt.* 8: 2; *Luke* 5: 12.

86. (*RSV*). Cf. *Matt.* 17: 15.   87. *Mark* 11: 3 (*RSV*).

88. P. Vielhauer, *Aufsätze zum Neuen Testament*, p. 154, explains the use of the address, which he considers unhistorical, by Jesus' advance knowledge of the existence and whereabouts of the animal. In his view, it is *qua* Hellenistic divine man that Jesus is referred to here as 'lord'. It seems not to have occurred to him that the same title is appropriately applied to a Jewish charismatic or prophet.

89. *Mark* 7: 28; *Matt.* 8: 6–8; *Luke* 7: 6.

90. On the paucity of the examples in *Mark*, see the excursus on pp. 127–8.

91. *Matt.* 8: 2; *Mark* 1: 40; *Luke* 5: 12. – *Matt.* 15: 22–7; *Mark* 7: 28. – *Matt.* 17: 15; *Mark* 9: 22. – *Matt.* 20: 30–3; *Mark* 10: 51; *Luke* 18: 41.

92. *Matt.* 8: 6–8; *Luke* 7: 6; cf. *John* 4: 49. – *Matt.* 9: 28, possibly a duplicate for *Matt.* 20: 29–34.

93. *Matt.* 8: 25 (*RSV*); *Luke* 8: 24. 94. *Matt.* 14: 28.

95. *Matt.* 14: 30. 96. *Matt.* 8: 21.

97. *Matt.* 13: 51 var. 98. *Matt.* 18: 21 (*RSV*).

99. *Matt.* 26: 22 (*RSV*). 100. *Matt.* 17: 4.

101. *Matt.* 16: 22. 102. *Matt.* 7: 21–2.

103. *Luke* 5: 12; *Mark* 1: 40; *Matt.* 8: 2. – *Luke* 18: 41; *Mark* 10: 51; *Matt.* 20: 33. – *Luke* 7: 6; *Matt.* 8: 8.

104. *Luke* 5: 8. 105. *Luke* 9: 54.

106. *Luke* 10: 17.

107. *Luke* 6: 46; 9: 57 var., 59, 61; 10: 40; 11: 1; 12: 41; 13: 23; 17: 37; 19: 8; 22: 33, 38, 49. – It is of interest to note that the reference in *Matthew* 7: 22 to prophecy, exorcism and healing is completely eliminated from the parallel in *Luke* 6: 46: 'Why do you keep calling me "lord, lord" – and never do what I tell you?'

108. *Luke* 23: 42 (*RSV*). Most manuscripts read 'Jesus', instead of 'lord'.

109. Cf. G. D. Kilpatrick, '*Kurios* in the Gospels', pp. 66–8.

110. *Luke* 1: 43; 2: 11. – *Luke* 24: 3, 34.

111. *Luke* 7: 13, 19.

112. *Luke* 10: 1; 13: 15; 17: 5, 6; 22: 61 (twice).

113. *Luke* 10: 39, 41; 11: 39; 12: 42; 18: 6; 19: 8.

114. *John* 4: 49; *Matt.* 8: 8; *Luke* 7: 6.

115. *John* 4: 11; 5: 7, etc. – *John* 6: 68; 13–14.

116. *John* 11: 27 (*RSV*). 117. *John* 20: 28.

118. C. E. B. Cranfield, *The Gospel according to St Mark*, p. 15.

119. Ibid., p. 91 (italics mine).

120. A comparison of the Hebrew account of the call of Samuel with its Greek re-edition by Josephus demonstrates this kind of stylistic difference more extensively.

1 Samuel 3: 3–5	*Ant. 5, 348*
Samuel slept in the Temple of the Lord where the Ark of God was. Before the lamp of God had gone out, the Lord called him, and Samuel answered, 'Here am I', and ran to Eli saying, 'You called me; here am I.'	One night as he slept God called him by name; but he, supposing that he had been summoned by the high priest, went off to him.

Chapter 6: Jesus the Messiah

1. Cf. *Acts* 11: 26. 2. *Acts* 26: 28.

3. According to the *Concise Oxford English Dictionary*: 'Christ=

Messiah or Lord's anointed of Jewish prophecy; (*title, now treated as name given to*) *Jesus as fulfilling this*' (my italics).

4. G. Sevenster, *De Christologie van het Nieuwe Testament* (Amsterdam, ²1948), p. 76.

5. M. de Jonge, 'The Use of the Word "Anointed" in the Time of Jesus', *NT* 8 (1966), p. 141.

6. 'The prayers of Israel were originally folk creations' – J. Heinemann, *Prayer in the Period of the Tanna'im and Amora'im* (Magnes Press, Jerusalem, 1964), p. 29 (Hebrew); cf. p. II (English).

7. Cf. R. H. Charles, *Apocrypha and Pseudepigrapha* II (Oxford University Press, London, 1913), pp. 629–30; O. Eissfeldt, *The Old Testament – An Introduction* (Blackwell, Oxford, 1965, and Harper & Row, New York), pp. 610–13, 773–4; A.-M. Denis, *Introduction aux pseudépigraphes grecs d'Ancien Testament*, pp. 60–4. The numbering of the verses varies according to the editions. Both current systems will be indicated in the references.

8. *Ps. Sol.* 17: 23–36 (21–32).

9. M. de Jonge, 'The Use of the Word "Anointed" in the Time of Jesus', p. 136.

10. Cf. I. Elbogen, *Der jüdische Gottesdienst in seiner geschichtlichen Entwicklung* (Frankfurt am Main, ³1931; repr. G. Olm, Hildesheim, 1967), pp. 27–41; D. Hedegard, *Seder R. Amram Gaon* I (Linstedt, Lund, 1951), pp. 70–3.

11. For the text see I. Elbogen, op. cit., p. 518.

12. For the text see D. Hedegard, op. cit., p. 37 (Hebrew).

13. D. Barthélemy – J. T. Milik, *Discoveries in the Judaean Desert* I (Clarendon Press, Oxford, 1955), pp. 127–8; *DSSE*, pp. 208–9.

14. Cf. J. M. Allegro, *JBL* 75 (1956), pp. 174–6; *DSSE*, p. 224; *Scripture and Tradition*, p. 53.

15. J. M. Allegro, *Discoveries in the Judaean Desert* V, p. 161; *DSSE*, p. 227. – If the Aramaic text published by J. Starcky is Messianic at all, it also belongs to the royal category. See 'Un texte messianique araméen de la grotte 4 de Qumrân', *Ecole des langues orientales anciennes de l'Institut Catholique de Paris – Mémorial du cinquantenaire 1914–1964* (Bloud et Gay, Paris, 1964), pp. 51–66; cf. J. A. Fitzmyer, *Essays on the Semitic Background of the New Testament* (Chapman, London, 1971), pp. 127–60.

16. *yTaan.* 68d. Cf. *Scripture and Tradition*, pp. 165–6.

17. Cf. E. R. Goodenough, *By Light, Light* (Yale University Press, New Haven, 1935), pp. 81–2; *Introduction to Philo Judaeus* (Blackwell, Oxford, ²1962, and Barnes & Noble, New York), p. 46.

18. *De praemiis* 95. See *Scripture and Tradition*, p. 159.

19. M. de Jonge, 'The Use of the Word "Anointed" in the Time of Jesus', p. 147.

20. There is no evidence to indicate the existence of any developed form of Messianism in Hellenistic Jewish writings. Josephus carefully

avoids the term, although he ascribes royal aspirations to various Zealot chiefs. In his entire work, the term 'Christ' occurs only in relation to Jesus and his brother, James (*Ant.* 18, 64; 20, 200). He was doubtless reluctant to associate his principal villains, even remotely, with a concept which might have enhanced their standing. The title does not appear in Philo either, despite his occasional allusion to a Redeemer figure (cf. above, p. 134). In fact, if Philo had been pressed, he would probably have conceded that in his opinion the Messiah would come only second to Moses, 'the greatest and most perfect of men' (*De vita Mosis* I, 1). Yet on the popular level the ferment must have existed in North Africa also, as is apparent from the arrogation to himself of the royal title by Andrew, known as Lucuas, who led the Jewish revolt in Cyrene in AD 115–17. Cf. Schürer-Vermes-Millar, *History* I, p. 531.

21. Among recent monographs on the subject, the following may be singled out: S. Mowinckel, *He that Cometh* (Blackwell, Oxford, 1956, and Abingdon Press, Nashville); J. Klausner, *The Messianic Idea in Israel* (Allen & Unwin, London, 1956); A. S. van der Woude, *Die messianischen Vorstellungen der Gemeinde von Qumran* (Vangorcum, Assen, 1962).

22. *1 Macc.* 14: 4–15.   23. *1 Macc.* 14: 10–15 (*RSV*).

24. For the various opinions, see A.-M. Denis, *Introduction aux pseudépigraphes grecs d'Ancien Testament*, p. 58. The best edition of the Greek text is by M. de Jonge, *Testamenta XII Patriarcharum* (Brill, Leiden, 1964).

25. *Test. of Levi* 18: 2–7.

26. *1Q Ser.* 9: 11; *DSSE*, p. 87. – *CDC* 6: 7; 7: 18; *DSSE*, pp. 102, 104. – *4Q Flor.* 1: 11; *DSSE*, p. 247. – *1Q Ser^a* 2: 11–14, 19–20; *DSSE*, p. 121. – *1Q Ser^b* 3: 1–21; 5: 20–9; *DSSE*, pp. 207–9; cf. *CDC* 7: 20; *DSSE*, p. 104.

27. See the above quoted passages, and *DSSE*, p. 49.

28. *CDC* 12: 23–13: 1; 14: 19; MS.B 2: 1; *DSSE*, pp. 106, 115, 117.

29. *1Q Ser.* 9: 11; *DSSE*, p. 87.

30. *4Q Test.* 5–20 (*DJD* V, p. 58); *DSSE*, pp. 247–8. For further evidence concerning the prophetico-Messianic function of *Geber* (Man) and his possible identification, at a later moment of the sect's history, with the Teacher of Righteousness, see *DSSE*, pp. 49–50; *Scripture and Tradition*, pp. 55–66.

31. The only possible Qumran example in which the word 'Messiah' and the prophetic office seem to be connected is a fragment dealing with the heavenly being, Melchizedek. Cf. M. de Jonge – A. S. van der Woude, '11Q Melchizedek and the New Testament', *NTS* 12 (1966), pp. 301–8; J. T. Milik, '*Milkî-ṣedeq* et *Milkî-reša*' dans les anciens écrits juifs et chrétiens', *JJS* 23 (1972), pp. 95–144.

32. Cf. *bSanh.* 98a, quoted above, p. 116. See also *Exod. R.* 1: 31: 'As Moses, who was to chastise Pharaoh, was reared by Pharaoh's

daughter, so the King Messiah, who is to chastise Edom (=Rome), dwells among them in the capital.' – It is from Rome that he is to come on the final Passover night: cf. *Palestinian Targums on Exod.* 12: 42; *Scripture and Tradition*, p. 217; *DSSE*, p. 51.

33. *yBer.* 5a.   34. *Dialogue with Trypho* 8.

35. *bPes.* 54a; cf. *Targ. Mic.* 5: 1; *Zech.* 4: 7.

36. See on the subject P. Volz, *Eschatologie der jüdischen Gemeinde im neutestamentlichen Zeitalter* (J. C. B. Mohr, Tübingen, ²1934), p. 206. Cf. E. Sjöberg, *Der verborgene Menschensohn in den Evangelien* (Gleerup, Lund, 1955), p. 59.

37. Cf. *2 Bar.* 40: 1; 72: 2–6; *4 Ezra* 12: 32. See also *Rev.* 5: 5.

38. *4 Ezra* 7: 29.

39. Rabbi Dosa probably dates to mid-second century AD. 'The rabbis' represent the common opinion.

40. *bSuk.* 52a.   41. Ibid.

42. A discrepant note is heard in the *Ps.-Jonathan Targum on Exod.* 40: 11, where no idea of defeat is linked to the Ephraimite Messiah: 'The Messiah son of Ephraim, who will descend from him (Joshua), it is by his hand that the house of Israel will vanquish Gog and his horde at the end of days.'

43. The conflict between Akiba, who hailed Simeon as the Messiah, and Yohanan ben Torta, who predicted that the son of David would come a long time after Akiba's death, may imply that Yohanan would have accepted Simeon as the Ephraimite, but not as the Davidic, Messiah. See above, p. 134.

44. Jesus echoes Jewish tradition in recognizing David as the actual author of the Psalm; without this, the whole argument would be meaningless.

45. *Mark* 11: 28–33; *Matt.* 21: 23–7; *Luke* 20: 1–8.

46. *Mark* 13: 6, completed by *Matt.* 24: 5; cf. *Mark* 13: 21–2; *Matt.* 24: 23–4; *Luke* 17: 23; 21: 8.

47. Cf. above, p. 98.

48. The words of warning are endowed with significance only if the speech presupposes a belief in the reappearance of the Messiah; but, as will be argued in the next chapter, such a conception can hardly be traced back to Jesus.

49. *Luke* 24: 26, 46; cf. *Acts* 17: 3; 26: 23.

50. (*AT*). Cf. E. Klostermann, *Das Markusevangelium* (J. C. B. Mohr, Tübingen, ⁴1950), p. 95; C. E. B. Cranfield, *The Gospel according to St Mark*, pp. 312–13; D. E. Nineham, *The Gospel of Mark*, p. 258, etc.

51. *Mark* 14: 65; *Matt.* 26: 67–8.

52. *Mark* 14: 65; *Luke* 22: 63.

53. *Matt.* 26: 68 (*RSV*); *Mark* 14: 65.

54. The words attributed to the high priest, 'Are you the Messiah, the son of the Blessed One?' possess a religious rather than political

emphasis; they constitute, in addition, a question, not a statement. See below, pp. 147–8.

55. *Luke* 23: 2.

56. *Mark* 15: 9. – *Mark* 15: 12. – *Matt.* 27: 17, 22.

57. *Mark* 15: 26; *Matt.* 27: 37; *Luke* 23: 38.

58. *Mark* 15: 18; *Matt.* 27: 29; *Luke* 23: 37. – *Matt.* 27: 42. – *Mark* 15: 32. – *Luke* 23: 39.

59. Cf. above, pp. 50–1. See *Luke* 23: 5.

60. *Luke* 4: 41.

61. Cf. *Matt.* 1: 16, 17; 2: 4; *Luke* 2: 11, 26. – *Matt.* 11: 2. – Cf. *Mark* 1: 1; *Matt.* 1: 1; see also *Matt.* 1: 18.

62. The phrase 'Jesus Christ' is very rare in the Synoptics.

63. *Mark* 10: 37; *Matt.* 20: 21.   64. *Acts* 1: 6 (*RSV*).

65. *Mark* 8: 29; *Matt.* 16: 16; *Luke* 9: 20.

66. Cf. *Jesus and the Gospel Tradition* (S.P.C.K., London, 1967, and Fortress Press, Philadelphia), p. 23.

67. *Matt.* 21: 7. Although 'on them' can refer to the cloaks placed on the she-ass and her colt, it can equally relate to the two mounts. The rendering of the verse in the New English Bible, 'they laid their cloaks on them and Jesus mounted', is described as 'a translation which smooths out the awkwardness' (A. E. Harvey, *Companion to the New Testament* (Oxford and Cambridge University Presses, 1970), p. 82). Some ancient manuscripts show the same tendency when they substitute 'on it' for 'on them'.

68. Cf. above, pp. 22–4.   69. Cf., e.g., *Mark* 1: 21–5.

70. *Luke* 4: 41.   71. Cf. above, p. 145.

72. *Mark* 8: 30.   73. *Matt.* 16: 20.

74. *Luke* 9: 21.   75. *Mark* 8: 33; cf. *Matt.* 16: 22–3.

76. C. K. Barrett, *Jesus and the Gospel Tradition*, p. 23.

77. Cf. G. Dalman, *Die Worte Jesu*, p. 253.

78. Cf. F. Blass – A. Debrunner, *Grammatik des neutestamentlichen Griechisch* (Vandenhoeck & Ruprecht, Göttingen, ⁹1954), §441, 3, p. 274. The Aramaic phrase, 'you have said it', is neither entirely unconnected, nor fully relevant. It is part of a cleverly manipulated conversation in which the speaker induces the other party to put into words something unpleasant which he himself prefers not to formulate; but when the question is asked by the others, he simply retorts: 'You have said it' (cf. *yKil.* 32b). The only Gospel example clearly pointing to such linguistic usage is Jesus' 'It is as you say', in reply to the question of Judas, 'Rabbi, can you mean me (to be the one to betray you)?' (*Matt.* 26: 25) See O. Cullmann, *The Christology of the New Testament*, p. 118.

79. *tKel.* I, 1: 6.   80. *Die Worte Jesu*, p. 254.

81. Cf. I. Abrahams, *Studies in Pharisaism and the Gospels* II, pp. 1–3.

82. The rabbinic formula, 'You say' or 'You have said', introducing an exegetical argument, might be seen as the best parallel. It does not

imply that the speaker agrees or disagrees with the interpretation cited. 'You say' is equal here to 'This is what you infer'. Cf. W. Bacher, *Die exegetische Terminologie der jüdischen Traditionsliteratur* (Georg Olm, Hildesheim, repr. 1965), I, p. 6.

83. *Luke* 22: 68.
84. *Mark* 15: 2; *Matt.* 27: 11. *Luke* 23: 3; cf. *John* 18: 33–7.
85. *Luke* 23: 4.
86. *Acts* 3: 20; 5: 42; 24: 24. – *Acts* 8: 12, 37 var.; 9: 34; 10: 36.
87. *Acts* 2: 36.
88. See my paper, 'The Qumran Interpretation of Scripture in its Historical Setting', *Dead Sea Scroll Studies 1969, Ann. of Leeds Univ. Or. Soc.* VI (Brill, Leiden, 1969), pp. 90–5.
89. *Acts* 4: 26–30.
90. *Acts* 8: 5; 9: 22; 18: 5, 28.
91. *Acts* 3: 17–18.
92. Cf. *Acts* 17: 3; 26: 23.
93. *Acts* 17: 3; 26: 22.
94. *Acts* 2: 29–31.
95. *Acts* 2: 34–5; 3: 21.
96. *Acts* 17: 6–7.
97. *John* 20: 31.
98. *John* 1: 41.
99. *John* 1: 49; 6: 15; 7: 25–31, 40–4; 9: 22.
100. *John* 17: 3.
101. *John* 4: 25.
102. 'There is no doubt that for the Synoptic tradition the life and work of Jesus had nothing Messianic according to the customary Messianic idea; neither did Paul and others understand it as Messianic' – *Theologie des Neuen Testaments*, p. 28.
103. 'Even if Jesus did not himself intend to raise the issue of messiahship, it will almost certainly have been raised by others as a result of his actions' – C. K. Barrett, *Jesus and the Gospel Tradition*, pp. 23–4.
104. Cf. *Luke* 1: 5, 36. See J. T. Milik, *Ten Years of Discovery in the Wilderness of Judaea* (SCM Press, London, 1959, and Allenson, Naperville, Ill.), p. 128.
105. Cf. above, pp. 138–9. Note, however, that all the sources relating to this Messianic concept are posterior in their redaction to AD 70 and probably reflect a change in Jewish Messianic speculation following the collapse of the First War. But these ideas may throw light on several later stages of Gospel tradition regarding such issues as Messianic secrecy in the Synoptics, and the combination of such pre-existent entities as the name of the Messiah and the *Shekhinah* (divine Presence) in the Word-Logos become flesh of the Johannine Prologue.
106. Cf. above, pp. 139–40.
107. This recalls a friend renowned for his understanding of the Old Testament although his knowledge of Hebrew was next to nothing. Yet each time he confessed this, people only smiled and no one believed him. The more he protested, the greater grew his reputation as a Hebrew scholar!
108. F. Hahn, *The Titles of Jesus in Christology*, p. 169.

109. *Acts* 7: 51–3.
110. *1 Thess.* 2: 14–16. – In *Rom.* 9–11, Paul is more moderate and poetic.
111. *John* 8: 44.
112. *Mark* 10: 48. See *Mark* 10: 47–8; *Luke* 18: 38–9; *Matt.* 20: 30–1; cf. 9: 27.
113. Cf. *Mark* 10: 51; *Matt.* 20: 33; *Luke* 18: 41; cf. *Matt.* 9: 28.
114. *Mark* 11: 9; *Luke* 19: 38; cf. *John* 12: 13.
115. Cf. K. Stendahl, *The School of St Matthew* (Gleerup, Lund, 1954), p. 66.
116. Cf. J. Jeremias, *Jerusalem in the Time of Jesus* (SCM Press, London, 1969, and Fortress Press, Philadelphia), pp. 276–7.
117. Cf. *yKil.* 32b; *yTaan.* 68a; *bKet.* 62b; *bSanh.* 5a; *bHor.* 11b; Origen, *De principiis* 4: 3. In *yKil.* 32b the Patriarch Judah the Prince admits that paternally he is descended from Benjamin, his line from Judah being maternal only, whereas the exilarch's descent from Judah was traced on the male side.
118. See Eusebius, *Ecclesiastical History* III, 12, 19–20, 32. The information is borrowed from the second-century AD writer, Hegesippus.
119. *Siphre on Num.* 117 (ed. H. S. Horovitz, p. 135).

Chapter 7 : *Jesus the* son of man

1. The phrase will be printed without capitals in italics except in quotations from other authors.
2. *Neotestamentica et Semitica – Studies in Honour of Matthew Black*, ed. by E. E. Ellis and M. Wilcox (T. & T. Clark, Edinburgh, 1969), p. 87.
3. *The Titles of Jesus in Christology*, p. 15 (my italics).
4. For a discussion, see N. Perrin, *Rediscovering the Teaching of Jesus* (SCM Press, London, 1967, and Harper & Row, New York), pp. 176–81. Note also a similar attribution of Jesus' words to James the brother of the Lord according to Hegesippus, quoted by Eusebius in *Ecclesiastical History* II, 23.
5. *Skizzen und Vorarbeiten* VI (G. Reimer, Berlin, 1899), p. 197.
6. *John* 12: 34. Note that 'the Messiah' and 'the *son of man*' appear to be synonyms.
7. *John* 18: 32. Cf. W. A. Meeks, 'The Man from Heaven in Johannine Sectarianism', *JBL* 91 (1972), p. 62 and n. 62.
8. *1Q Ser.* 11: 20 offers the only exception known to me in the form of a variant reading introduced by a second copyist into the Community Rule. Cf. *DSSE*, p. 94.
9. For a fuller treatment, see my study, 'The use of *bar nash/bar nasha* in Jewish Aramaic', Appendix E in M. Black, *An Aramaic Approach*

to the Gospels and Acts, pp. 310–28. Cf. Excursus II, pp. 188–91 below.

10. For the nominal and indefinite pronominal use, see 'The use of *bar nash* . . .', pp. 315–19.

11. See in particular, A. Meyer, *Jesu Muttersprache* (J. C. B. Mohr, Freiburg i.B., 1896), pp. 92–7; J. Y. Campbell, 'The Origin and Meaning of the Term Son of Man', *JTS* 48 (1947), pp. 152–4; R. E. C. Formesyn, 'Was there a Pronominal Connection for the Bar Nasha Selfdesignation?' *NT* 8 (1966), pp. 1–35.

12. *Gen. R.* 48: 12. The speaker does not wish to draw attention to the fact that he has been favoured with a supernatural revelation.

13. *Gen. R.* 100: 5.   14. *yMSh.* 55c.

15. *yMK* 81d. – On the idiom, see G. Dalman, *Grammatik des jüdisch-palästinischen Aramäisch*, p. 108; H. Odeberg, *The Aramaic Portions of Bereshit Rabba* II (Gleerup, Lund, 1939), §5, p. 3.

16. E. Sjöberg, *Der verborgene Menschensohn in den Evangelien*, p. 239, n. 3.

17. 'The use of *bar nash* . . .', pp. 320–6.

18. *yBer.* 5c.

19. For a more thorough treatment of this objection, see Excursus II, p. 188 below.

20. *yKet.* 35a.   21. *yBer.* 3b; cf. *yShab.* 3a.

22. Cf. '*Ben adam* und *bar 'enash* im Hebräischen und Aramäischen', *Acta Orientalia* 21 (1950–1), p. 94, n. 66.

23. Cf. *yKid.* 66c.

24. In Aramaic: *kol bar nash* or *kol bar nash we-bar nash.*

25. See *yShab.* 3a: *haden bar nasha*. The *editio princeps* offers a slightly different reading: 'this, the *son of man*'.

26. See *ySheb.* 38d; *Gen. R.* 79: 6; *Eccles. R.* 10: 11. Cf. H. Odeberg, *The Aramaic Portions of Bereshit Rabba* I, pp. 92, 155–7.

27. *ySheb.* 38d.   28. *Gen. R.* 79: 6.

29. J. Theodor – C. Albeck (*Midrash Bereshit Rabba*, pp. 941–2) cite the following decisive reading: '*my* soul' (*naphshi*), instead of 'the soul of the *son of man*' (*nephesh de-bar nasha*). The source is an Oxford manuscript (MS. Opp. Add. 3, fol. 142 verso) which I have checked personally in the Bodleian Library.

30. A similar conclusion, though without fresh evidence and occasionally on dubious grounds, is reached independently by R. E. C. Formesyn, art. cit., *NT* 8 (1966). He postulates a phrase, 'that *son of man*' (*hahu bar nasha*), to explain the Greek phrase, and claims that it was both a pronominal substitute and a Messianic title. See, in particular, pp. 30, 34.

31. *Dan.* 7: 13–14 (*AT*).   32. Cf. *Dan.* 7: 15–27.

33. H. E. Tödt, *The Son of Man in the Synoptic Tradition* (SCM Press, London, 1965, and Westminster Press, Philadelphia), p. 23.

34. *bHag.* 14a; *bSanh.* 38b. Rabbi Yose the Galilean's criticism that

Akiba was 'profaning the Shekhinah' is patently a rhetorical exaggeration. To see there, as D. R. Catchpole does (*The Trial of
Jesus*, p. 141), a serious possibility of a real blasphemy (applying
also to *Mark* 14: 62) is unwarranted.

35. *bSanh.* 98a.

36. *Midrash Tanhuma*, ed. S. Buber (Romm, Wilna, 1885), I, p. 140.

37. Cf. R. Le Déaut – J. Robert, *Targum des Chroniques* (Biblical
Institute Press, Rome, 1971), I, p. 47; II, p. 18.

38. *Amos* 9: 11. The title, *bar niphle*, is linked to the Hebrew verb 'to
fall' (*naphal*).

39. This one-sidedness of the exegetical picture – confirmed, as will be
seen, by *1 Enoch* and *4 Ezra* – seems to have been overlooked by
those New Testament scholars who attempt to introduce an element
of suffering into the image of the *son of man*.

40. Quite apart from its late date, the *Targum of Psalm* 80: 16, 18, cannot
be adduced as evidence for the titular employment of *bar nash*
because the expression is accompanied by a specifying clause: 'the
son of man whom thou hast strengthened for thyself'. An anti-
Christian exegesis of *Numbers* 23: 19 by the early-fourth-century AD
Palestinian Rabbi Abbahu is occasionally quoted in this respect: 'If
a man says to you, "I am God", he lies; "I am a *son of man*", he will
regret it at the end; "I will go up to heaven", he says so but will not
fulfil it' (*yTaan.* 65b). Two points are to be observed. (1) There is
no connection whatever with *Daniel* 7: 13. (2) The contrast between
God and the *son of man* derives from *Numbers* and is interpreted
by Abbahu as expressing the difference between the divine and the
human. The mention of sorrow at the end alludes to death, untimely
and humiliating in this case. The rabbi from Caesarea seems to
attack the Patristic claim that *son of man* describes the humanity
of Jesus as opposed to the divinity expressed by *son of God*.

41. If the reader's faith in *son of man* as a title still remains unshaken,
he might care to explain why the *Targum of Ezekiel* never translates
the Hebrew *son of man* (*ben adam*), with which God addresses the
prophet, as *bar enash* or *bar nash*, but always as 'son of Adam'. Is
this not an external confirmation of the present argument, since it
shows *son of man* to be unacceptable even as a mode of address?

42. Cf. also N. Perrin, *Rediscovering the Teaching of Jesus*, p. 171. It
should also be noted that the Latin version of the work never
employs the phrase, '*filius hominus*'.

43. *1 Enoch* 60: 10 is not considered here. It is modelled on the *Ezekiel*
use and differs from the other examples.

44. *Son of man: 1 En.* 46: 2, 3, 4; 48: 2; 'son of the male': 62: 5; 69: 29
(twice); 71: 14; 'son of the child of the mother of all the living':
62: 7, 9, 14; 63: 11; 69: 26, 27; 70: 1; 71: 17.

45. R. H. Charles, *The Book of Enoch or 1 Enoch* (Oxford University
Press, London, 1912), p. 86.

46. E. Ullendorff, 'An Aramaic "Vorlage" of the Ethiopic Text of Enoch', *Atti del Convegno internazionale di Studi Etiopici*, Accademia Nazionale dei Lincei 357 (1960), p. 265.

47. R. H. Charles, *The Book of Enoch*, pp. 86–7.

48. 'On reexamining the question in conjunction with G. Vermes's . . . study . . . , it now appears to me that the Ethiopic evidence has little or nothing to contribute and that it remains essentially an Aramaic (Hebrew) issue' – E. Ullendorff, *Ethiopia and the Bible* (Oxford University Press, London, 1968), p. 61.

49. *1 En.* 46: 1–4.

50. *1 En.* 48: 2–3, 10. See pp. 138–9 above and p. 255, n. 105, below.

51. Some manuscripts read 'son of the woman'.

52. Cf. also *1 En.* 63: 11.   53. *1 En.* 69: 26–9.

54. *1 En.* 70: 1.   55. *1 En.* 71: 14.

56. Cf. G. Dalman, *Die Worte Jesu*, p. 200; W. Bousset, *Die Religion des Judentums im späthellenistischen Zeitalter* (J. C. B. Mohr, Tübingen, ⁴1966), p. 353; R. Otto, *Reich Gottes und Menschensohn* (C. H. Beck, Munich, ³1954), p. 161; E. T. *The Kingdom of God and the Son of Man* (Lutterworth, London, 1943), p. 208.

57. Without wishing to enter into controversy on the etymology of Metatron the celestial scribe (cf. G. Scholem, *Major Trends of Jewish Mysticism* (Thames & Hudson, London, 1955, and Schocken, New York), pp. 69–70), I should underline that the *Palestinian Targum* preserves a tradition that echoes the *Enoch* speculation. 'And Enoch served God in truth; and behold, he was no more with the inhabitants of the earth. For he was led away and raised up to the firmament by the Word of the Lord; and he called his name Metatron, the appointed (or: great) scribe' (*Ps.-Jonathan on Gen.* 5: 24).

58. Cf. *CBQ* 30 (1968), p. 428.   59. *1 En.* 46: 3; 71: 14.

60. This point was made already half a century ago by N. Messel, *Der Menschensohn in den Bildreden des Henoch* (Töpelmann, Giessen, 1922), p. 3.

61. *The Book of Enoch*, p. 73: 94–64 BC.

62. *Der Menschensohn im äthiopischen Henochbuch* (Gleerup, Lund, 1946), p. 39.

63. J. T. Milik, *Ten Years of Discovery in the Wilderness of Judaea*, p. 33.

64. 'Problèmes de la littérature Hénochique à la lumière des fragments araméens de Qumrân', *HTR* 64 (1971), pp. 373–8. His major study, *The Books of Enoch, Aramaic Fragments of Qumran Cave 4*, is to be published shortly by the Clarendon Press, Oxford.

65. Cf. above, pp. 137–9.

66. Cf. *ySanh.* 26b: 'Whoever says, Here are five (coins), give me something worth three, he is a fool. But he who says, Here are three (coins), give me something worth five, he is *bar nash*.' It is worth

noting that in modern Hebrew this Aramaic loan-word connotes contempt.

67. *Theologie des Neuen Testaments*, pp. 31–2; E. T. *Theology of the New Testament* I (SCM Press, London, 1952, and Scribner, New York), p. 30.

68. *An Outline of the Theology of the New Testament*, pp. 135–6. See also P. Vielhauer, *Aufsätze zum Neuen Testament*, pp. 55–91.

69. *Jesus and the Gospel Tradition*, p. 32.

70. The leading critic, among New Testament specialists, of these axioms is N. Perrin, *Rediscovering the Teaching of Jesus*, pp. 164–73. See lately R. Leivestad, 'Exit the Apocalyptic Son of Man', *NTS* 18 (1972), pp. 243–67.

71. Cf. *Mekh.*, ed. Lauterbach, III, p. 197. The speaker is Rabbi Simeon ben Menasiah.

72. Ibid., p. 198. See also pp. 39–40.

73. Cf. above, pp. 37–8.

74. The same meaning is to be attributed to *Matt.* 26: 22; *Luke* 22: 48; 24: 7.

75. The probably secondary resurrection idea is also hinted at in the sign of Jonah.

76. *Matt.* 8: 20=*Luke* 9: 58.

77. *Luke* 12: 10=*Matt.* 12: 32. – *Matt.* 11: 19=*Luke* 7: 34.

78. Cf. above, pp. 98–9.

79. For a good discussion, see N. Perrin, *Rediscovering the Teaching of Jesus*, pp. 173–81.

80. Cf. above, pp. 141–2.

81. For further discussion see N. Perrin, op. cit., pp. 173–81; *NTS* 12 (1965–6), pp. 150–5; H. E. Tödt, *The Son of Man in the Synoptic Tradition*, pp. 33–6.

82. N. Perrin, op. cit., p. 186.

83. *Matt.* 24: 27, 37, 44=*Luke* 17: 24, 26; 12: 40. – *Matt.* 24: 30= *Luke* 17: 22, 30.

84. *Matt.* 24: 27, 37, 39.

85. Cf. *Matt.* 16: 28 and *Mark* 9: 1; *Luke* 9: 27; *Matt.* 19: 28 and *Luke* 22: 30. See N. Perrin, op. cit., pp. 16–17.

86. E.g. the sower: *Matt.* 13: 37, 41; the sheep and the goats: *Matt.* 25: 31.

87. *Matt.* 10: 23. Cf. *Mark* 9: 1: 'There are some of those standing here who will not taste death before they have seen the kingdom of God already come in power.'

88. *Luke* 18: 8; cf. *Luke* 21: 36.

89. See N. Perrin, op. cit., pp. 175–6.

90. Only the Fourth Gospel envisages a journey from earth to heaven. Cf. *John* 6: 62; 3: 13–14. See also 1: 51. Note that the phrase, apart from these instances, figures only twice in an eschatological context (5: 27; 6: 27).

91. P. Winter, *Deutsche Literaturzeitung* 89 (1968), col. 784. For the latest comprehensive treatment of the subject, see C. Colpe, '*ho huios tou anthrōpou*', *TDNT* VIII (1972), pp. 400–77.

92. Cf. above, p. 170.   93. *bYoma* 4a.

94. *PR* 20: 4. The same image, suitably reshaped, forms the substance of Josephus's account of the final departure of Moses (*Ant.* 4, 326).

95. *Acts* 1: 9. Cf. *Rev.* 11: 12. For further examples, see G. H. Boobyer, *St Mark and the Transfiguration Story* (T. & T. Clark, Edinburgh, 1942), p. 83.

96. See *Ps.-Jonathan, Fragm. Targ.* and *Targ. Neofiti*.

97. Cf. above, pp. 138–9.

98. Cf. *Scripture and Tradition*, p. 217, n. 1.

99. *Acts* 1: 11.   100. *John* 3: 13.

101. *John* 6: 62.   102. Op. cit., p. 328, n. 1.

103. Ibid., pp. 328–30.   104. Op. cit., p. 23 and n. 4.

105. *ZNW* 58 (1967), p. 165, n. 9. See also *New Testament Theology* I (SCM Press, London, 1971, and Scribner, New York), p. 261, n. 1.

106. Cf. above, p. 165.   107. *Lam. R.* 1: 5, 31.

108. A misconception regarding the equivalence of 'I' and *son of man* underlies also R. Le Déaut's valuable review in *Biblica* 49 (1968), pp. 397–9.

109. *CBQ* 30 (1968), p. 427.

110. The illogicality of Fitzmyer's thesis has not escaped Morton Smith's critical acumen: see *JBL* 90 (1971), p. 247.

111. *CBQ* 30 (1968), pp. 420, 426–7.

112. J. T. Milik, *DJD* II, pp. 104ff.; *Gli scavi del 'Dominus Flevit'* I (Tipografia dei PP. Franciscani, Jerusalem, 1958), p. 92.

113. Not so the Qumran *Genesis Apocryphon* 22: 34: Eliezer!

114. M. Schwabe – B. Lifshitz, *Beth She'arim* II, no. 177, p. 73; no. 93, p. 34. There is one *Lazar* of undisclosed origin in Josephus (*BJ* 5, 567) but another twenty-two biblical and contemporary figures with the name spelt Eleazar. Cf. A. Shalit, *A Complete Concordance to Flavius Josephus*, Suppl. I (Brill, Leiden, 1968), p. 42.

115. See *The Founder of Christianity*, pp. 110–13, 178, n. 25. Cf. also T. A. Burkill, *New Light on the Earliest Gospel* (Cornell University Press, Ithaca and London, 1972), p. 36, n. 27.

Chapter 8: Jesus the son of God

1. Cf. above, pp. 146–8; for Jesus' supposed answer to the high priest, see pp. 147–9.

2. V. Taylor, *The Names of Jesus*, p. 65.

3. *Mark* 13: 32; *Matt.* 11: 27; *Luke* 10: 22.

4. '*Der Sohn*' *in den synoptischen Jesusworten* (Brill, Leiden, 1961), p. 183.

5. *Jesus and the Gospel Tradition*, pp. 25–7.

6. *An Outline of the Theology of the New Testament*, pp. 128–9.

7. *Theologie des Neuen Testaments*, p. 53. Cf., however, the objections raised by G. Dalman, *Die Worte Jesu*, p. 223.

8. *The Titles of Jesus in Christology*, pp. 284–307.

9. For the latest full discussion, see *TDNT* VIII (1972), pp. 340–62.

10. *Gen.* 6: 2, 4; *Deut.* 32: 8; *Ps.* 29: 1; 89: 7; *Dan.* 3: 25.

11. *Exod.* 4: 22; *Jer.* 31: 20; *Hos.* 11: 1; *Deut.* 32: 5–6, 18–19.

12. *2 Sam.* 7: 14.   13. *Ps.* 2: 7 (*RSV*).

14. *Ps.* 89: 26–7.

15. *Ecclus.* 4: 10 (*AT*) (Hebrew). The Greek version (*RSV*) reads: 'You will then be like a *son of the Most High*, and he will love you more than does your mother.'

16. *Wisd.* 2: 17–18.

17. *Jub.* 1: 24–5.

18. *Ps. Sol.* 17: 26–7 (28–9); cf. also 13: 8 (9); 18: 4.

19. *1Q Ser.* 11: 8; *1Q Hod.* 3: 22, etc. Cf. *DSSE*, pp. 93, 158.

20. *1Q Milh.* 17: 8; *1Q Hod.* 6: 29–30; 7: 29–30; 9: 35, etc. Cf. *DSSE*, pp. 146, 171, 175, 182.

21. *1Q Hod.* 4: 32–3; 11: 9; cf. *DSSE*, pp. 164, 186.

22. *De specialibus legibus* 1, 318. Cf. also F. H. Colson, *Philo* (Loeb) VII (Heinemann, London, 1958), p. 622, on the Stoic terminology involved. Here Philo foreshadows the rabbinic view that the good man who imitates Abraham is like one who has 'registered God as his father and become by adoption his only son' (*De sobrietate* 56).

23. *mAb.* 3: 14.   24. *yKid.* 61c.

25. Philo may be cited again in this connection: 'If there is any as yet unfit to be called son of God, let him press to take his place under God's firstborn, the Word (*Logos*), the elder among the angels, an archangel as it were' (*De confusione linguarum* 146). This Alexandrian speculation on the sonship *par excellence* of the Word cannot, however, be considered customary, or even as having left any noticeable imprint on ordinary Judaism.

26. *Die Worte Jesu*, p. 223. It might be pointed out that the quotation of *Psalm* 2 to illustrate Pharaoh's ill-treatment of Israel, God's firstborn son in *Mekhilta* (ed. Lauterbach, II, pp. 57–8), discloses a collectivizing tendency in the exegesis of *son of God*.

27. *4 Ezra* 7: 28; 13: 22, 37, 52; 14: 9.

28. *TDNT* VIII, p. 361.

29. J. M. Allegro, *DJD* V, pp. 53–4; cf. *DSSE*, pp. 246–7.

30. *1Q Ser*ᵃ 2: 11–12; cf. D. Barthélemy – J. T. Milik, *DJD* I, pp. 110, 117–18; *DSSE*, pp. 246–7.

31. Y. Yadin renders the section as follows: 'The session of the notables called to the stated meeting of the council of the community, on the occasion of their meeting (YW'DW).' Cf. 'A Crucial Passage in the Dead Sea Scrolls', *JBL* 78 (1959), pp. 240–1. I myself have taken it

to be a sectional heading: '[This shall be the ass]embly of the men of renown [called] to the meeting of the Council of the Community when [the Priest-] Messiah shall summon (YW'YD) them.' Cf. *DSSE*, pp. 246–7.

32. Cf. J. A. Fitzmyer, *Essays on the Semitic Background of the New Testament*, p. 121, n. 10.

33. Cf. W. von Martitz, *TDNT* VIII, pp. 336–40.

34. Cf. Philostratus, *Life of Apollonius* 1: 6; 4: 31; 5: 24, etc.

35. E. Schweizer, *TDNT* VIII, pp. 372–3; C. K. Barrett, *Jesus and the Gospel Tradition*, p. 24; F. Hahn, *The Titles of Jesus in Christology*, p. 316.

36. Cf. above, pp. 183–4.   37. *The Names of Jesus*, pp. 64–5.

38. *Jesus and the Gospel Tradition*, pp. 25–6. Both Hahn, op. cit., p. 313, and Schweizer, op. cit., p. 372, ascribe the verse not to Jesus, but to Palestinian Judeo-Christianity.

39. Cf. C. K. Barrett, op. cit., p. 27.

40. Cf. below, pp. 210–11.   41. *Matt.* 16: 16.

42. *Mark* 14: 61; *Matt.* 26: 63.

43. (*RSV*). Cf. above, p. 197. See also *Acts* 13: 33.

44. An autonomous occurrence of the *son of God* title cannot be argued from the account of Paul's activity in Damascus – 'And in the synagogues immediately he proclaimed Jesus, saying "He is the son of God" ' (*Acts* 9: 20 (*RSV*)) – because two verses later Saul is described as proving to the Jews that 'Jesus was the Christ' (*Acts* 9: 22 (*RSV*)).

45. Cf. above, pp. 145–9.   46. *Luke* 1: 31–2 (*RSV*).

47. *Luke* 1: 35 (*RSV*).   48. *Rom.* 1: 4.

49. Cf. the excursus at the end of the chapter.

50. There are altogether twenty-two texts representing ten distinct statements.

51. *Mark* 3: 11.   52. *Luke* 4: 41.

53. *Mark* 5: 7; cf. *Luke* 8: 28.   54. *Matt.* 8: 29.

55. *Matt.* 4: 3; *Luke* 4: 3.   56. *Matt.* 4: 5–6; *Luke* 4: 9.

57. *Matt.* 14: 33.   58. *Mark* 15: 39; *Matt.* 27: 54.

59. Cf., e.g., R. Bultmann, *History of the Synoptic Tradition*, p. 282.

60. *Luke* 23: 47 (*RSV*).   61. Cf. above, p. 71.

62. *Matt.* 27: 40 (*RSV*).   63. *Matt.* 27: 42–3 (*RSV*).

64. It was commonly held among Jews of the inter-Testamental and early rabbinic period that a disincarnate vocal communication of this kind (*bath kol*) had taken the place of prophecy and that one of its purposes was to testify to the righteousness of God's elect. Cf. above, p. 92. In addition to the examples quoted, see *Test. of Levi* 18: 6–7 (despite its ultimate Christian formulation): 'The heavens shall be opened, and sanctification shall come upon him from the Temple of glory with a father's voice as from Abraham to Isaac. And the glory of the Most High shall be proclaimed over him,

and the spirit of understanding and sanctification shall rest on him in the water.'

65. *Matt.* 3: 17 (*RSV*).   66. *Mark* 1: 11 (*RSV*); *Luke* 3: 22.
67. *Mark* 9: 7; *Matt.* 17: 5; *Luke* 9: 35.
68. The saying consists of a composite Bible quotation from *Gen.* 22: 2 and *Isa.* 42: 1. Cf. *Scripture and Tradition*, pp. 222–3.
69. Cf. F. Hahn, *The Titles of Jesus in Christology*, pp. 288–98.
70. *Theologie des Neuen Testaments*, pp. 132–3.
71. V. Taylor, *The Names of Jesus*, pp. 59–60; O. Cullmann, *The Christology of the New Testament*, p. 272, etc.
72. *TDNT* VIII, p. 377. For the most recent discussion, see M. Smith, *JBL* 90 (1971), pp. 174–99.
73. Cf. above, p. 92.
74. The fact that these traditions belong to a period later than that of Jesus does not disqualify them from being used as terms of comparison. For a historical evaluation, see my paper in *JJS* 24 (1973), pp. 51–64.
75. *bTaan.* 24b; *bBer.* 17b; *bHul.* 86a.
76. *bHag.* 15b.   77. *bHag.* 16a.
78. Literally 'transgressors of transgression', an expression often denoting unlawful sex.
79. *bKid.* 81a.   80. Ibid.
81. Cf. above, p. 76.   82. *bBer.* 43b.
83. Cf. above, p. 70.   84. *mTaan.* 3: 8.
85. Cf. A. Büchler, *Types of Jewish–Palestinian Piety*, p. 203.
86. In singling out two words from *Proverbs* 23: 23 and neglecting the rest, rabbinic tradition sees in Honi's story the fulfilment of a quasi-biblical prophecy: 'Scripture refers to you when it says, Your father and mother rejoice, and she that bore you is glad' (*yTaan.* 67a).
87. See most recently F. Hahn, *The Titles of Jesus in Christology*, pp. 307–17.
88. *Mark* 14: 36. Cf. *Matt.* 26: 39; *Luke* 22: 42.
89. *Gal.* 4: 6.   90. *Rom.* 8: 15.
91. F. Hahn, op. cit., p. 307.
92. Cf. B. M. F. van Iersel, *'Der Sohn' in den synoptischen Jesusworten*, p. 183.
93. *mBer.* 5: 1.   94. Cf. above, pp. 69–72, 118–19.
95. *bTaan.* 23b.
96. Cf. also D. Flusser, *Jesus*, pp. 93–5; I. Abrahams, *Studies in Phari-aism and the Gospels* II, pp. 201–2.
97. Cf. above, pp. 138–9.
98. *Gal.* 4: 4–5 (*RSV*); cf. *Rom.* 8: 3.
99. *John* 11: 27.   100. *John* 1: 1, 14, 18 (*AT*).
101. O. Cullmann, *The Christology of the New Testament*, p. 314.
102. *2 Cor.* 4: 4; *Col.* 1: 15; *Heb.* 1: 3.
103. *Ephesians* 1: 1; *Smyrnians* 1: 1.

104. F. Hahn, *The Titles of Jesus in Christology*, pp. 295-7, 303-4.
105. *Matt.* 1: 18, 23; *Luke* 1: 32-3, 35.
106. The Qumran *Gen. Ap.* 2 tells the story of Lamech who was worried that the child, Noah, borne to him by his wife, may have been fathered by a fallen angel. He sought reassurance from the heavenly Enoch, his grandfather, who knew all things. Cf. *DSSE*, pp. 216-17.
107. Cf. Schürer-Vermes-Millar, *History* I, pp. 399-427, against the historicity of Luke's account.
108. The notion of Mary's virginity is introduced into Matthew by means of the quotation of the apposite Greek version of *Isaiah* 7: 14, 'Behold the virgin shall conceive and bear a son' (*Matt.* 1: 23 (*AT*)). It is notorious that the term used in the original Hebrew text of Isaiah does not mean *virgo intacta* but a nubile girl who may or may not be a virgin. The New English Bible renders the verse correctly: 'A young woman is with child.' Cf. G. R. Driver, 'The New English Bible', *JJS* 24 (1973), pp. 6-7. On the Greek use of *parthenos*, see below, p. 218.
109. The dilemma was noticed at an early stage, and already in the second century AD clumsy attempts were made to solve it by ascribing Davidic descent to Mary also (reflected in the Lucan genealogy). Cf. *Protoevangelium of James* 10: 1; Justin, *Dialogue with Trypho* 43, 45. See also the doctrinal variant introduced into a few manuscripts of *Luke* 2: 4, reading 'because they were of the house and family of David', instead of the masculine singular form applicable to Joseph alone.
110. F. C. Grant, 'Jesus Christ', *Interpreter's Dictionary of the Bible* (Abingdon Press, Nashville, 1962), II, p. 879.
111. *Luke* 3: 23.
112. Cf. the style in *Matt.* 1: 3, 5-7.
113. For a useful collection of the Patristic evidence, see J. Weiss, *Earliest Christianity* II (Harper, New York, 1959), pp. 731-2, n. 47.
114. Cf. *Gen.* 20: 18; 29: 31; 30: 22; *1 Sam.* 1: 5-6.
115. G. Delling, *TDNT* V (1967), p. 827.
116. H. J. Leon, *The Jews of Ancient Rome* (Jewish Publication Society, Philadelphia, 1960), pp. 130, 232, 274-5 (no. 81), 299 (no. 242), 311 (no. 319).
117. Cf. *Gen.* 24: 16, 43. For the rest of the Bible, the Septuagint always translates *bethulah* as *parthenos*.
118. *Gen.* 24: 16; *tSheb.* 3: 15.   119. *mNid.* 1: 4.
120. *tNid.* 1: 6.   121. *yNid.* 49a.
122. *mNid.* 10: 1.   123. Cf. Josephus, *BJ* 2, 161.
124. Cf. *De posteritate Caini* 134.   125. *De mutatione nominum* 131.
126. *De legum allegoria* 3, 218-19; cf. *De cherubim* 45: 'For (Moses) shows us Sarah conceiving at the time when God visited her in her solitude; but when she brings forth it is not to the author of her visitation, but to . . . Abraham.'

127. See above, p. 220.
128. *Matt.* 1: 18–25 (*RSV*). Note that the Sinaitic version of the Old Syriac Gospel, which in *Matt.* 1: 16 (*AT*) reads, 'Joseph . . . begot Jesus', renders *Matt.* 1: 25, 'he did not know her until she had borne *him* a son'.
129. *Luke* 1: 34 (*AT*).
130. Cf. *mKid.* 2: 1 giving as the *terminus ante quem* for a girl's betrothal the age of twelve years, six months and one day.
131. *Luke* 1: 36–7 (*RSV*).

Acknowledgements

The author and publishers wish to acknowledge their indebtedness for permission to reproduce copyright material as follows: from the New English Bible, second edition © 1970, by permission of Oxford and Cambridge University Presses; from the Revised Standard Version Bible, copyright 1946, 1952 and © 1971 by the Division of Christian Education, National Council of the Churches of Christ in the U.S.A.; from the Loeb Classical Library edition of *Josephus*, © The President and Fellows of Harvard College, translated by H. St. J. Thackeray, R. Marcus and L. H. Feldman, and published by Heinemann, London, and Harvard University Press, Cambridge, Mass.; and from the Loeb Classical Library edition of *Philo*, © The President and Fellows of Harvard College, translated by F. H. Colson and G. H. Whitaker, and published by Heinemann, London, and Harvard University Press, Cambridge, Mass.

Reference index

Where references are to notes the numbers of these are given in brackets after the page numbers

THE MIDRASHIM

Aboth de-Rabbi Nathan a
27, 238 (68)
28, 243 (112)

Deuteronomy Rabbah
3: 10, 1, 245 (58)
5: 15, 240 (32)

Ecclesiastes Rabbah
10: 11, 257 (26)

Exodus Rabbah
1: 31, 252 (32)

Genesis Rabbah
13: 2, 248 (48)
13: 7, 241 (61)
48: 12, 257 (12)

56: 1, 234 (162)
75: 5, 248 (55)
79: 6, 257 (26, 28)
89: 5, 248 (59)
94: 9, 237 (49), 249 (70)
100: 5, 257 (13)

Lamentations Rabbah
1: 5, 31, 261 (107)

Mekhilta de-Rabbi Ishmael
   (ed. Lauterbach)
I, *115–16*, 245 (61)
II, *57–8*, 262 (26)
II, *183*, 242 (93)
III, *39–40*, 260 (72)
III, *197*, 260 (71)
III, *198*, 260 (72)

Midrash Tanna'im
Deut. *26: 13*, 238 (78)

Pesikta de-Rab Kahana
40ab, 239 (29)

Pesikta Rabbathi
20: 4, 261 (94)

Siphre on Numbers
99, 246 (81)
117, 256 (119)

Song of Songs Rabbah
2: 9. 3, 245 (61)

Tanḥuma [Buber]
I, *140*, 258 (36)
IV, *118–19*, 239 (29)

THE NEW TESTAMENT

Matthew
1: 1, 254 (61)
1: 3, 265 (112)
1: 5–7, 265 (112)
1: 16, 254 (61), 266 (128)
1: 17, 254 (61)
1: 18, 254 (61), 265 (105)
1: 18–25, 266 (128)
1: 23, 265 (105, 108)
1: 25, 266 (128)
2: 4, 254 (61)
3: 14, 233 (120)
3: 17, 244 (33), 264 (65)
4: 2, 244 (22)
4: 3, 231 (36), 263 (55)
4: 5–6, 263 (56)
4: 6, 231 (36)
4: 12, 232 (99)
4: 15, 231 (42)
4: 17, 232 (83)
4: 23, 230 (19), 232 (85)
4: 25, 233 (109)
5: 11, 179, 182
5: 44–8, 237 (44)
6: 1–4, 242 (101)
6: 25–33, 242 (94)
6: 28–9, 236 (33)
7: 6, 237 (39)
7: 21–2, 247 (24), 250 (102)
7: 22, 239 (27), 250 (107)
7: 29, 232 (87)
8: 1–3, 231 (46)
8: 2, 107, 128, 249 (85, 91), 250 (103)
8: 3, 231 (57)
8: 4, 239 (6)
8: 5–13, 231 (51), 237 (41), 242 (79)
8: 6–8, 249 (89), 250 (92)

8: 8, 247 (18), 250 (103, 114)
8: 13, 231 (66)
8: 14–15, 231 (47)
8: 15, 231 (56)
8: 16, 230 (18), 231 (41)
8: 20, 179, 242 (96), 260 (76)
8: 21, 250 (96)
8: 25, 250 (93)
8: 26–7, 232 (74)
8: 28–31, 230 (20)
8: 29, 231 (38), 263 (54)
8: 34, 233 (110)
9: 1, 237 (36)
9: 1–8, 241 (51)
9: 2–8, 231 (40)
9: 3, 234 (151)
9: 6, 179, 180
9: 8, 180
9: 10–13, 232 (82)
9: 11, 234 (150)
9: 18, 236 (9)
9: 20, 231 (60)
9: 20–2, 231 (48)
9: 25, 231 (71)
9: 27, 256 (112)
9: 27–31, 231 (45)
9: 28, 250 (92), 256 (113)
9: 29, 231 (58, 65)
9: 32–4, 230 (24)
9: 34, 239 (26)
9: 35, 232 (85)
10: 1, 230 (25)
10: 1–4, 232 (100)
10: 4, 237 (52)
10: 5–6, 237 (41)
10: 6, 232 (81)
10: 7–11, 230 (25)

10: 14, 230 (25)
10: 23, 179, 260 (87)
10: 37, 233 (143)
11: 2, 233 (126), 242 (104), 254 (61)
11: 2–3, 233 (121)
11: 3, 233 (125)
11: 6, 233 (127)
11: 7–15, 233 (124)
11: 19, 179, 260 (77)
11: 27, 201, 261 (3)
12: 1–6, 181
12: 2, 234 (150)
12: 8, 179, 180
12: 9–13, 231 (49, 67)
12: 14, 233 (144)
12: 24, 234 (151), 239 (26)
12: 27, 239 (25)
12: 32, 179, 260 (77)
12: 38, 128
12: 40, 179, 182
12: 43–4, 231 (33)
13: 10–17, 232 (84)
13: 24–8, 236 (33)
13: 34–5, 232 (84)
13: 37, 179, 260 (86)
13: 41, 179, 260 (86)
13: 51, 250 (97)
13: 55, 230 (4, 11)
13: 55–6, 230 (5)
13: 57, 233 (139), 243 (16)
13: 58, 231 (44), 243 (18)
14: 1–2, 233 (118), 235 (183)
14: 3–12, 237 (47)
14: 5, 243 (10)
14: 13–21, 244 (21)
14: 15–21, 232 (75)
14: 22–7, 232 (77)

Index of names and subjects

Where references are to notes the numbers of these are given in brackets after the page numbers